Mapping
Multiple
Literacies

ALSO AVAILABLE FROM BLOOMSBURY

Bilinguality and Literacy (2nd edition), edited by Manjula Datta
Educating the Postmodern Child, Fiachra Long
Literacy on the Left, Andrew Lambirth
Rethinking the Education Improvement Agenda, Kevin J. Flint and Nick Peim

Mapping Multiple Literacies

An Introduction to Deleuzian Literacy Studies

DIANA MASNY AND

DAVID R. COLE

BLOOMSBURY

LONDON · NEW DELHI · NEW YORK · SYDNEY

Bloomsbury Academic

An imprint of Bloomsbury Publishing Plc

50 Bedford Square
London
WC1B 3DP
UK

1385 Broadway
New York
NY 10018
USA

www.bloomsbury.com

Bloomsbury is a registered trade mark of Bloomsbury Publishing Plc

First published in 2012 by the Continuum International Publishing Group Ltd
Paperback edition first published by Bloomsbury Academic 2014

© Diana Masny and David R. Cole 2012

Diana Masny and David R. Cole have asserted their rights under the Copyright, Designs
and Patents Act, 1988, to be identified as Authors of this work.

British Library Cataloguing-in-Publication Data
A catalogue record for this book is available from the British Library.

ISBN: HB: 978-1-4411-4920-6
      PB: 978-1-4725-6914-1
      ePDF: 978-1-4411-8695-9
      ePUB: 978-1-4411-5768-3

Library of Congress Cataloging-in-Publication Data
Masny, Diana.
Mapping multiple literacies: an introduction to Deleuzian literacy studies/Diana Masny
and David R. Cole.
p. cm.
Includes bibliographical references and index.
ISBN-13: 978-1-4411-4920-6
ISBN-10: 1-4411-4920-1
ISBN-13: 978-1-4411-8595-2
ISBN-13: 978-1-4411-8695-9
1. Literacy–Philosophy. 2. Deleuze, Gilles, 1925–1995. I. Cole, David R. II. Title.
LC149.M28 2012
302.2'244–dc23
                              2012003516

Typeset by Fakenham Prepress Solutions, Fakenham, Norfolk NR21 8NN
Printed and bound by CPI Group (UK) Ltd, Croydon, CR0 4YY

CONTENTS

FOREWORD: THE MULTIPLE, THE LETTER, AND THE THEORIST

Claire Colebrook

There is a crisis, today, in literacy. This despair concerns not only the capabilities of marginal and disenfranchised groups, but the human species as a whole. The USA's 'No Child Left Behind' Act of 2001, aimed at raising standards in public schools is one of many worldwide governmental campaigns designed to restore numeracy and literacy to disempowered populations. But alongside these restorative gestures there has been a less sanguine articulation of a far more profound illiteracy: it is not only publicly schooled children but humanity in general that is losing its basic human capacity to read. It is assumed that man is a reading animal, and that a current atrophy of the reading brain is the beginning of the end of 'our' humanity.

Widespread lament and preliminary mourning is being articulated with regard to a loss of the reading and critical brain in the face not only of an increasingly visual culture, but of a society of such intense and multiple stimuli that individuals are losing their very distinction. According to the neurologist Susan Greenfield we are becoming increasingly entranced by a screen culture of isolated and short-term stimuli, at the expense of the sophisticated reading skills that are constitutive of our sense of self (Greenfield Derrida, J., 2008). Ours is a culture of shallow, distracted, increasingly over-taxed and threateningly myopic attention (Carr, 2010; Gallagher, 2009; Jackson, 2008).

Now, more than ever, claims might be made for a strong campaign for literacy, not just in this or that specific discourse or canon, so much as a basic commitment to the sustained reading eye and its capacities to synthesise and process complex systems (Hayles, 2007). Now, it seems, would not be the time to celebrate the wilder imperatives of Deleuzian theory, such as the claim to retreat from the 'order words' that typify classroom teaching but are structural for a political mode in general that calls 'us' all to recognize ourselves as legitimate speaking subjects (Deleuze and Guattari, 1987: pp. 106–07). Now would not be the time to celebrate a literary retreat from sense and communication to move towards a stammering, stuttering or aphasia

(Deleuze 1997: p. 15). Perhaps it would be more prudent to focus on a mode of *literary theory* – where the reading of texts and the sense of textual systems and their complexity would be part of a broader training in cultural, political and historical rhetoric. If it is true that we are shifting from an era of deep attention (or the modes of focus required for the close reading of complex texts) to hyper attention (or the fast, shifting and multi-tasking modes of alertness cultivated by gaming culture) then an integration of reading with stimulus culture would seem to be more requisite than the types of affirmative self-annihilation advocated by post-avant-garde theory (Hayles, 2007).

If Deleuzian theory today has a market, it is precisely to the extent to which it has allowed a move away from textual and literary models of culture and politics towards the body, affects, living systems and virtual powers that operate above and beyond constituted systems (such as languages). And if we wanted to think about *literacy* or about saving our faculty to read, judge, remain recognizably coherent and competent among the political and cultural milieu of the present, would it really serve us well to turn to a theorist who celebrated Artaud's imperative to 'have done with the judgment of God,' and who saw 'becoming-imperceptible' and going beyond actualized systems as the only genuine ethics? But I would suggest that it is precisely now, at a time of literacies in the plural, that Deleuze offers an approach that charts beyond the false opposition of anarchic relativism on the one hand and a pragmatic subjection to already established norms. Deleuxe's concept of the differential or the claim that system of differences are actualisations of powers to differ – powers that we can sense whenever there is deviation, deflection or mutation – allow us both to recognize that judgment and speaking take place through constituted systems, *and* that each event of speech and judgment bears its own expressive relation of emergence to the life of which it is one of multiple instances. There is a truth and force to this relativity: each speaker expresses one aspect of a life and force that is given in all its different perspectives and modes.

If ethics is not to be an arbitrarily moral system that reactively conserves some already constituted norm, then surely – Deleuze argues – we need to direct our attention to 'the powers of the false', or to the virtual tendencies and potentials from which organized systems have emerged. When Deleuze and Guattari examined language, they made two key maneuvers: first, language is just one system of differences among many and should not be seen as the system through which all other systems ought to be coded; second, language possesses (like all systems) a power of *higher* deterritori-alization. Language, as such, is deterritorialising, for it allows systems to operate independent of individuals; language is *reterritorialised* when it is deemed to be the proper mode of human expression or articulation, and when a single dominant and ordering language is assumed to be centre from which deviation or *il*literacy is generated. 'Higher deterritorialisation' occurs when the differential elements from which language was composed – such as phoneme differences or etymological resonances – are varied beyond speakers' and writers' intentionality. One can think here of the ways in which high modernist or avant-garde texts start to explore the 'machinic' qualities of writing – such as type-face – which operate in a radically material manner.

But this *literary* theory in which one no longer sees language as flowing forth from human intentionality but as bearing a rogue structural force – a theory which allowed literary studies to carve out some autonomous space for the study of texts – does not help us with *literacy*. Indeed, there is one reading of post-structuralism generally (if such a category has any unity) that would locate a valorization of illiteracy in late twentieth-century French thought. Julia Kristeva, for example, argued that the symbolic order (where language operates as a unified and unifying system of judgment) could – in a manner that was directly revolutionary – be disturbed by the anarchic and non-semantic disruptions of the sounds and rhythms of high modernist texts (such as those of Joyce) (Kristeva, 1984). Also celebrating Joyce, Derrida explores those aspects of Joyce's writing that create resonance between the sounds of different words or even the physical appearance of text on the page, even if there is no coherence of sense: what is literary about Joyce's work is not any communication or informational dimension but a halting of understanding via the primacy of sound: 'what remains …inaudible, although visible is the literal incorporation of the *yes* in *eyes*' (Derrida, J., 1992: p. 42). Foucault, too, argued that it was literature (especially as it approached the modern era) that would liberate language from the rationality of sense and communication (Foucault, 2002: p. 326).

On the one hand Deleuze would seem to be at the extreme end of this seeming celebration of the anarchic destruction of linguistic competence. Whereas the literary theory that emanated from writers as varied as Jacques Derrida, Michel Foucault, Julia Kristeva and Jacques Lacan focused on the radical implications of linguistic structuralism – such that we can only work at the limits of language – Deleuze was perhaps *the* French theorist who focused on non-linguistic powers. Deleuze criticized Derrida and Foucault for remaining at the limits of language; with Guattari he wrote of the 'despotism of the signifier' or the tyranny of the modern notion that one becomes a subject by submitting to the order of symbolic systems, and his anti-Oedipal theory of life was committed to tracing the emergence and proliferation of life beyond the bounds of both texts and structures of meaning. On the other hand, whereas post-structuralism tended to celebrate those high modernist or avant-garde texts – such as Joyce, Mallarme, Celine or Roussel – that attended to the forces of linguistic sound and script, Deleuze and Guattari provided complex arguments regarding the politics of language. Theirs was not a theory that would see 'the subject' *either* lining up and submitting to the symbolic order *or* falling into psychosis: that theory, they argued, was possible because of capitalism's oedipal structure (Deleuze and Guattari, 1983). Submit to the one unifying, quantifying, general and formal system of exchange, or fall back into the dark night of the undifferentiated.

Here, we can begin to see why Deleuze was at once a theorist – in contrast with other post-structuralists – of *illiteracy,* at the same time as he enabled a thought of multiple literacies. First, illiteracy is a refusal of the letter, an active annihilation of the already inscribed and constituted system. This is in accord with Deleuze's celebration of the differential calculus: not a destruction of differentiated systems, but the refusal of already inscribed units in favour of increasingly refined and infinitesimal differences (Deleuze, 1994). This then takes us to a higher, deterritorialised – or, as this volume would have it – *multiple* literacies. For it is not the case that deviations from the literate norm are negations and losses of refinement so much as increasingly refined, nuanced, mobile and dynamic differentials. This, in turn, is what ties multiple literacy to a radical and productive (or intensive) conception of the multiplicity.

Normative notions of literacy (whereby populations are measured against a single standard) operate in terms of extensive multiplicities: There is a linguistic standard deemed to be crucial to effective communication and the transmission of sense; the project is to include as many persons as possible within this standard. The more individuals who attain literacy (so the story goes) the more enabled and empowered they and the public sphere of democratic communication will be. By contrast, Deleuze's differential and multiple approach operates from an intensive concept of multiplicity: each new attainment of literacy introduces difference into what counts as literacy. At certain thresholds – such as the populations of Tasmania (noted by David R. Cole in this volume) who are deemed by the common standard to be illiterate – new modes of literacy are constituted. Intensive multiplicities alter their nature with increasing quantities, and require us to consider sense not so much as information to be communicated via the letter but as an *event.*

Deleuze and Guattari describe sense as an 'incorporeal event': on the one hand the world is composed of bodies and states of affairs, and these can be denoted by linguistic systems (Deleue and Guattari, 1987, 106). Sense occurs neither in the fixity of the system, nor in the concrete matter of the world. If I can refer to something like the 'invasion' of Australia then I take one constituted system (standard English) and create a combination that might then cause us to question the legitimacy of that same system. What other ways of speaking, referring, denoting, differentiating or including might create new multiple literacies? If 'Australia' were to speak with these other modes of literacy writings – such as the multiple lines of language that enter into *supposedly* failing populations – how might 'we' speak, what might we be able to sense?

At first glance the theorization of literacy would appear to be anathema to everything that has come to be known as Deleuzian. If 'theory' is today often criticized or rejected it is because of its supposed textualism and abstraction, with an insufficient attention paid to the complexities and differential intensities of life. Many of the post-theory fads have included various returns to life (whether in the form of history, bodies, Darwinian evolution, politics, or identity). The most recent wave of post-theoretical grounding has taken the form of a 'turn' towards cognitive science (Zunshine, 2010). In general, critical theories of literacy would need to be wary of *any* attempt to provide a foundation for linguistic systems; but the turn to cognitive science might give us special pause precisely because of the assumption that language and reading are tied not just to competence but to a general human competence. Cognitive science can, and should, (we are told) help us in theories of reading precisely because the reading of texts is generated from of a universal human ability for sense-making, understanding and the attribution of mind and motives to the behaviour of characters (Zunshine, 2006). What this 'turn' to cognitive science in a range of disciplines – such as evolutionary archaeology, Darwinian literary theory, and economics, politics and social science – presupposes is an assumption of something like *human* competence. What a focus on multiple literacies would add to this widespread turn is twofold: there is no such thing as human competence, for each system of differences constitutes its own field and expertise; *and* what might be required is not a reading of language as competence but a positive attention to *incompetence.* Various modes of distortion, deflection, and the refusal of common communication create new – and not necessarily adaptive or life-furthering – deviations. What Deleuze offers to an understanding of the multiple and literacy is a new mode of literary theory. It is true that Deleuze celebrates the great texts of traditional modernism; but what he finds in the great works is what he and Guattari refer to as *minor* literature (Deleuze and Guattari, 1986). Like the minor mode in music, minor literature begins with a tonal deviation that is not that of a full measure, in the way that a slight accent, deviation or inflection might be introduced into the dominant. If, for example, Kafka is a great writer it is because he is minor: speaking his 'home' language as though he were a foreigner, an illiterate. So it is not the case that reading and writing should aspire to the grand, human, cognitive and majoritarian aim of attaining maximum coherence and pattern-inference. On the contrary, one would read supposed great, human, founding and normative systems *as though they were rogue systems without a population.* If we learn to read with a sense of the multiple, with a sense that we do not know in advance who is speaking or how one ought to speak then communication (in the sense of conveying information) is thwarted, but communication (in the way a virus is communicated) is intensified.

A viral model of literacy opens new domains: rather than restore deviation by including illiterates within an already constituted standard, the standard itself is open, dynamic and *productive of sense.* For it is only a question of literacy – or of how modes of writing and reading enable orientations, differences and the creation of minor deflections – that truly enables the possibility of reading and writing *not as modes of replication* (tracing a pattern) but as modes of mapping – marking out new spaces, new dimensions, new lines of filiation.

References

Carr, N. (2010). *The Shallows: What the Internet is Doing to Our Brain*. New York: Norton.

Deleuze, G. (1994). *Difference and Repetition*. (p. Patton trans.). New York: Columbia.

—(2007). *Essays: Critical and Clinical*. (D.W. Smith & M.A. Greco, trans.). Minneapolis: University of Minnesota Press.

Deleuze, G. & Guattari, F. (1983). *Anti-Oedipus: Capitalism and Schizophrenia* (R. Hurley, M. Seem & H. R. Lane, trans.). Minneapolis: University of Minnesota Press.

—(1986). *Kafka: Towards a Minor Literature*. (D. Polan, trans.). Minneapolis: University of Minnesota Press.

—(1987). *A Thousand Plateaus*. (B. Massumi, trans.). Minneapolis: University of Minnesota Press.

Derrida, J. (1992). *Acts of Literature* (D. Attridge, ed.). London: Routledge.

Gallagher, W. (2009). *Rapt: Attention and the Focused Life*. Harmondsworth: Penguin.

Greenfield, S. (2008). *I.D.: The Quest for Meaning in the 21st Century*. London: Sceptre.

Foucault, M. (2002). *The Order of Things: An Archaeology of the Human Science*. London: Routledge.

Hayles, N. K. (2007). 'Hyper and Deep Attention: The Generational Divide in Cognitive Modes.' *Profession* 13 (2007): 187–99.

Jackson, M. (2008). *Distracted: The Erosion of Attention and the Coming Dark Age*. Amherst, N.Y.: Prometheus Books.

Kristeva, J. (1984). *Revolution in Poetic Language*. (M. Waller & L. Roudiez, trans.). New York: Columbia.

Zunshine, L. (2006). *Why We Read Fiction*. Columbus: Ohio State University Press.

—(ed.) (2010). *Introduction to Cognitive Cultural Studies*. Baltimore: Johns Hopkins.

ACKNOWLEDGMENTS

David Cole would like to thank the editors of *Educational Philosophy & Theory* for giving permission to use: Cole, D. R. (2011). The Actions of Affect in Deleuze: Others using language and the language that we make … In: D. R. Cole and L. J. Graham (eds), *The Power in/ Of language, Special Issue of Educational Philosophy & Theory*, 43(6), August, pp. 549–61 (Wiley-Blackwell) as Chapter Three. Also, sections of D. R. Cole (2007). Teaching Frankenstein and Wide Sargasso Sea Using Affective Literacy, *English in Australia*, 42(2), pp. 69–75 have been used in Chapter Three. Chapter Six is an adapted version of Cole, D. R. (2009). The power of emotional factors in English teaching, *Power and Education*, 1(1), pp. 57–70, and is used here with the permission of editor Michael Watts. Sections of Chapter Seven have appeared in D. R. Cole and V. Moyle (2009). Cam-capture Literacy and Its Incorporation into Multiliteracies, *Multiliteracies and Technology Enhanced Education: Social Practice and the Global Classroom*, IGI Global, Darren L. Pullen and David R. Cole (eds). Hershey, PA, pp. 116–33.

Diana Masny would like to to thank Monica Waterhouse for her invaluable comments and to Brenna Quigley for her technical knowledge. Also to the MLT–Deleuze study group of the Multiple Literacies Research Unit, who provided much inspiration during discussions of literacies research and concept creation. The study that appears in the form of vignettes came about because of the generosity and research interest in minority language education of the French Language Public Board of Greater Ottawa, its principals, teachers and daycare educators; Diana would like to say many thanks for their collaboration. Finally, Diana wants to express her gratitude to the families, parents and children, who graciously gave of their time and contributed significantly to this study. Funding for this study was granted to Diana Masny by the Social Sciences and Humanities Research Council of Canada and the Official Languages Support Program, Heritage Canada.

ABBREVIATIONS

ECC   Deleuze, G. (1997). Essays critical and clinical (D. W. Smith and M. A. Greco, trans). Minneapolis: University of Minnesota Press (original work published 1993).

EPS   Deleuze, G. (1992). *Expressionism in philosophy: Spinoza*.(M. Joughin, trans.). New York: Zone Books (original work published 1968).

DEP   Deleuze, G. and Parnet, C. (2007). Dialogues II: European Perspectives (H. Tomlinson and B. Habberjam, trans). New York: Columbia University Press (original work published 1977).

DR   Deleuze, G. (1994). *Difference and repetition*. (P. Patton, trans.) New York: Columbia University Press (original work published 1968).

FB   Deleuze, G. (1981). *Francis Bacon: Logique de la sensation*. Paris: Editions de la différence.

LS   Deleuze, G. (1990). *The logic of sense* (M. Lester and C. Stivale, trans.). New York: Columbia University Press (original work published 1969).

NG   Deleuze, G. (1995). *Negotiations: 1972–1990*. (M. Joughin, trans). New York: Columbia University Press.

SPP   Deleuze, G. (1988). Spinoza: Practical philosophy (R. Hurley, trans.). San Francisco: City Lights (original work published 1970).

TP   Deleuze, G. and Guattari, F. (1988). *A Thousand Plateaus: Capitalism and schizophrenia II* (B. Massumi, trans.). London: The Athlone Press.

WP   Deleuze, G. and Guattari, F. (1994). What is philosophy? (H. Tomlinson and G. Burchell, trans). New York: Columbia University Press (original work published 1991).

LIST OF FIGURES

CHAPTER ONE

Introduction to mapping multiple literacies

David R. Cole and Diana Masny

DELEUZIAN LITERACY STUDIES (PART I)
David R. Cole

Introduction

I was recently (2009) invited to a literacy summit on the island of Tasmania. The island had faired badly at nationally orchestrated literacy tests. The summit therefore had the air of an emergency meeting to discuss the literacy problems of the local children. Why couldn't they do well at these tests? Why were they lagging behind the other states in Australia in reading, writing and spelling? The summit organizers had brought in a principal from the mainland who was in charge of a school where the literacy results were substantially ahead of those in Tasmania. The principal spoke against whole language literacy, Nativism, and notions of immersive language learning. Instead, the principal advocated phonics instruction and a back-to-basics approach to literacy. Included in his presentation was the slide shown in Figure 1.1.

I wondered, why was reading represented as an entwined rope? How do the elements of reading come together? Where is the notion of time

Big Ideas in Beginning Reading

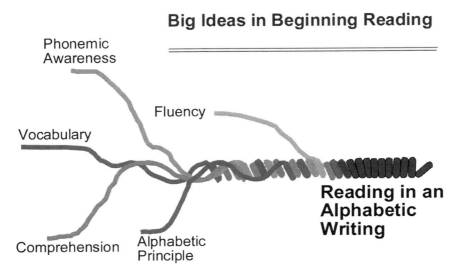

Figure 1.1 Big ideas in beginning reading (Fleming, 2009: slide 34)

in this image? The answers to these questions were not forthcoming at this summit. Rather, as an audience we were left with the impression that we must tie together ropes to help our children to become literate. This process is presumably a matter of practice and dexterity with the various 'entwinements' that one has to deal with as a teacher. I mused further: does every child require its own rope? Could one rope maybe cover half a class? Of course, there is a serious side to these reflections, one that this book on multiple literacies will address, and one that was not covered at the summit. This is that the speaker was not talking about literacy, but illiteracy. The rope that is conjured above works in reverse to explain illiteracy, i.e. when the rope becomes untwined. The summit established a false power relationship between the principal's school and Tasmania, in that the 'solution' to the literacy problems in Tasmania did not lie in exterminating deviant or lax literacy pedagogy amongst some of the island's teachers. Rather, the literacy questions embedded in the population of the island lie in deeply engrained social/cultural perceptions of themselves as other to the mainstream. Tasmanians often pride themselves in their eccentric and perhaps erratic sense of communication, which can lead to cutting themselves off from normative, mainstream practices. This wouldn't be such a bad thing if they didn't have to take part in these national literacy tests, yet this issue was not discussed at the summit. Instead, universal evidence of literacy improvement was sought; practical, proven methods that were known to work across the board to help children read, write and spell were examined. This book engages with such a discourse, yet from a Deleuzian perspective, where literacies are multiple, normativity is not imposed, and literacy concepts are treated creatively and fully involved with the unconscious.

Mapping multiple literacies

Kaustuv Roy (2005) has suggested that deploying Deleuze in literacy studies could help to derail the current literacy wars between opposing camps. On one side, the evidence-based 'scientists' advocate phonics and strict literacy structures tied to increased levels of phonemic competence. On the other side, critical literacy theorists and the new literacies base their analyses on social/cultural forces. Deleuze is useful here, because the philosophical framing of literacy does not exclude questions to do with educational psychology and literacy, whilst simultaneously providing a basis for literacy in the sociology of education. For example, the literacy scores of the children in Tasmania could be mapped cognitively, and in terms of the psychometrics that the test results reveal; however, this information should be aligned with sociological and cultural information about the participants. The results would therefore not be a comparative disaster compared with the rest of Australia, but reflect the ways in which use of Standard English has drifted and changed in the island context. Similarly, standardized English testing of Aboriginal children in Australia should take account of their first language skills, as well as the specific relationships with English language learning that populations have developed through time due to colonialization and schooling. For example, many Aboriginal populations were 'settled' in reserves and taught English by missionaries (see Goodall, 1988). This displacement of peoples and culture meant that not only did the Aboriginal Australians often struggle to come to terms with the geographical disorientation; they also had to imbibe missionary Christian values (through English literacy). The result was a double disjunction away from learning English, and away from their original cultures. Australian society is still coming to grips with this double disjunction, 250 years after it began.

The mapping of multiple literacies as offered by this book therefore allows the literacy theorist, teacher and researcher the freedom to look simultaneously at micro and macro factors in language learning. The base fact behind this examination is that literacy is multiple. This fact cuts away at any assumptions or prejudices that one might have about the unified nature of the context under analysis. Unlike the early explorers of Australia, such as James Cook, who mapped the coastline in 1770, the maps that we may produce about literacy teaching and learning should not be single lines on a page. Rather, the cartography of multiple literacy learning that happens over time is responsive to change and has various dimensions (even non-dimensions). Mapping multiple literacies is about representing complexity in the literacy process, even if one might not want to designate the process as a stable form of representation. As soon as one designates the representation of literacy learning as something else, a hole in the actual experience has appeared. The transcendental possibility of a perfect representation (of literacy learning) has henceforth been suggested. The unconscious will start to work overtime to make associations with this ideal other, thus draining the real of its emergent qualities, which we are in fact at pains to understand. The hole therefore has to be attended to with questions such as: What devices have we used to make the map – language, diagrams, schema or numbers? Who was making the map and why? How do the mapmakers relate to the subject and objects of their map? Who is going to use the map? For what purposes will the map be employed? In the case of Cook, the map of Australia was designed in terms of possession and occupation of the territory; the map was a geopolitical claim of the land for Britain. In the case of mapping multiple literacies, the maps are designed to bridge social/cultural/psychological gaps between learners, and to connect the creative unconscious with the textual objects of study. Mapping multiple literacies is about producing material records of the literacy events as they unfold, enfold and (con)fold. This is a non-restrictive practice, one that does not stop with educational research, or with the words of the teacher, or with the products of the students. Mapping multiple literacies is about continually reinventing the process of mapping as new ways to do literacy become apparent in context; this is a non-normative approach to practice (see Cole and Hager, 2010).

This book is therefore full of maps. A discarded necklace is a map of love. A dagger is a map of betrayal. Make your own maps. Let the children amaze you with their mapping abilities. Develop unexpected places whereby maps can communicate and take on an inhuman life of their own. Allow the random multiplicity of literacies to take over, submit yourself to the map …

Deleuzian literacy studies

Why should one consider the use of Deleuzian theory in literacy studies? The edited book, *Literacy as Snake Oil* (Larson, 2001), documents the ways in which literacy practice has recently been under siege due to governmental, commercial and societal concern. The 'Snake Oil' book shows how literacy practice in the US has suffered due to external influences on what children and teachers do in the literacy classroom. Autonomy and self-determination are drained by the stresses and impositions of external agents, such as commercial literacy product makers, who may try to sell their latest 'quick fix' to problems in literate development. The book on literacy as snake oil stands in opposition to these outside influences, which can make the work of the literacy teacher riven with decisions that come from outside of their control. The danger of such a perspective is that it valorizes literacy teachers as heroes, fighting against the encroachments of capitalist exploitation, that signifies a commodification and standardization of literacy mores. Contrariwise, this book on mapping multiple literacies and Deleuzian literacy studies does not reify the subjectivity of ant-capitalist literacy teachers, fending off their practice against commercial invasion. Deleuzian literacy studies analyze the context for the ways in which literacy is becoming other (often to itself). The teacher's subjectivity is not projected as a saviour to the ubiquity of commercial culture according to Deleuzian literacy studies. Rather, the literacy classroom is full of hybrid human and non-human subjectivities that can interrelate, overlap and contradict each other in text-based activities. Deleuzian literacy studies do not pre-determine or project subjectivity into context, as the field is enlivened through pre-personal affects, which are multiple and happen in time, often without the rational overtures of literacy development or instrumental 'improvementism'. This is not to say that Deleuzian literacy studies only sides with irrationality or the utterly chaotic, yet the unconscious, with its concomitant drives, should be an equal party in any literacy programme with rational order; associative powers should be valued alongside logic.

So, what is the Deleuzian solution to literacy problems (of illiteracy)? In the case of Tasmania, the solution would be to fully understand the ways in which Standard English has evolved in the context of island life. A new form of speech has developed as a hybrid of settler, convict, immigrant and international English (since global communications). Tasmanian language has incorporated the influence of Aboriginal Australians, who were officially declared extinct in 1876, yet successfully interbred with new arrivals, therefore continuing their bloodlines under the disguise of white-skin offspring. The Tasmanian spoken variety of English should be transcribed and discussed by poets, writers and educators, and taught in schools as a living record of Tasmanian history. With pride restored and understanding of the non-standard English language abilities of Tasmanians, the literacy testing exam results would improve, and should become on a par, if not better than, the rest of Australia. The case of Aboriginal Australians is perhaps more complicated with respect to the perhaps narrow goal of raising literacy scores. The first and most crucial point is to teach and learn about Aboriginal language, culture and history in schools. The difficulty here is that the Aboriginal lore was handed down through oral transmission. Compared to the British literary culture of the colonialists, the oral transmission of the Aboriginal Australians was easily broken. Communities were separated, children were sent off and fostered, people were assimilated and brainwashed through Christianity. Reclaiming Aboriginal Australian cultures through education is therefore not a straightforward task, yet educators such as David Rose *et al.* (Harrison, 2011) have started this difficult process. Deleuzian literacy studies necessitate planes of immanence between literacy events and learnings, where disparate and multiple cultures and traditions in the population are respected, revived and understood. In the case of the Aboriginal Australians, this means reversing the processes of otherness in British colonial rule, and attending to the linguistic impairments that imposed English literacy have had on the wills to power of the Aboriginals.

In the US, the situation of commercial takeover in education is perhaps even more intractable, yet comparable to that of the Aboriginal Australians. This is because contemporary capitalism transforms all cultural input as a quantity, so that these quantities can be exchanged for money or floated on the stock exchanges against other quantities. For example, if the raising of the literacy scores of the first Americans (in English) is understood and explained as giving equal value to first American culture, society and language in schools, this act of Deleuzian literacy study can henceforth be codified and packaged by commercial interests. The resultant set of educational practices would be valued according to their requisite market value, that can be worked out easily by looking at the demographics of first Americans in US schools. The same process could be repeated with African Americans, Latin Americans and Chinese Americans. Therefore capitalism deals with cultural diversity in terms of the creation of surplus value, and the ways in which difference can be represented and exploited to make a profit. Contrariwise, Deleuzian literacy studies do not insert an undisclosed, or 'revolutionary' other into the workings of capitalism in education. Rather, Deleuzian literacy studies work at the level of non-literacy, parallel to Laruelle's non-philosophy (1996). This means that one does not describe literacy as other, or create surplus value about literacy that could be encoded by capitalism as an enhancement process. In Deleuzian literacy studies, one strictly follows the material flows in literacy process through multiple mappings that work as forms of non-representation, or the differentiation of contextual affects as they transmit elements of life. In other words, Deleuzian literacy studies demonstrate a rigorous scepticism about normatively determined forms of literacy, whether they are commercial, skills based, psychological, sociological or governmental. In the wake of such scepticism, one is left with what Derrida calls 'a certain experience and experiment of the *possibility of the impossible*; the testing of the aporia from which one may invent the only possible invention, *the impossible invention*' (Derrida, 1992: p. 41; italics in original).

Cole's chapters in the book

Chapter Three examines the Deleuzian notion of affect and its application in literacy studies. Deleuze wrote about and analyzed the philosophy of Spinoza, who made affect an integral part of his *Ethics*. The point of the

Spinozist influence on literacy studies is to affect and be affected, causing fluctuations in the substance of the textual lesson. However, it is clear that Deleuze did not rest with a conformist or literal uptake of Spinoza, especially in his writing with Félix Guattari. This resulted in affect having social and cultural consequences, as has been extensively described in recent affect theory applications in cultural studies. To take account for the double articulation of affect in Deleuze, I have designed a two-role model of affect. The first role deals with the word of the teacher, curriculum or truth of textual and linguistic analysis. The first role, for example, takes into account the Freudian analysis of dreams, and the ways in which instinctive drives interact with spoken language. Any time that an educator engages with research or explains their pedagogy to an audience, the first role of affect becomes active, and will mediate notions of textual authority as affect and sense. The second role of affect is determined by the uptake of power and language, and involves the social and cultural consequences of meaning making. For example, children will have their own pre-determined circuits of affect that the teacher has to plug into so that the curricula textual practice can make an impact in that context. These affects have recently been enhanced and accelerated by gains in online social networking such as Facebook, making curricula choice perhaps at odds with the plethora of electronically mediated texts available online. Teachers need to use the second role of affect in conjunction with the more accustomed first role, and Chapter Three explains how this may be achieved. Chapter Three also includes a section on affective literacy, which is a textual practice designed to enhance functioning with affects.

Questions about power are extremely important to Deleuzian literacy studies. Chapter Six addresses questions related to power and literacy by examining empirical data from a case study of English teachers in Tasmania (Australia). The state had recently initiated a process of curriculum change, and implemented a new curricula model called *The Essential Learnings*. This constructivist model (Figure 6.1) of teaching and learning had questioned traditional models of literacy by headlining critical literacy as a practice, and by replacing the 'cheese slice' curriculum, where English has its component and segmented place, with the idea of 'Becoming Literate'. Such changes in literacy provision are in line with Deleuzian literacy studies, and concur with many of the findings in this book. However, this study found that teachers in Tasmania were divided and polarized by the introduction of the Essential Learnings. Such a case study therefore gives vital information as to how to implement a new Deleuzian literacy structure without creating the reactionary backlash as happened in Tasmania. This chapter also looks at data from the study of practising English teachers that relates to affect and emotion, and that were studied under the rubric of affective literacy.

Chapter Seven is the most speculative one in the book, as it maps the literacy of digital futures. This is not an easy task, as the pace of development in digitally mediated text is accelerating, recombining and fanning out as technology extends communicative options to all corners of the globe. Yet a concern for the future is critical to Deleuzian literacy studies, as it also helps to explain what is happening in today's educational environment. Chapter Seven is divided up into sections that examine digital machines and connectivity, cyber-revolutions, science fiction landscapes in education, cam-capture literacy in middle schools, young Muslims in Australia on Facebook and the 'digito-sphere'. The sections of Chapter Seven define a new option that is distinct from the New Literacies or Multiliteracies, as the ways in which the future is impinging upon the present through educational provision remain differentiated beneath the Deleuzian inspired Multiple Literacies Theory (MLT). This chapter challenges teachers and parents to become other to what they currently understand about literacy, and to fully embrace the future, as it works from the inside to pierce notions of stability and hegemony.

DELEUZIAN LITERACY STUDIES (PART II)
Diana Masny

I approach this book as an assemblage. In this assemblage, 'literacies education', Diana Masny and David R. Cole plug into concept creation by disrupting the traditional concept of 'literacy education' in order to create different concepts related to literacies education.

    For this introduction, I asked myself how I should enter this chapter. Mapping literacies relates to cartography. The concept of cartography I am referring to is Deleuzian, a rhizomatic cartography. As you will read in Chapter 2, *Cartographies of multiple literacies*, a rhizome has no beginning, no end, just a middle. Therefore, the introduction has no beginning, no end. I enter the chapter in the middle, that is, a continuous interplay between concept creation and mapping multiple literacies. I want to enter this book with its title, *Mapping Multiple Literacies: An Introduction to Deleuzian Literacy Studies*. However I would like to interrupt the linearity of the title by flipping it and considering *An introduction to Deleuzian Literacy Studies* as an entry and then attending to the topic of *Mapping Multiple Literacies*.

An introduction to Deleuzian Literacy Studies

Deleuze and Guattari never wrote on the topic of literacy/literacies. How is it that Deleuze and literacies are connected? This connection is not about applying Deleuze to literacies. I would like to enter with the question: what is concept creation?[1] What Deleuze and Guattari contributed, not only to philosophy but also to life and living, is concept creation. Deleuze associates doing philosophy with creating philosophical concepts, to push thinking beyond what is known or assumed. With Deleuze and Guattari, concept creation is a process. In this book, we also are involved in concept creation (our own) in the context of literacy studies. While we are informed by concepts such as becoming, affect, immanence, and power, we disrupt these concepts to create our own concepts as they relate to literacies. What is the importance of concept creation? Concept creation in the words of Colebrook creates a different path for thinking. Concept creation creates a potential, the *thought of* ... immanence. A concept provokes us and opens experiences to new intensities: ways of seeing differently. Concept creation 'is an encounter with life that opens life to its potentialities, how experience of life could be extended from what is to what could be' (Colebrook, 2002: p. 20).

An important aspect of this book on mapping multiple literacies is creating concepts of reading, reading the world and self and connecting these concepts with other concepts. For example, take the word literacy. With a definition of literacy, literacy is fixed or bounded as in a territory. In concept creation, the definition or territory of literacy is disrupted. The disruption opens up potentialities for viewing literacy as a different concept, putting literacies to new uses. This is what this book is about. Reading, reading world and self become newly created concepts, and it is from concept creating that thinking happens. In this instance, what happens when literacy is unhinged/disrupted from its current territory as the ability to read and write? The concept reterritorializes. It has, however, little connection with the previous concept of literacy. The new concept of literacy is different. The reterritorialized concept is a different concept until it is disrupted. Then the concept finds a different territory as it is now reterritorialized. The concept of multiple literacies referred to in MLT (Multiple Literacies Theory) is one such example. The process is one in which the school-based literacy that is related to reading and writing is deterritorialized and reterritorialized as multiple literacies: reading, reading the world and self (cf. Chapter Four, *What is reading?*).

The difference in literacy concepts is due to the deterritorialization that happens in this process. Moreover, deterritorialization links with becoming. To deterritorialize is to create different becomings (TP). Deterritorialization then opens up potentialities for what could happen. Because we are in the realm of the potential, Deleuze (DR) speaks of virtual difference.

Concept creation is precisely creating concepts to push thinking beyond what is assumed or given, to what could be. One way in which Deleuze and Guattari go about doing concept creation involves a process of territorialization, deterritorialization and reterritorialization. The concept of territory is linked to geography. When combined with philosophy, Deleuze and Guattari created the concept of geophilosophy.

Geophilosophy

Deleuze and Guattari (WP) state that Earth is sometimes a virtual realm, and because of the virtualness attributed to Earth, Deleuze and Guattari create a concept, transcendental geophilosophy, the study of the space of empirical/material systems (Protevi, 2001). Geophilosophy refers to mapping rhizomatic cartographies (cf. Chapter Five, *Cartographies of Talking Groups*; Bonta and Protevi, 2004). This book is titled Mapping Multiple Literacies. The concept of mapping is not a metaphor. It is a process whereby mapping takes place in conjunction with how de- and reterritorialization functions. While I want to focus on deterritorialization, I cannot write about it unless reterritorialization is included and it is difficult to imagine de- and reterritorialization without making connections with cartography, rhizome, and becoming. This points to the very notion that Deleuze and Guattari advance: that we cannot talk about concepts in isolation. Concepts enter in a relation with each other. A cartography (cf. Chapter Two, *Cartographies of multiple literacies*) is considered rhizomatic when it is made up of overcoding/institutionalized social practices (e.g. regulations about when to water the garden, where to park) and deterritorialization practices that create lines of flight or becoming and transform an assemblage. Here we go again making another connection: this is 'the assemblage'. In the parking example, there is an assemblage: the driver, the parking zones, financial costs, other drivers, road code, etc.). In Chapter Five I explore what an assemblage does and how it functions. The subject is part of an assemblage and the role of rhizomatic cartography is to deterritorialize this assemblage, deterritorialize overcodings. In the process of deterritorialization, transformations happen and becoming is created. An interesting aspect of transformation is that we do not know where it will go, what it will do and how it will do it. Deleuze and Guattari refer to the untimely.

Components of Rhizomatic Mapping (summary)

- Geophilosophy,
- de/re/territorialization,
- Concept creation

Masny's chapters in the book

What follows is a brief summary of each chapter. With regard to the first half of the title: *Mapping Multiple Literacies*, what comes to mind is the rhizome and cartography. Chapter Two, *Cartographies of multiple literacies*, focuses on how conventional cartography is conceptualized and then moves on to de/reterritorialize the concept of cartography as rhizomatic. Deleuze and Guattari were concerned about how the social sciences as well as natural sciences explored problems in terms of closed hierarchical systems, which they refer to as a tree or an arborescent system (tracings). They were interested in open, rhizomatic systems/maps. They could not and would not underestimate the power of arborescent systems/tracings. How to live with the latter? This was their response: 'The important point is that the root-tree and canal-rhizome are not two opposed models: the first operates as a transcendent model and tracing, even if it engenders its own escapes; the second operates as an immanent process that overturns the model and outlines a map ...' (TP: p. 2). Tracing and maps are not a dualism; rather, the relationship of the tracing and the map refers to 'paradoxical forces at work together in an assemblage' (TP: p. 12). There exist tree or root structures in rhizomes; conversely, a tree branch or root division may begin to burgeon into a rhizome (TP: p. 15). Chapter Two continues to examine literacies research based on the Cartesian (autonomous thinking subject), research that is representational and includes empirically grounded data. This is followed by an exploration of literacies research studies that would qualify as part of Deleuzian Literacy Studies. The chapter continues with its focus on talking groups and collective enunciations in relation to a study on multiple literacies.

The study in question appears in the chapters and includes vignettes taken from research that focuses on how perceptions transform reading, reading the world and self. In this study multilingual children (five to seven years old) were learning multiple writing systems simultaneously. This study was conducted over a two-year period. Data collection includes: (1) observations of literate events in class, a daycare center and at home, (2) interviews with the teachers, parents and daycare educators, (3) observations of each child-participant teaching their mother tongue to peers, and (4) texts produced by the children. While this chapter disrupts concepts, they also reterritorialize. What are the mappings for multiple literacies? What do they produce? Mapping literacies takes us to a tracing of literacy and literacies segmented and overcoded as a territory of socially institutionalized practices. The rupture happens when the tracing is put back on the map and deterritorialization of literacy/literacies happens. This describes rhizomatic cartography and what this book is about, Mapping Multiple Literacies.

In Chapter Four, *What is reading?*, reading, reading the world and self as concepts are created and elaborated on. Each concept is accompanied by a vignette based on the study with multilingual children that was presented in the preceding paragraph. This chapter reminds the reader that reading and how it happens is about mapping literacies through a rhizomatic cartography in which reading is intensive and immanent. Moreover, reading is a process that deterritorializes and reterritorializes differently each time. The assemblage has a particular combination that is unique to a particular context. The chapter exits on the relation of reading, reading the world and self in relation to teaching, learning, assessment and curriculum.

Chapter Five, *Cartographies of Talking Groups*, focuses on the social character of language. Deleuze and Guattari (TP) propose that there are no individual enunciations but rather collective assemblage of enunciation. By appealing to the collective, Deleuze and Guattari highlight the importance of the dominant social order that frames how language works. They refer to language as 'the set of all order words (*mots d'ordre*), implicit presuppositions, or speech acts current in a language at a given moment' (TP: p. 79). Joughlin, the translator of *Negotiations* (NG), has translated *mots d'ordre* by precepts underlining their normative and prescriptive character. The notion of social obligation enters into the equation in its relationship to the dominant social order and order words. The second half of Chapter Five is devoted to the study described in the previous paragraph. The vignettes selected explore the links between collective enunciations and order words.

Multiple Literacies Theory (MLT) (summary)

- Reading, reading world, and self,
- Reading intensively and immanently,
- Becoming (i.e. transformation)

Becoming literate and pedagogy

In education, as in other domains, we tend to want to focus more on solutions than on the problems at hand. In other words, there is an acknowledgement of a problem based on an assessment and then solutions are proposed. While solutions may be important, what is the problem? Best practices and effective practices have become solution buzz words. Is there one size that fits all? Can we generalize practices in the name of a solution?

According to Deleuze, 'we are led to believe that problems are given ready-made and that they disappear in the responses or the solution. ... We are led to believe that the activity of thinking ... begins only with the search for solutions' (DR: p. 158). From this statement, I would suggest the following: Take a problem in life, explore its tracings and put the tracings on the map. For example, literacy levels of a country are an important statistic. It is an economic benchmark of a country to the world. The reports are filed in terms of literacy rates, quoted in percentages. What could the implications be for mapping multiple literacies? We live in societies in which literacy is institutionalized by the overcoded practices associated with assessment of literacy (OECD, 2009). Putting the tracing of literacy on the map of multiple literacies is to deterritorialize a definition of literacy (ability to read and write and process information) and to reterritorialize this notion as: reading, reading the world and reading self. What mapping literacies through concept creation does is to deterritorialize the definition of literacy and to reterritorialize it as a different concept – in this instance: reading, reading the world and self. The aim of Multiple Literacies Theory (MLT) is to deterritorialize overcoded literacy practices. MLT itself is designed to deterritorialize through concept creation. And MLT will reterritorialize as overcoded literacies (it has happened!). But then again it will undergo deterritorialization. Each time there is deterritorialization and reterritorialization, the repetition will not be identical; each time the assemblage changes, the repetition is not the same. It is different each time (DR).

In other words, focusing on a problem is an opportunity for concept creation. Problem-becoming concepts provide a different way of thinking about pedagogy. The importance of untimely transformations of the individual in pedagogical experiences as becoming 'does not mean becoming the other', but *becoming-other* (Semetsky, 2003: p. 214). Concept creation is also a 'way of creating a future' of education (Colebrook, 2002: p. 21). What could it produce?

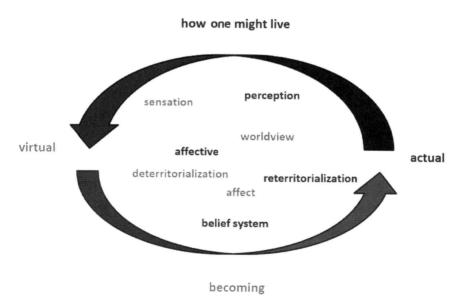

Figure 1.2 Actual – Virtual

References

Bonta, M. and Protevi, J. (2004). Deleuze and Geophilosophy: A guide and a glossary. Edinburgh: Edinburgh University Press.

Cole, D. R. and Hager, P. (2010). Learning-practice: The ghosts in the education machine. *Education Inquiry*, 1(1) 21–40.

Colebrook, C. (2002). *Gilles Deleuze*. New York: Routledge.

Derrida, J. (1992). *The Other Heading: Reflections on Today's Europe* (P.-A. Brault and M. Naas, trans). Bloomington: Indiana University Press.

Fleming, J. (2009). Tasmanian Literacy Summit (presentation). Hobart: Edrington Precinct.

Goodall, H. (1988). Crying out for land rights. In V. Burgmann and J. Lee (eds), *Staining the wattle* (pp. 163–85). Fitzroy, Vic.: McPhee Gribble/Penguin.

Harrison, N. ed. (2011). *Teaching and Learning in Aboriginal Education* (2nd edn). Melbourne: Oxford University Press.

Larson, J. ed. (2001). *Literacy as Snake Oil: Beyond the quick fix*. New York: Peter Lang.

Laurelle, F. (1996). *Prinçipes de la Non-Philosophie*. Paris: P.U.F.

May, T. (2005). *Gilles Deleuze: An introduction*. Cambridge: Cambridge University Press.

Organization for Economic and Cultural Development (OECD) (2009). *Programme for International Student Assessment*. Paris: OECD.

Protevi, J. (2001). *The geophilosophy of Deleuze and Guattari*. Available online at http://www.protevi.com/john/research.html (accessed 9 February 2011).

Roy, K. (2005). On Sense and Nonsense: Looking Beyond the Literacy Wars. *Journal of Philosophy of Education* 39(1), 99–111.

Semetsky, I. (2003). The problematics of human subjectivity: Gilles Deleuze and the Deweyan legacy. *Studies in Philosophy and Education, 22,* 211–25.

St. Pierre, E. A. (2004). Deleuzian concepts for education: the subject undone. *Educational Philosophy and Theory*, 36(3), 283–96.

Note

1   I want to use the concept of 'plugging in' that St. Pierre (2004) popularized. It has reduced the anxiety level in many readers who do not grasp aspects of Deleuzean philosophy at some point or other. The notion of plugging in can take us to Deleuze, who said: 'doing philosophy is like reading a book. … and the only question is "Does it work, and how does it work?" How does it work for you? … something comes through or it doesn't. There's nothing to explain, nothing to understand, nothing to interpret. It's like plugging in to an electric circuit' (NG: p. 8).

CHAPTER TWO

Cartographies of multiple literacies

Diana Masny

Introduction

This book is about making connections between Deleuze and literacies. This chapter is entitled Cartographies of Literacies. What could the relation be between literacies and maps (as in the title of this book)? Cartographies are central to the work of Deleuze and Guattari. Therefore, it is important to understand what cartographies do and how cartographies relate to literacies. A map has no beginning, no end (TP). You enter a map in the middle. Moreover, a map has multiple entry ways. All the chapters in the book I have authored the structure of a map, with each section considered an entry.

Cartography in the received or conventional view is presented in order to understand Deleuze and Guattari's move to disrupt a conventional view of cartography. Cartographies in the conventional way refer to mapping out representations of what is actually there within a territory.

Cartography according to Deleuze and Guattari is explored in this chapter. Cartography plays a key role in their work on *geophilosophy* (WP). Earth and territory produce problems from life and concept creation becomes a response to problems in the world. Instances of concept creation in *geophilosophy* are rhizomes, territorialization, deterritorialization and reterritorialization. These concepts are woven throughout this chapter.

The literature review brings together the conventional notions of literacy and cartography although, to my knowledge, I do not think that this connection has been made. The conventional notions of literacy and cartography refer to the humanist mode of representation and the Cartesian-centered (autonomous thinking) subject that creates maps and learns reading and writing skills. Accordingly, literacy and maps, in this context, operate within a closed system and territory. The review enters at the notion of autonomous and ideological models of literacy (Street, 1984). The former is the domain, though not exclusively, of psychology and has overtaken the field of literacy research. It has had a tremendous impact in how assessment of literacy is done (Luce-Kapler and Klinger, 2005; Marshall, 2009), in its emphasis on the role of phonological awareness in determining success in learning to read (Cardosa-Martins *et al.*, 2011; Prior *et al.*, 2011; Saiegh-Haddad *et al.*, 2011) and in school-readiness (Berninger *et al.*, 2010; Romano *et al.*, 2010). In addition, it is the psychological concept of literacy that pervades government policies on literacy (e.g. Programme for International Student Assessment [PISA], 2011). That said, the social aspects in literacy research have not gone unnoticed. The ideological model highlights literacy/literacies as socially situated practice. The latter has given rise to New Literacy Studies (Barton and Hamilton, 2005), Multiliteracies (Cope and Kalantzis, 2009), and New Literacies (Lankshear and Knobel, 2008).

Deterritorialization focuses on disrupting the concepts of literacy and cartography and creating them differently (reterritorializing) as cartographies and literacies within an open rhizomatic (non-linear) system. Characteristics of cartography are presented throughout various literacies studies working with cartographies. The characteristics of cartography stemming from transcendental empiricism are: assemblage, decentered subject and immanence. What is critical in reterritorialization is the notion of assemblage and the relation (or relationality) of the elements or machines to each other in the assemblage. Research studies on literacies are reviewed that take into account the disrupting of literacy as multiple literacies and involving concept creation (TP).

This entry reports on a study exploring the perceptions of multilingual children learning more than one writing system simultaneously. Data is deterritorialized as transgressive (moving away from conventional forms of data reporting) and reterritorialized as vignettes. The vignettes constitute openings for concept creation (i.e. reading as intensive and immanent) in the context of multiple literacies conceptualized within MLT (Multiple Literacies Theory: Masny, 2009a).

This chapter exits in the middle by considering the potentialities of reading, reading the world and self as part of an assemblage in which reading disrupts the assemblage. The assemblage reconfigures. In turn, the assemblage disrupts reading. The assemblage provides a different way on reading the world and self. These disruptions function within a rhizomatic cartography and deterritorialize on a virtual plane, referred to as a plane of consistency. Deterritorialization not only disrupts the assemblage but also reading, and reading the world. Reterritorialization is the effect or response to problems in life.

What is cartography (the conventional view)?

Cartography in the conventional way refers to maps designed to represent what is actually there, be it landscape such as forests, deserts, or subways systems for example. Cartography is the art of mapping that lends itself to describing closed spatial systems. Establishing boundaries or markers are characteristics of cartography. These are considered identity markers created for social, economic, political and historical reasons. These markers are fixed unless there is new information that requires a revision of the map.

What does cartography involve? Here is a quote from the Canadian Cartography association (http:www.cca-acc.org/careers-3.asp):

> A basic decision has to be made about the study area and the subject matter. Data have to be obtained and evaluated, and if necessary processed. A scale has to be chosen, and possibly a map projection (a mathematical transformation that flattens out the curved surface of the earth, necessary for maps of high accuracy or large areas). Decisions have to be made about generalization, the process whereby unnecessary detail (for instance, small settlements or minor sinuosities in stream) is omitted in order to keep the map clear and uncluttered. In addition, a host of design choices is required, such as shapes, sizes and colors of symbols, the sizes and styles of lettering, and the overall layout of the map (the positioning of the title, legend, scale bar and so on). Frequently these things are set down in a detailed list of specification, or are incorporated into a compilation, a preliminary drawn map that serves as a guide for the actual final process.

Accordingly, it is decided *a priori* what the area is to be studied. Data is empirically gathered and assessed for its reliability and validity. Decisions are made about the information to be included on the map. The criteria for including information are based on 'keeping the map clear and uncluttered'. Framed this way, cartography can been seen in relation to literacy education as the ways in which curriculum may be developed for universal application with particular content included, particular outcomes clearly defined, and criteria for assessment defined in advance of any encounter with the learner. A predetermined path to successful literacy learning becomes established. What does this kind of curricular cartography for literacy education mean for individual learners, for people?

Quite often, a bounded territory represented by a map is an empirical documented display that defines a people. Is it possible to say that a territory affirms a people? For a human to say that he or she is Talantian, for example, is to assume that the person is born in a modern-day imaginary territory, one possibly drawn by political and governmental institutions, called Talantia. Talantia was built on kingdoms based on tribal regions.

Tribes were differentiated by particular cloths or fabrics. From a Deleuzian perspective, there were colors and fabrics that then began to be used by tribes. There was an investment of different tribes in the combinations of different colors and fabrics. These colors and fabrics transformed into overcoding signifiers. They began to stand in lieu of a particular tribe or ruled over Talantia. This is how territorializations happen in conventional cartography. In addition, each tribe invests in some geographic formation that then is elevated to a territory associated with that tribe. These investments produce an assemblage of bodies that then become identified as Talantia. Individuals within the assemblage become Talantian.

However, naming a fixed territory Talantia masks the tribal aspects and the accompanying territories or regions upon which Talantia is constituted. There are also social and cultural elements that are part of a territory to which a person relates.[1] Yet this seems like a generalization, dismissing details. The importance of having maps that draw out territories seems to derive from the need to order (classify and categorize) the world, what is included and what is excluded according to certain criteria. Maps and territories are efficient in this regard. In education a closed system operates in such areas as exceptionalities and inclusive education: what maps are drawn up? What are the criteria established *a priori*? They must meet the criterion of a closed system, 'omitting unnecessary detail'. Such systems are constituted as a fixed territory (TP). Deleuze and Guattari would consider this approach to cartography as tracings or decalcomania (TP).

In education, take the example of school achievement. The students have participated in various performance assessments. The participants rally around the results and these results designate the school and as a lighthouse school[2] (schools that have displayed superior performance in academic achievement). The school has been territorialized as a lighthouse school. While assessments were performed, it was not pre-given that this school was a lighthouse school.

What about non-humans? Territories exist for them as well. They are created sometimes by man, at other times by nature and sometimes by themselves. What would the mappings look like? How would they function? Take communities of bodies (human and non-human) that live, for instance, in rain forests unknown to the rest of the world. How are their territories constituted? Animals have territories. Plants have territories as well.[3] Could the mappings or cartography of these territories be nomadic?

In sum, conventional cartography relates to an arborescent tracing/ cartography and is a fixed territory. In a similar way, so is identity, fixed and operating within a closed system. Deleuze and Guattari (TP) in line with the notion of an open system would acknowledge the necessity for deterritorializations (lines of flight) as part of a rhizomatic cartography. The lines of flight are characteristic of a rhizome.

What is cartography (Deleuze and Guattari)?

The concept of maps as representation of a closed system conceived by man did not appeal to Deleuze and Guattari. Rather, they were interested in open systems and trajectories and becomings in relation to each other. '… Becomings belong to geography, they are orientations, directions, entries and exits' (NG: 2).

Mapping that composes us, that is non-linear lines, is of tremendous significance to a Deleuzian ontology of difference. There are many lines (lines of flight, molar and molecular lines) that pass though life. Deleuze and Guattari saw the potential in rhizomatic cartography as an open system. A rhizomatic cartography consists of lines of flight which intersect and disrupt molar lines and possibly molecular lines[4] thereby deterritorializing and reterritorializing.

The following quote from Deleuze and Guattari is poignant: 'It is an affair of cartography. They compose us, as they compose our map. They transform themselves and may even cross over into one another. Rhizome' (TP: p. 202). What are 'they'? The concept of the rhizome is a valuable component of MLT (Masny, 2009b). First though, what is a rhizome (TP)?

> A rhizome as subterranean stem is absolutely different from roots and radicals. Bulbs and tubers are rhizomes (p. 6) … Any point of a rhizome can be connected to anything other, and must be … A rhizome continuously establishes connections between semiotic chains, organizations of power, and circumstances relative to the arts, sciences, and social struggles: (p. 7). There are no points or positions in a rhizome, such as those found in a structure, tree, or root. There are only lines. (p. 8)

Multiplicities are rhizomatic and flat (non-hierarchical). Deleuze and Guattari propose *a plane of consistency* of multiplicities.

> Multiplicities are defined by the line of flight or deterritorialization according to which they change in nature and connect with other multiplicities … A rhizome may be broken, shattered at a given spot, but it will start up again on one of its old lines, or on new lines. … Every rhizome contains lines of segmentarity according to which it is stratified, territorialized, organized, signified, and attributed, etc., as well as lines of deterritorialization down which it constantly flees. There is a rupture in the rhizome whenever segmentary lines explode into a line of flight, but the line of flight is part of the rhizome. (p. 9)

> The rhizome is a *map and not a tracing*. … The map is entirely oriented toward experimentation in contact with the real. … The map constructs the unconscious … The map is open and connectable in all of its

dimensions … It can be drawn on a wall, conceived of as a work of art, constructed as a political action or as a meditation …

Perhaps one of the most important characteristics of the rhizome is that it always has multiple entryways. (p. 12)

As we will see in the subsequent section, the concept of cartography has important implications for the way literacy is conceived and how literacy education may be transformed.

Map and tracing: 'Putting the tracing back on the map'

A map refers to a rhizome, lines of flight, a deterritorialization. A tracing refers to a territory and reterritorialization, lines of segmentarity, molar. The relation between a map and a tracing is close. Deterritorialization ruptures/disturbs territories by shooting lines of flight through the tracing, the territory, lines of segmentarity. The process involves blowing apart the tracing and turning it into a map. Once there is derritorialization, the map turns into a tracing and reterritorialization happens with lines of segmentarity that segment and overcode. A tracing (territory) is arborescent. It is about determinacy, representation, and hierarchy positioning one territory over another. The relationship between a map and a tracing is that of a discourse not about binaries. It is not about tracings or maps. Rather it is about rhizomes and trees, maps and tracings, lines of flight and lines of segmentarity, multiple and multilayered. 'This is not a dualism, it is paradoxical forces at work together in an assemblage' (TP). 'If it is true that it is of the essence of the map or rhizome to have multiple entryways, then it is plausible that one could even enter them through tracings or the root-tree, assuming the necessary precautions are taken. Thus, there are very diverse map-tracing, rhizome-root assemblages, with variable coefficients of deterritorialization. There exist tree or root structures in rhizomes; conversely, a tree branch or root division may begin to burgeon into a rhizome' (TP: p. 15). The rhizome is always in motion, constantly transforming.

Accordingly, what is of interest is the rhizomatic map and the arborescent tracings which make up segmentary lines (rigid lines or territories) that lines of flight disrupt and deterritorialize on a plane of immanence,[5] and becoming that transforms reading, reading the world and self as texts. Each time it is different. What once was could be no longer.

In sum, tracings are arborescent, operate within a closed system and constituted by segmentary lines. Rhizomatic mapping with lines of flight brings about different ways of thinking and reading. However, rhizomatic mapping cannot happen without lines of segmentarity as well. Otherwise, cartography would operate in perpetual deterritorialization and that would destabilize an open system. Rhizomatic cartography and becomings offer potential for creativity. Just as a line of flight causes a concept to reterritorialize it might do so creating trees and root; the converse is also possible: a territory deterritorializes and a rhizome comes through the tree:

> If it is true that it is of the essence of the map or rhizome to have multiple entryways, then it is plausible that one could even enter them through tracings or the root-tree, assuming the necessary precautions are taken. Thus, there are very diverse map-tracing, rhizome-root assemblages, with variable coefficients of deterritorialization. There exist tree or root structures in rhizomes; conversely, a tree branch or root division may begin to burgeon into a rhizome. (TP: p. 14)

However, before producing rhizomatic maps in relation to multiple literacies, the next section explores ways in which literacies in the received (humanist and modern) view are considered arborescent overcoded territories.

Knowledge about cartography and literacies

The concern of this chapter is about map and tracing. This entry focuses mainly on the tracing where models and theories are arborescent in nature because of the ontological stance and epistemological stance of these models and theories relying on the centered subject, representation and fixed knowledge (determinacy). In other words, the research presented in this section deals with transcendent empiricism which is different from what Deleuze and Guattari called transcendental empiricism, which will be elaborated in the next section of this chapter, entitled Multiple literacies: a Deleuzian perspective. Transcendent empiricism is concerned with knowing the world directly as it is given, or experienced. It emphasizes the centered subject in that the data collected is grounded in the subject. It is the subject who does. This approach to research is foundational in that the research seeks to discover essences or origins that contribute to the interpretations of data as findings or results. Moreover, in the data analysis, the notion of representation allows for analyzing the data to determine what it represents and this is performed by way of interpretation of the data, again the centered subject (the researcher) becoming the voice of the data, in which case it is reading the data and discovering truth(s) through interpretations. In transcendent empiricism, there is world out there to be discovered and experienced. This view of research involving transcendent empiricism is a backdrop to the presentation of literacy research.

What is literacy? It can be viewed within an autonomous model or an ideological model (Street, 1984). As autonomous, literacy has a fixed determinate definition and has universal truth-value applied across and within disciplines. Many studies in applied linguistics (Serrano and Howard,

2007), and psycholinguistics (Bialystok, 2007), for instance, view literacy as the ability to read, write and process information. Literacy in this context gives primacy to the printed text often referred to as school-based literacy. It is interesting to note that until recently, and in some fields still, reading has been the term to denote a skill; it was a technical approach. Literacy or reading is still connected to the binary world in terms of literate/illiterate. It is a concept steeped in postpositivism which derives its traditions from the natural sciences with its desires for replication, laboratory-like controls, generalizeable results and universal appeal (Gort, 2006). It is not uncommon for meta-analyses on literacy research (Juzwik *et al.*, 2006) to be conducted in order to develop a meta-narrative on what literacy is.[6]

Within an ideological model, school-based literacy became unhinged by pointing out that there is more to literacy than what happens with the printed text in the classroom. In New Literacy Studies (NLS), literacy became socially, culturally, and politically situated in time and place (Barton *et al.*, 2000). Literacy and oral traditions were mixed and not treated as distinctly separate (Stephens, 2000). In addition, literacy has come to be regarded in terms of multiplicities involving local meanings of literacy. Applying the term 'multiple' signals a greater openness to more social and value-laden notions of literacy (Lankshear and McLaren, 1993; Luke, 1991, 2003). Literacies as meaning-making and different ways of knowing are situated in context (Gee, 1990). The NLS range across paradigms informed by sociocultural perspectives, but also crossing over into the paradigmatic realms of constructivisms and critical theory. It is not uncommon to see such NLS theoretically grounded in the work of Vygotsky, Bakhtin, and Freire (e.g. Dagenais *et al.*, 2006; Dyson, 2003, 2005). McCaffrey (2005), for instance, stemming from experiences in Guinea, Sierra Leone and South Sudan, explores ways in which the methodology and modalities of community-based participatory literacy interrelate and combine with those of conflict resolution and peacebuilding. The three projects described integrated literacy, numeracy, conflict resolution, peacebuilding, and community development through activities such as: discussions, role play, mapping, transect walks, interviews, conflict and seasonal calendars, timeline construction (pre-conflict, conflict, post-conflict), and 'real-world' numeracy activities ranging from 'counting the number of plots or doors required, to assessing agricultural yields, measuring areas and calculating quantities of building materials' (2005: p. 458). While literacy activities included written and oral modes, ultimately they tended to return to 'print-based' literacies; texts (which sometimes included drawings) were inscribed in the dirt with a stick and then transferred to paper. The study is firmly situated within the NLS tradition with the focus on the social situatedness of literacy practices (citing Barton and Hamilton's *Local Literacies*, and Street). As well, there is a strong emphasis on 'transformative models of literacy' (citing Freire's [2000] seminal *Pedagogy of the Oppressed*) aimed at adult literacy and community development. In addition, the approaches advocated are informed by 'the humanist model [which] stresses the autonomy, agency and interaction of the learner with the environment' (McCaffrey 2005: p. 451). Moreover, there are literacy studies concerned with contesting relations of power by problematizing what counts as literacy, which literacy dominates and which ones are marginalized or disenfranchised (Masny and Ghahremani-Ghajar, 1999; Street, 2003). Multiliteracies created by the New London Group took on significant importance starting in the late 1990s (The New London Group, 1996; Cope and Kalantzis, 2009). Multiliteracies called for a different perspective on literacy that takes into account cultural and linguistic diversity and multimodality. Strangely, Multiliteracies has come to be equated with technology. However, Multiliteracies include oral, written, and gestural. Cope and Kalantzis (2009) cite the following example:

> Marion Drew and Kathleen Wemmer's work with first-year audiology students had the students studying textbooks and visiting local sangomas (traditional doctors). Joni Brenner and David Andrew based their class assignments for visual literacy students on local craft forms, such as the Minceka, a traditional cloth worn by women in the Limpopo province. (p. 189)

As Cope and Kalantzis (2009) state:

> Traditionally, literacy teaching has confined itself to the forms of written language. The new media mix modes more powerfully than was culturally the norm and even technically possible in the earlier modernity that was dominated by the book and the printed page. Through the theorizations and curriculum experimentations of the past decade and a half, we have reconfigured the range of possible modalities. We have separated written and oral language as fundamentally different modes (Kress, 2003), added a tactile mode and redefined the contents and scope of the other modes. (p. 178)

In another example, Cumming-Potvin (2007) published an Australian qualitative case study of a grade-7 boy's literacy identity and Multiliteracies development (at home and school) from a social constructivist perspective on learning. The analysis included a Multiliteracies framework, that is, multimodal texts (especially computer and technology-based are highlighted), situated practice, overt instruction, critical framing, transformative practice, and design – cornerstones of Multiliteracies (The New London Group, 1996; Cope and Kalantzis, 2009).

Emerging new spaces for literacy was the role of digital technology and a different approach called New Literacies (Lankshear and Knobel, 2003) was created. Morgan (2010) identifies 'some current elaborations on the theme of participation and digital literacy in order to open further debate on the relationship between interaction, collaboration and learning in online environments'. Motivated by an interest in using new technologies in the context of formal learning, the author draws on in-school and out-of-school work in Web 2.0 spaces. This work is inflected by the New Literacies approach (Lankshear and Knobel, 2008). Merchant's study (2009) focuses on the experience of introducing blogs in an English literature alternative education classroom, the ways in which students reconstructed the blog into a third space for identity construction, and the effects of student online literacies in the classroom. Merchant is particularly interested in the relationship between participation, learning, and digital literacies in Web 2.0 spaces. Citing Lankshear and Knobel's work on new literacies as well as Gee's work on video games and literacy learning, he begins by indexing four features of Web 2.0 spaces: presence, modification, user-generated content, and social participation. These features presume a centered subject is in control as the subject embraces more fluid conceptualizations of identity (e.g. avatars). Merchant's conceptualizations of knowledge move away from 'hierarchically organized forms of knowledge that are somehow to be transferred to individual learners' (2009: p. 117) towards knowledge as socially constructed through participation in Web 2.0 communities and online cultures. Several examples from around the world are offered in relation to students' class blogging. In each case, these students are using New Literacies 'to participate in a digitally mediated culture as they become involved in online communicative interaction in a shared space related to a joint endeavour' (p. 112).

In sum, these approaches to literacies call upon different theoretical frameworks: social constructivism (Vygotsky), critical pedagogy (Freire, Giroux, and Bourdieu). To what extent have we moved away from the binary world of literate/illiterate? What is the role of subjectivity? In most cases, the Cartesian subject is at the center. A consequence of the centered subject is the notion of reader as *agent* of meaning-making. Agency is particularly evident in New Literacy Studies that focus on what people do (agency) with literacy practices and also Multiliteracies where people are agentive designers of social futures. These approaches to literacies research are also reviewed in Masny and Waterhouse (2011).

New Literacy Studies (NLS) and Multiliteracies are predominantly connected with tree-tracing, that is, the application of a fixed theory. 'All of tree logic is a logic of tracing and reproduction. It consists of tracing, on the basis of an overcoding structure or supporting axis, something that comes ready-made. The tree articulates and hierarchizes tracings ...' (TP: pp. 12–15). It is overcoded because it has been taken up by institutions and applied in determinate ways such as in school curriculum and policy. However, a theory can deterritorialize. One possible example is the deter-ritorialization of the 1996 version of Multiliteracies as some conceptual shifting in the 2009 version of Multiliteracies has taken place. Cope and Kalantizis see three key shifts, as follows:

Since the publication of the initial Multiliteracies paper, we have attempted to articulate further and to apply the pedagogy of design and multimodality. Since that time, our tone and emphasis have changed. Three major innovations over that time have been to focus less on the teachable specificities of meaning-system and more on the heuristics of learners' discovering specificities amongst the enormously varied field of possibly-relevant texts; to develop a theory of semiotic transformation as a theory of learning itself; and to reconfigure the modalities of multi-modality. (Cope and Kalantzis: p. 174)

It could be conceivable that this shift is a case of 'the tracing should always be put back on the map' for disruption to happen. In addition to the shift, Cope and Kalantzis acknowledge that the outcomes of 'a pedagogy of multi-literacies as design' are not guaranteed. They don't know how multiliteracies get taken up; how transformations happen. They use the term 'agnostic' in the quote below to express this. Nevertheless, Cope and Kalantzis maintain a controlling subject that makes 'choices' and 'represents'.

In a pedagogy of multiliteracies, all forms of representation, including language, should be regarded as dynamic processes of transformation rather than processes of reproduction. (Cope and Kalantzis: p. 175)

However ...

A pedagogy of multiliteracies can be agnostic about the stance learners and teachers may wish to take in relation to changing social conditions. For example, they might take the route of compliance or that of critique. If they take the former route, education will help them develop capacities that will enable them to access the new economy and share in its benefits. Or they may reject its values and their consequences in the name of an emancipatory view of education's possibilities. Whichever stance they take, their choices will be more explicit and open to scrutiny. (p. 174)

As well, there are teachers in classrooms and researchers, for example, that plug into NLS or Multiliteracies when teaching-as-event or research-as-event effects a deterritorialization. One such instance is that of Maybin (2007). According to Maybin, NLS has a tendency to dichotomize literacy in terms of school and home and qualifies these literacy practices as schooled and vernacular respectively. This perspective is deterritorialized by what Maybin calls the messy world of literacies-in-practice in which official and unofficial literacies regularly appear heterogeneously. This can be a kind of mapping that might effect a becoming for NLS.

In sum, the contributions from NLS, Multiliteracies and New Literacies have been significant in providing alternate avenues for the conceptual-ization, teaching and learning within an ideological model of literacies.

They differ, however, from what a Deleuzian perspective could offer. In NLS, for example, literacy practices are linked to identity. Multiliteracies are still concerned with representation, and both NLS and Multiliteracies consider a primary role for the centered subject.[7]

Up to now, literacy practiced within institutions is a static and arborescent concept and considered an overcoded social practice:

> Once a rhizome has been obstructed, arborified, it's all over, no desire stirs; for it is always by rhizome that desire moves and produces. Whenever desire climbs a tree, internal repercussions trip it up and it falls to its death; the rhizome, on the other hand, acts on desire by external, productive outgrowths. That is why it is so important to try the other, reverse but nonsymmetrical, operation. Plug the tracings back into the map, connect the roots or trees back up with a rhizome. (TP: p. 14)

Institutionalized literacy practices are fixed in the way literacy is defined. Literacy has categories to organize life. Categories within literacy make literacy a candidate of accountability (cf. OECD, 2009).

In this context, literacies are tracings and part of a closed system. To consider literacies as rhizomatic, literacies are conceptualized differently. They are processes in reading, reading the world and self. Literacies relate to becoming, to lines of flight that disrupt rigid arborescent lines. In order for becoming to happen, rhizomatic cartography operates in an open system where the outcome is unpredictable. The next entry focuses on rhizomatic cartographies and multiple literacies.

Multiple literacies: a Deleuzian perspective

In the previous entry, literacy as well as literacies was produced within a paradigm called transcendent empiricism. It is different from what Deleuze and Guattari refer to as transcendental empiricism.

Transcendental empiricism

Transcendental empiricism (TE) as conceived by Deleuze was vital to his perspective on life as becoming and to the place of experience in life, and therefore critically relates to the mapping of multiple literacies. His approach departs from those of other philosophers. First, experience is not an event ascribed to the autonomous thinking subject, which means that experience is not grounded in the individual. Experience is conceived in terms of the thought of an experience. In what follows are key words that characterize TE. These keys words help us understand how experiences of mapping literacies are multiple, and non-linear. The characteristics of Deleuzian transcendental empiricism are that it is:

1 Anti-representational;
2 Interpretosis (non-interpretation);
3 Involves 'decentered subject' and
4 Is about immanence.

In Deleuze's conceptualization of transcendental empiricism, the premise is that experience is anti-foundational. TE is not interested in the autonomous thinking subject that grounds experience through explanation. The subject is decentered in that the subject becomes part of an assemblage. The reading that goes on is a result of an assemblage. The experience of life is about becoming. Representation limits experience to the world as we know it – and not as a world that could be. The act of representation also considers that there is an object present, and that it has another meaning. An example is looking for meaning in a piece of abstract art (what does it represent? Or giving it a meaning) instead of looking at the painting purely in terms of the power of affect. Representation and interpretation are closely linked. Looking for meaning in the artwork is also seeking an interpretation. Deleuze refers to interpretation as an illness, interpretosis (there is more on this notion in Chapter Four, *What is reading?*). Deleuze is interested in what a thing does and therefore proposes experimentation. To experiment is to create. It is from a multiplicity of experiences that the human and non-human are effected. When considering maximizing life to its potential, calling for experimentation and creation, Deleuze appeals to immanence. Immanence refers to the *thought of* ... Immanence is set off at the moment a disruption happens. What will happen cannot be predicted. For example, in cinema, the scene of a car rapidly driving down a narrow wet road might bring on the thought of an accident, the thought of a nearby final destination around the corner, the thought of ... an experience. What happens next is an actualization whereby the film provides one response to that scene. Immanence allows thinking to take off and it is from experiences of becoming that thinking happens.

Ontology of difference

Deleuze was interested in doing philosophy that would be concerned with how one lives (ontology or the nature of being). It is not surprising, since experience, experiment, concept creation and life were key concepts for Deleuze and Guattari. Deleuzian ontology, according to May (2005), is about concepts of difference. The world according to Deleuze is virtual and actual. In the virtual, the world is made up of multiple prepersonal forces (entities) that are then actualized according to a particular space and time. The premise is that the world is complex and made up of multiple free-flowing forces and it is from these prepersonal unattached forces that actualization happens. For example, the disruption of a concept of literacy calls upon a becoming in the virtual, drawing on the potential of what literacy could be and not knowing in advance how it will actualize until a sense of literacy actualizes in a particular space and time in which it operates. Chapter Four refers to reading that disrupts, deterritorializes in order to open up potentials for what reading might be in a particular situation.

The important ontological question of how one might live is in relation to difference. There is a constant flow of forces between the virtual and the actual. There is the appearance of repetition yet in the movement between the virtual and actual, there is the 'in-between-ness' that characterizes becoming. Becoming transforms each time and therefore a territory can never be the same. Difference relates to how one might live. Multiple Literacies and creating concepts such as reading, reading the world and self provides opportunities for expanding our lives beyond what is to what they could be.

Deleuzian characteristics of Transcendental Empiricism (summary)

- Anti-representational
- Interpretosis
- Decentered subject
- Immanence: virtual, actual, prepersonal, and
- Difference

An important characteristic of transcendental empiricism is its relation to that of the assemblage of whom the subject is a part and that it is from encounters within the assemblage that transformations happen. It is an event; the change brings on new paths. In addition, these transformations cannot be predicted *a priori* because as they happen they do so in an untimely way. You cannot predict what will happen because of immanence, another characteristic of transcendental empiricism. Immanence is a creative process that happens when encounters within the assemblage disrupt the assemblage and it is the *thought of* what might happen next that is immanent to the event. These transformations happen when lines of flight deterritorialize segmentary lines familiar with arborescent tracings. However, if you put the tracing on the map, then transformations happen. What this process says is that it is not a rhizome or tree, not a map or tracing. Dualisms are not part of the equation. In the studies that follow, it is not a question of tree or rhizome. It is both in variation that matters:

> The important point is that the root-tree and canal-rhizome are not two opposed models: the first operates as a transcendent model and tracing, even if it engenders its own escapes; the second operates as an immanent process that overturns the model and outlines a map. (TP: p. 20)

A number of scholars are engaging these kinds of experimentations with Deleuzian perspectives within education (cf. Semetsky, 2008). Here I foreground instances from literacies research in particular. Dufresne (2006) creates cartographies of multiple literacies by exploring literacies as processes (not pre-established endpoints) through the lens of Deleuzian–Guattarian rhizoanalysis. Her cartographies enable a shift away from conventional views of literacy still informing school practices. Institutionalized concepts of literacy prevail as segmentarity lines. Following Deleuze and Guattari, Dufresne asserts that 'The subject is effected from experience. ... Experience is a group of sensations composed of percepts and affects' (2006: p. 348). By considering the affects at work in the classroom interactions between native English speaking students and French Immersion teachers during French second language literacies lessons, she sheds light on the epistemological aspects of literacies and language learning. Bringing in the notion of belief systems, that is worldviews, she shows how the collision of worldviews (the teacher's and the student's) can be one effect of literacies learning which in turn may produce resistance to new knowledge, resistance to change, in short, resistance to learning. To design rhizomatous cartography, Dufresne created the concept of Telling Maps, a process. From experience within a system that is multi-layered, non-linear, and non-determinate and operating in a specific time and space, connections are made and transformations happen. Dufresne works with the concept of a fractal in which iterations of experience are effected and each iteration is different each time. Given the necessarily linear nature of the written form of reporting data, telling maps take the shape of assembled data bits on a page which brings them into a rhizoanalytic relation where reading data texts intensively and immanently enables the production of new kinds of ideas and/or thinking. In other words, telling maps create an assemblage which produces thought.

In his study of power and literacies in Christian faith-based education space (school and museum sites), Eakle (2007) turns his attention to multiplicity – 'multiple practices, strategies, and concepts' (p. 472) – to disrupt given territories of literacies research. Eakle acknowledges that 'the occidental Cartesian concept involving a split between human subject and object has influenced how many people [including literacies researchers arguably] transact with the world' (p. 475). However, Eakle operates in a different mode, disrupting the autonomous Cartesian subject through Deleuze and Guattari's concepts of desiring machines, space, power, and collectives. Analysis of literacies spaces and the lines of power relations moving through them involve what Eakle calls mapping. Mapping entails assembling 'texts as an affirmation of the possible, of accidents, and of unpredictability' (p. 482). These assemblages are expressed in dramatizations: scripted scenes with blocking notes. This mode of reporting research (as mapping) offers an alternative to what has been typical of the literacies field.

Leander and Rowe (2006) focus their attention on the common literacy practice of the student presentation in high school; however, they disrupt and map this territory differently by taking seriously the complexity of the classroom space as an open system. They argue that 'even a cursory review of some of the complexities of student presentations reveal that they are composed of diverse types of texts, objects, and bodies and that power and meaning within them are stretched across diverse media, performers, and audience members' (2006: p. 428). Thus, Leander and Rowe do not view literacies as the cognitive activity of a single individual, but rather they look at the potentially transformative, affective forces at work within an assemblage that is the event by drawing on Deleuzian–Guattarian concepts: collective expressions of enunciation (order-words, social processes that influence what is said) and machinic assemblages of bodies (social, human and non-human bodies come together and the relations between them in an assemblage; elaborated in Chapter Five, *Cartographies of talking groups*). In their rhizomatic analysis of student presentations as performance, they give up on ideas of interpretation 'as reading for meaning' (p. 429) and instead 'follow the emergence of relations and differences by mapping performances-in-motion' (p. 429).

Masny (2009b) plugs into Multiple Literacies Theory (MLT), a theory-practice which engages Deleuzian–Guattarian concepts and engages in concept creation to see how multiple literacies may be de/reterritorialized, mapped differently as processes of becoming. A case study of a multilingual child (Spanish–French–English) is presented as a series of rhizoanalytic vignettes. Writing becomes art in connection with the concept of affect and aesthetics. Invented words are viewed as instances of creativity (forming novel connections across languages) that disrupt language territories, and the child's conceptualization of 'extraterrestrials' (those words that do not follow the rules of their language). These vignettes become a way to understand perceptions of competing writing systems. The cartographies produced unsettle the privileged position of school-based ways of being literate and attend to the untimely effects of literacies as processes of becoming.

Waterhouse (2011a) foregrounds the Deleuzian–Guattarian concept of becoming to disrupt received conceptualizations of what literacies and language learning produce within a federally funded programme to teach English to adult newcomers to Canada. She focuses on how a multitude of transformations take place – through reading, reading the world and self – in ways that cannot be contained by the mandated outcomes of the language instruction program and its curriculum. Waterhouse deploys diagrammatic assemblages to resist representing data in terms of what literacies mean or how they might develop. Instead, the diagrammatic assemblages attempt to 'maintain a fluid thinking space' (2011a: p. 185) by mapping the connections and untimely transformations that are produced by events in the language classroom.

Cartographies in the form of vignettes can be visually presented. Waterhouse (2011a, 2011b), in a study of multiple literacies as a means to explore peace education in an immigrant English-as-a-Second-Language classroom, deploys the rhizome to analyze how teachers, adults, and the curriculum as part of an assemblage reconfigure as moments rupture and Waterhouse maps lines of flight. Rhizoanalytic cartographies highlight the ruptures when the government policy of multiculturalism is deterritorialized and immigrant lives transform. In the Figure 2.1, Waterhouse, based on a rhizoanalysis of her 'data', arrives at five rhizomatic cartographies which she renders in the following visual way:

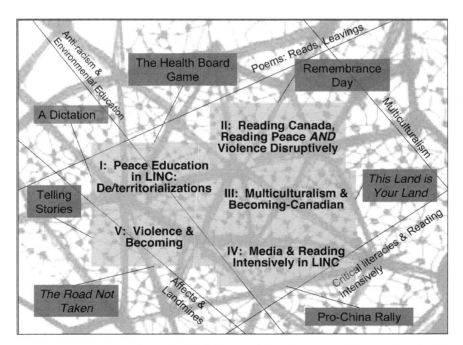

Figure 2.1 Five cartographies of multiple literacies (Waterhouse, 2011b). Reproduced with permission of the author.

As for the elements that move around and shoot through the five cartographies … The shaded boxes are titles relating to empirical 'transgressive data', that is, classroom events observed and/or discussed during the research. For example, Cartography V connected the classroom practice of students 'telling stories' (about the circumstances of their coming to Canada) and the practice of reading the Robert Frost poem 'The Road Not Taken' as one teacher's way to engage her students in conversations about homesickness and feelings of regret post-immigration.

In sum, these studies provide avenues for exploring cartographies of literacies in multitudinous ways. In a way rhizoanalysis might be considered a methodology in that a methodology puts forward a paradigm that frames the research questions and the manner in which data are treated. Rhizoanalysis refers to a Deleuzian-Guattarian paradigm with its adherence to transcendental empiricism. However, because of transcendental empiricism, methodology cannot have the same conceptual lens when it is steeped in transcendent empiricism. The latter is a conventional view in which the methodology involves a paradigm that is subject-centered, representational and foundational. Methodology is a territory which is deterritorialized and reterritorialized as transcendental empirical rhizoanalysis. In addition, methodology and method or technique for collecting and analysing data go hand in hand. Rhizoanalysis is a non-method. The studies presented in this section point to as many ways of doing rhizoanalysis as there are studies using rhizoanalysis. Rhizoanalysis is a non-method that is transgressive, involves immanence, assemblages and a decentered subject as part of the assemblage.

Vignettes

Cartography is to map out, mapping out different literacies which may be considered as multiple yet one, that is the nature of the rhizome. There is no endorsement of the type of silo effect that has permeated the field of literacies: computer literacy, math literacy, finance literacy, etc. This silo effect tends to have an arborescent, linear perspective.

> … We're tired of trees. We should stop believing in trees, roots, and radicles. They've made us suffer too much. All of arborescent culture is founded on them, from biology to linguistics. Nothing is beautiful or loving or political aside from underground stems and aerial roots, adventitious growths and rhizomes. (TP: p. 15)

Despite the impact/influence of arborescent linear literacy/literacies, the concept of multiple literacies (MLT, Masny 2006) is to conceptualize multiple literacies rhizomatically. Accordingly, rhizomatic cartography integrates lines of flight/becomings that destabilize arborescent linear systems in order to reveal an open system complex and multi-layered.

'To be rhizomorphous is to produce stems and filaments that seem to be roots, or better yet connect with them by penetrating the trunk, but put them to strange new uses' (TP: p. 15). In other words, to put literacies to new uses in terms of how literacies function and what they produce. Literacies – that is, reading – reading the world and self, produce rhizomatically in unpredictable ways. Reading refers to a combination of assemblages (experiences) in life that happen to us and impact how reading goes on. Reading is disruptive and brings on the *thought of* what could happen possibly next. For example, when reading a novel or seeing a film, an image presents itself which leads to reading the scene in a singular way based on experiences in life and a reading of what could possibly happen and relate that possibility to one's own life. In the end, a cartography is mapped out, a rhizome. At that moment, a territory explodes with a line of flight shooting through a territory deterritorializing lines of segmentarity. This is what multiple literacies do (Masny, 2009a).

When reading, reading the world and self happens, bodies as territories interact with other bodies in relation with the power to affect and be affected. When territories explode, lines of flight deterritorialize territories on a plane of immanence and reterritorialize as a different territory. 'We know nothing about a body until we know what it can do, in other words, what its affects are, how they can or cannot enter into composition with other affects, with the affects of another body, either to destroy that body or to be destroyed by it, either to exchange actions and passions with it or to join with it in composing a more powerful body' (TP: p. 257; see also FB: pp. 39–41). Literacies do not have an end/outcome in itself precisely because life is not something personal. The only aim of literacies is life, through the combinations it draws (NG).

Rhizomatous cartography/mapping is taken up in the form of vignettes that attempt to disrupt overcoded literacies by introducing the role of desire in the rhizome and the productive power of affect. The vignettes are part of a two-year longitudinal research study exploring multilingual children's learning of writing simultaneously. The five participants, aged between five and seven years old, were filmed in class (language arts, mathematics, science, and social sciences), at home (meals, homework, reading, recreational time), and where applicable, in the day-care center (library, computer, games). Each filmed session was followed by an interview. In addition, each child was filmed participating in a mini-lesson in which she gave a lesson on how to write in the home language (Spanish, Mandarin, Afar, and English). Finally each child received a disposable camera and the child took pictures of people, places and things that were linked to her perspective of literacy (music, road signs, animals, flags, etc.). Each filmed session and the photo session were followed by an interview. Each of these activities happened twice during the school year.

Cristelle's grade 3 teacher, Mrs. Connor (year 2 of the study)

Cristelle lives in a predominantly English-speaking part of the city in the vicinity of hi-tech industry. Her mother's mother tongue is French, though she also grew up speaking English. She works as a civil servant with the federal government. Cristelle's father is a unilingual English speaker who works in the hi-tech sector. It was particularly important for the mother that Cristelle go to a nearby school where French is the sole language of instruction. Mrs. Conner, Cristelle's grade 3 teacher, is bilingual, French and English. Her first language is French and she came from Western Canada and settled in Ottawa because of a job opportunity for her husband. She had been teaching for eight years at the time she participated in the study.

> *Teacher:* Calligraphy seems to be less important according to the curriculum. I found that this year, there was not enough time to work on sentences. What is a sentence? To analyze it: subject–verb–object. We spent so much time on text genres. It is ridiculous to spend so much time on this in grade 3 when they can learn it later. They need the basics in writing. I am not satisfied. They mix up everything when it comes to sentence writing. I didn't have enough time. They also had to learn how to write a song, and do a poster. A poster to me is not about writing a text. There are few words. There are few sentences. This they can learn later when they have the basics in writing: Writing a sentence.

Could this be a territorialization of literacies? Mrs. Connor expresses a particular stance with respect to what literacies are about. What counts as writing? These discourses are set within particular structures of power as *pouvoir* in which literacy is a word-order. Moreover, there is the added thrust of institutional power when grade 3 teachers are preparing children for their first round of large-scale, province-wide standardized tests in reading and writing. Prior to assessment, teachers tend to set aside the official curriculum and pull out the unofficial curriculum with its complete focus on test-taking. What does this technology of state combined with reading, reading, reading the world and self produce? In the next vignette, the cartography is also that of a tracing with its arborescent logic.

Cristelle in the classroom (year 2 of the study)

> *Researcher:* When do you do your drawings?
> *Cristelle:* When I am in my house.
> *R:* Yes, at the house? And anywhere else?
> *Cr:* Um, in the class.

R: You draw in the class?

Cr: Humm. (agreeing)

R: Yes? And, does Madame [teacher] say, 'Oh Cristelle, another
    beautiful drawing!' No? What does she say?

Cr: Um, 'It is not the time to draw.'

R: It is not the time to draw? It is the time for what?

Cr: Reading.

Putting the tracing back on the map as Deleuze and Guattari suggest would
involve a line of flight, a creative becoming that disrupts the tracing in an
untimely manner and in unpredictable ways as rhizomatic cartography.
In this vignette, would creativity become possible as a line of flight with
drawing? This becoming changes the assemblage as reading, reading the
world and self happens. The assemblage is transformed through a flow of
forces between actual and virtual in which there is a movement between
reading and drawing both virtual and actual. This repetition may occur and
each time it will be different.

In the first vignette, Cristelle's teacher would like to see a curriculum
that highlights the basics of writing. She dismisses writing songs and doing
posters as writing. By extension, doing stories in the manner Cristelle
produced in Figure 2.2 would probably not constitute writing. During the
two years of the study when she was seven and eight years old, Cristelle
liked to read, though perhaps not in class. At the daycare center after
school, when there was an activity linked to the school library, Cristelle
would select a cartoon book. With regard to writing, she often stated
that she did not like to write. The figure taken from year 1 below is her
response. Her drawing in class and the telling of the story of Anne and
Cristelle in the figure below are indicative perhaps of becomings happening
as the tracing of arborescent school ways of doing is put on the map with
its lines of flight that disrupt conventional reading and writing. In a way,
might Cristelle be happy at the *thought of* the teacher dismissing what the
assemblage (of which Cristelle is a part) produced as non-writing? Yet reterritorialization happens, as it appears to be a story of Anne and Cristelle in
a haunted castle. Both are described as bats, each having different qualities
(Anne is the inspector. In the first year of the study, Anne and Cristelle were
in the same class and worked together. When Cristelle would draw instead
of working on the exercise in question, Anne would often remind her to
focus on the task at hand.) In addition, the 'story' continues, as a third
figure later that day joins them for lunch and love is 'in the air'. Is this a
happy ending?

Translation: On the left side of the figure, Cristelle writes: 'Anne is a
very very bad bat. Cristelle is the most most gentle of bats'. In the castle
Cristelle draws a figure with the caption 'bad vampire'. At the bottom she
draws two figures and refers to Anne as the inspector. On the right side the
story continues, saying: 'the same day at noon'. There is a drawing of three

Figure 2.2 Cristelle tells a story of Anne and herself in a haunted castle.[8]

figures with a 'love line' drawn between the girl and the boy. At the bottom, once more there are drawings of Cristelle and Anne as bats. The 'haunted castle' text was created during an interview with both children after school at the daycare centre.

Estrella's mother (year 1 of the study)

In this vignette, the researcher sits down with Estrella and her mother to talk about the role of a parent in helping with school assignments at home. Estrella was born in Canada. Her mother came from Mexico and her father from a Canadian Portuguese-speaking family. When the family came to Ottawa, the father has accepted a job in the United States. Estrella spoke Spanish and Portuguese at home, French at school and English in the neighborhood. Estrella's mother wanted her daughter to attend a French school because what she would learn in terms of the structure of the French language was closest to Spanish.

> *Researcher:* She allows you to participate in reading, but does not allow you to participate in writing.
> *Mother:* Writing, no.
> *R:* Why is that?
> *M:* For now, before she would allow me, but now she's very particular. I think it's because Madame Matisse [Teacher] told them that they

have the right to be allowed for this time to let themselves go when they're exercising or writing this story.

R: And before when you were helping her write in Spanish, how would Estrella respond to this?

M: She would allow me to, she was receptive, and so she would allow me to correct her.

Estrella: But now no.

M: But now, you have to change because otherwise you won't learn to write properly, or read properly, so you have to. So usually it's during reading exercises that I can correct her. You know, I am not the best person to correct her, so I help her in French the best I can and in Spanish certainly I do it all the time. To correct her, but before I was able to correct her, during the writing process, that lately it's been two months or so that she doesn't let me to correct her.

R: Neither in French nor in Spanish.

M: Nor in Spanish and I think it was something to do with a technique that Madame Matisse wanted them just to, just let them feel free, so they just could write and worry about the little details later. And I think that's what stuck very much in their head, is that we'll write very well in *deuxième année* (grade 2), so I don't know what's gonna happen, I don't know if it's gonna turn into a disaster, but I think it's a good idea.

Estrella's mother is talking about Estrella's changing responses to her (the mother's) interventions/help in literacies activities. This assemblage – the mother, Estrella, the teacher (and her policies about letting the children 'have the right' to write freely without interference. There has been a shift: Estrella used to let her mother help, but now she won't. Estrella herself pipes up to confirm this and the mother responds that you have to correct your work to learn to write 'properly'. There are mother's beliefs about learning to write properly, and teacher and student beliefs about being free to write. There seems to be molar territorial forces at work (learn to write properly) as well as creative and affective forces (writing freely). From this assemblage, how are becomings affected? Are these transformations what are suggested when Estrella shifts from letting her mother help to refusing her participation in writing activities? To create a rhizomatous cartography, segmentarity lines are formed (writing properly) with lines of flight (writing freely) disrupting. In this process, transformations in the assemblage happen.

In sum, to put literacies to new uses as conceptual tools in relation to tracings and maps brings forth ways in which we can do literacies differently. Cartographies of literacies are made up of assemblages presented as tracings and maps, the latter involving rhizomatic (untimely) becoming. At that moment, a territory explodes with a line of flight deterritorializing the territory.

In the vignette with the teacher and the vignette with Cristelle, bodies interact with other bodies in relation with the power to affect and be affected. In the first vignette, the bodies of the human and non-human (curriculum) are in a relation of affect while, in the second vignette, it is the teacher and Cristelle. When territories explode, lines of flight deterritorialize territories on a plane of immanence and reterritorialize as a different territory. When territories disrupt and are disrupted, lines of flight and the directions they take are unpredictable and the reterritorialization as a different territory that happens is unknown until the bodies come together and relate to each in terms of the power to affect and be affected (TP; FB).

Reterritorialization

This chapter, indeed the entire book, is devoted to mapping and cartographies. These are concepts or territories related to geography. They are deterritorialized by Deleuze and Guattari in order to create concepts in life that are then reterritorialized differently. By bringing together philosophy and geography, Deleuze and Guattari have created a concept, geophilosophy. In turn, this chapter attempts to deterritorialize geophilosophy created by Deleuze and Guattari and reterritorialize the concept differently in the context of multiple literacies. The concepts that are the focus of this chapter are territorialization, deterritorialization and reterritorialization. Thus concepts such as text, discourse and reading are deterritorialized and reterritorialized differently each time within multiple literacies (MLT) in such a way that text, discourse, and reading relate to what they do, how they function, and and what they produce.

Moreover, rhizomatic cartography refers to open self-organizing systems. Just as a system is prepersonal, so is an assemblage, often referred to as a machinic assemblage. It actualizes and is comprised of assemblages: social, cultural, political, and economic, for example depending on the milieu in which the assemblage operates.[9] An assemblage deterritorializes (becomes prepersonal) and resonates with the flow of forces in the actual and virtual.

Now the relationship between earth and territory would look like this: While earth is virtual, it actualizes as a territory and the latter can deterritorialize on a plane of immanence, earth, and reterritorialize as 'the creation of a future new earth' (WP: p. 88). 'Becomings belong to geography, they are orientations, directions, entries and exits' (NG: p. 2).

Geophilosophy affords us different ways to talk about literacies in terms of territorialization, deterritorialization, and reterritorialization within open and self-organizing systems. Deterritorialization disrupts and creates lines of becoming, mapping the virtual. Emerging sense actualizes and reterritorializes. Mapping multiple literacies includes the virtual and the actual, and in this way maps complex and non-linear ways in which humans and non-humans participate in reading the world and self. Multiple literacies is a theory (MLT) in becoming and itself is constantly becoming (that is, transforming). It does so with the perspective that multiple literacies reterritorialize and tracings are formed – at which point the tracing is put on the map in order to deterritorialize. This process is desirable because it is only in this situation that change/transformation happens. Reterritorialization is a response to problems in life.

References

Barton, D. and Hamilton, M. (2005). Literacy, reification and the dynamics of social interaction. In D. Barton and K. Tusting (eds), *Beyond communities of practice: Language, power and social context* (pp. 14–35). Cambridge: Cambridge University Press.

Barton, D., Hamilton, M. and Ivanic, R. (eds) (2000). *Situated literacies: Reading and writing in context*. New York: Routledge.

Berninger, V. W., Abbott, R. D., Nagy, W. and Carlisle, J. (2010). Growth in phonological, orthographic, and morphological awareness in grades 1 to 6. *Journal of Psycholinguistic Research*, 39(2), 141–63.

Bialystok, E. (2007). Acquisition of literacy in bilingual children: A framework for research. *Language Learning*, 57(s1), 45–77.

Bonta, M. and Protevi, J. (2004). *Deleuze and geophilosophy: A guide and glossary*. Edinburgh: Edinburgh University Press.

Canadian Cartography Association (2009). *Cartography*. Available online at http://www.cca-acc.org/careers-3.asp (accessed January 21 2011).

Cardoso-Martins, C., Mesquita, T. C. L. and Ehri, L. (2011). Letter names and phonological awareness help children to learn letter-sound relations. *Journal of Experimental Child Psychology*, 109(1), 25–38.

Cope, B. and Kalantzis, M. (2009). "Multiliteracies": New literacies, new learning. *Pedagogies: An International Journal*, 4(3), 164–95.

Cumming-Potvin, W. (2007). Scaffolding, multiliteracies, and reading circles. *Canadian Journal of Education*, 30(2), 483–530.

Dagenais, D., Day, E. and Toohey, K. (2006). A multilingual child's literacy practices and contrasting identities in the figured worlds of French immersion classrooms. *International Journal of Bilingual Education and Bilingualism*, 9(2), 205–18.

Dufresne, T. (2006). Exploring the processes in becoming biliterate: the roles of resistance to learning and affect. *International Journal of Learning*, 12(8), 347–54.

Dyson, A. Haas. (2003). *The brothers and sisters learn to write: popular literacies in childhood and school cultures*. New York: Teachers College Press.

—(2005). Crafting "The Humble Prose of Living": rethinking oral/written relations in the echoes of the spoken word. *English Education*, 37(2), 149–64.

Eakle, A. J. (2007). Literacy spaces of a Christian faith-based school. *Reading Research Quarterly*, 42(4), 472–510.

Freire, P. (2000). *Pedagogy of the oppressed*. New York: Continuum.

Gee, J. P. (1990). *Social linguistics and literacies: Ideology in discourses*. New York: Falmer Press.

Gort, M. (2006). Strategic codeswitching, interliteracy, and other phenomena of emergent bilingual writing: Lessons from first grade dual language classrooms. *Journal of Early Childhood Literacy*, 6(3), 323–54.

Haas Dyson, A. (2008). Staying in the (curricular) lines: Practice constraints and possibilities in childhood writing. *Written Communication*, 25(1), 119–59.

Juzwik, M. M., Curcic, S., Wolbers, K., Moxley, K. D., Dimling, L. M. and Shankland, R. K. (2006). Writing into the 21st century: An overview of research on writing, 1999 to 2004. *Writing Communication*, 23(4), 451–76.

Kaufman, E. and Heller, K. J. (1998). *Deleuze and Guattari: Mappings in politics, philosophy and culture*. Minnesota: University of Minnesota Press.

Kress, G. (2003). *Literacy in the new media age*. New York: Routledge.

Lankshear, C. and Knobel, M. (eds) (2003). *New literacies: Changing knowledge and classroom learning*. Buckingham: Open University Press.

—(2008). *Digital literacies: Concepts, policies and practice*. New York: Peter Lang Publishing.

Lankshear, C. and McLaren, P. (1993). *Critical literacy: Politics, praxis, and the postmodern*. Albany: State University of New York Press.

Leander, K. M. and Rowe, D. W. (2006). Mapping literacy spaces in motion: A rhizomatic analysis of classroom literacy performance. *Reading Research Quarterly*, 44(4), 428–60.

Lotherington, H., Holland, M., Sotoudeh, S. and Zentana, M. (2008). Project-based community language learning: Three narratives of multilingual story-telling in early childhood education. *Canadian Modern Language Review*, 65(1), 125–45.

Luce-Kapler, R. and Klinger, D. A. (2005). Uneasy writing: The defining moments of high-stakes literacy testing. *Assessing Writing*, 10(3), 157–73.

Luke, A. (1991). Literacies as social practices. *English Education*, 23(3), 131–47.

—(2003). Literacy and the Other: A sociological approach to literacy research and policy in multilingual societies. *Reading Research Quarterly*, 38(1), 122–8.

Marshall, J. (2009). Divided against ourselves: Standards, assessments, and adolescent literacy. In L. Christenbury, R. Bomer and P. Smagorinsky (eds), *Handbook of adolescent literacy research* (pp. 113–25). New York: Guilford.

Masny, D. (2006). Learning and creative processes: A poststructural perspective on language and multiple literacies. *International Journal of Learning*, 12(5), 147–55.

—(2009a). *Bridging access, equity and quality: The case for multiple literacies*. Refereed paper presented at the National Conference of the Australian Association for the Teaching of English (AATE) for Teachers of English and Literacy, Wrest Point Conference Centre. Hobart, Tasmania. Available online at http://www.englishliteracyconference.com.au/files/documents/hobart/conferencePapers/refereed/MasnyDiana.pdf (accessed 17 January 2012).

—(2009b). Literacies as becoming: A child's conceptualizations of writing systems. In D. Masny and D. R. Cole, *Multiple literacies theory: A Deleuzian perspective* (pp. 13–30). Rotterdam: Sense Publishers.

—(2011). *International literacy testing: Powering the world*. Paper presented at the 4th International Deleuze Conference, Copenhagen, June.

Masny, D. and Ghahremani-Ghajar, S. (1999). Weaving multiple literacies: Somali children and their teachers in the context of school culture. *Language, Culture and Curriculum*, 12(1), 72–93.

Masny, D. and Waterhouse, M. (2011). Mapping territories and creating nomadic pathways with Multiple Literacies Theory. *Journal of Curriculum Theorizing*, 27(3), 287–307.

McCaffrey, J. (2005). Using transformative models of adult literacy in conflict resolution and peace building processes at community level: examples from Guinea, Sierra Leone and Sudan. *Compare*, 35(4), 443–62.

Maybin, J. (2007). Literacy under and over the desk: Oppositions and heterogeneity. *Language and Education*, 21(6), 515–30.

Merchant, G. (2009). Web 2.0, new literacies, and the idea of learning through participation. *English Teaching-Practice and Critique*, 8(3),107–22.

Morgan, B. (2010). New literacies in the classroom: Digital capital, student identity, and third space. Available online at http://www.youtube.com/watch?v=4g56fcYN9dE (accessed 17 January 2012).

Organization for Economic and Cultural Development (OECD) (2009). *Programme for International Student Assessment*. Paris: OECD.

Prior, M., Bavin, E. and Ong, B. (2011). Predictors of school readiness in five- to six-year-old children from an Australian longitudinal community sample. *Educational Psychology*, 31(1), 3–16.

Protevi, J. (2001). *The geophilosophy of Deleuze and Guattari*. Available online at http://www.protevi.com/john/research.html (accessed 9 February 2011).

Ranker, J. (2009). Redesigning and transforming: A case study of the role of semiotic import in early composing processes. *Journal of Early Childhood Literacy*, 9(3), 319–47.

Romano, E., Babchishin, L., Pagani, L. S. and Kohen, D. (2010). School readiness and later achievement: Replication and extension using a nationwide Canadian survey. *Developmental Psychology*, 46(5), 995–1007.

Saiegh-Haddad, E., Levin, I., Hende, N. and Ziv, M. (2011). The linguistic affiliation constraint and phoneme recognition in diglossic Arabic. *Journal of Child Language*, 38(2), 297–315.

Semetsky, I. ed. (2008). *Nomadic education: Variations on a theme by Deleuze and Guattari*. Rotterdam: Sense Publishers.

Serrano, R. and Howard, E. (2007). Second language writing development in English and in Spanish in a two-way immersion programme. *International Journal of Bilingual Education and Bilingualism*, 10(2), 152–70.

Stephens, K. (2000). A critical discussion of the 'New Literacy Studies'. *British Journal of Education*, 48(1), 10–23.

Street, B. (1984). *Literacy in practice*. Cambridge: Cambridge University Press.

—(2003). What's new in the New Literacy Studies? Critical approaches to literacy in theory and practice. *Current Issues in Comparative Education*, 5(2), 77–91.

The New London Group (1996). A pedagogy of multiliteracies: Designing social futures. *Harvard Educational Review*, 66(1), 60–92.

Waterhouse, M. (2011a). Deleuzian experimentations in Canadian immigrant language education: Research, practice, and policy. *Policy Futures in Education*, 9(4), 505–17.

—(2011b). *Experiences of multiple literacies and peace: A rhizoanalysis of becoming in immigrant language classrooms*. Unpublished doctoral dissertation, University of Ottawa. Available online at http://hdl.handle. net/10393/19942 (accessed 17 January 2012).

Notes

1   What comes to mind is the concept of identity linked to a territory. Identity is a concept based on the centered subject and on representation with already defined characteristics that represent a particular formation (social, cultural, etc.).

2   Student success lighthouse projects are beacons for over 10,000 struggling students. Government of Ontario. Available online at http://news.ontario.ca/ archive/en/2006/11/30/Student-Success-Lighthouse-Projects-Are-Beacons-for-Over-10000-Struggling-Studen.html (accessed 19 January 2012).

3   There are claims by governments for example of mineral and water rights, owning a "territory. However, water moves and deterritorializes

4   Molecular structure or lines are considered supple lines in that, depending on the context, at one time they can either be molar-like and at other times they be constituted as lines of flight.

5   Plane of immanence or consistency. Moving beyond what we actually know to a world of the virtual and what could be.

6   I acknowledge that allotting a brief space to literacy reifies the complex issues that are important to literacy.

7   Deleuze (DR) tackled the concept of identity by stating that the concept is tied up with representation (you are women, single, Canadian). These characteristics are fixed categories, that can change over time, but they still remain static. Identity also is associated with the centered subject.

8   Translation: On the left side of the figure, Cristelle writes: 'Anne is a very very bad bat. Cristelle is the most most gentle of bats'. In the castle Cristelle draws a figure with the caption 'bad vampire'. At the bottom she draws two figures and refers to Anne as the inspector. On the right side the story continues, saying: 'the same day at noon'. There is a drawing of three figures with a 'love line' drawn between the girl and the boy. At the bottom, once more there are drawings of Cristelle and Anne as bats. The 'haunted castle' text was created during an interview with both children after school at the daycare centre.

9   Every abstract machine is linked to other abstract machines, not only because they are inseparably political, economic, scientific, artistic, ecological, cosmic – perceptive, affective, active, thinking, physical, and semiotic – but because their various types are as intertwined as their operations are convergent (TP: 514).

CHAPTER THREE

Mapping literacies with affect

David R. Cole

Introduction

There is a growing literature on affect and its connections to education. The spectrum of studies in this literature take differing perspectives on affect that range from scientific framing, looking at affect as neuroscience and any consequent learning (see Damasio, 2003), to cultural studies that places affect as performance in culture, and adds education as a subset of these performances (e.g. Gregg and Seigworth, 2010). The advantage of using Deleuze as a basis for literacy study is that one may take evidence from science or culture on affect. Deleuze gives one a philosophical platform for understanding literacy as multiple literacies (MLT), as has been articulated in this book. Affect has been a habitual concern of philosophers, as it provides a link between desire, the irrational and the products of rationality. In terms of literacy studies, affect links the conscious use of language with the unconscious learning of language. This statement does not suggest that Deleuze's philosophical framework may be reduced to a psychoanalytical analysis of how one acquires and uses language. On the contrary, Deleuze counteracts any narrowing down to 'subject centredness' in much of his writing, whilst not excluding the power and influence of the unconscious drives (see Deleuze, 2001). Mapping literacies with affect includes understanding and using the key Deleuzian concept of becoming as a means to thinking through the changes in agency that happen as one changes in literacy skills. In this case, one can refer to a plural as well as a single subject. Becoming links the influences of the drives with external factors of change, and this can be determined through literacy testing. For example, a student or group of students may be tested on spelling, writing, reading and speaking. These skills have definite affects and processes attached to these affects, many of which relate to how well the student copes with particular practices of schooling (e.g. Youngblood, 2010) and their concomitant linguistic affects. However, below this surface of discernible language affects there is a substratum of material affects that also define change in the lives of these students. This substratum might include the financial position of the student's family, status worries, or the relationships between the student and his or her community. Affect here changes literacy skills, but in a manner that is difficult to test. One may perform qualitative research on the substratum; yet the relationship between this substratum and particular multiple literacy skills is in a constant flux. The focus of this chapter makes sense of this flux by linking changes in literacy (becoming), with questions about multiple literacies as a concept and the substrata of indeterminate, circulating affect.

Affecting and being affected through literacy

It has been argued that building relationships is the fourth 'r' of education (see David and Charlton, 1996). This chapter will explain how under-standing Deleuzian literacy studies adds to this claim, in terms of both how to build literate relationships in education, and when this process is actualized through literacy acts or affective literacy. This multiple literacies chapter builds upon feminist work in this area that has focused on pedagogy as a relationship (e.g. McWilliam, 1996). The body as conceptual and lived matter is reactivated in teaching and learning contexts through the relation-ships that it engenders, and these relationships depend, according to Gilles Deleuze, on affect. The actions of affect are prominent in the philosophy of Deleuze, and can be broken down for the purposes of education into two roles. The first alludes to the history of philosophy and the ways in which affect has been defined by Spinoza (Deleuze, 1992), Nietzsche (Deleuze, 1983) and Bergson (Deleuze, 1991). In this role, Deleuze reinvigorates and challenges definitions of affect that could be placed into systems of under-standing and initiate metaphysics or paradigms for capture in any further theorization of affect. For example, scholars might attest to the use of affect as defined by Spinoza in the *Ethics*. Deleuze (1992, 1991, 1983) attends to the ways in which scholarly understanding of affect has been broached in order to free up the idea for empirical studies and to show that the power of didactic language may be subverted through literacy. The second role of affect in the work of Deleuze comes from his first two co-authored books with Félix Guattari (Deleuze and Guattari, 1984, 1988). These publications have a distinct purpose from the scholarly work, which this chapter will examine in terms of literacy acts and affective literacy. This level of affect imbues the use of language in literate acts with an intense affective resonance and the multiple traces of becoming that could be present in any teaching and learning context. The two roles therefore define a way forwards in terms of building pedagogic relationships and literacy; the first role works with the search for the truth in education, the second focuses on the students' social and cultural context and the ways in which their language and power work. Deleuzian literacy studies incorporate the two roles of affect as a strategy to disrupt dualisms between teachers and students and separate and/or divided identities that are produced in the educative context.

This chapter adds to the deployment of the multiple in literacy. Affect is a non-representational aspect of teaching and learning that, according to Deleuze (1992), forms pre-personal circuits of becoming and change that can be trapped in institutes of education. Affect is a manner of reciprocation that includes imaginative responses to phenomena. Trying too hard to make education work can hinder affect, as factors such as the added stress of the imposition of overly high standards would cause retardation in literacy development. Affect involves establishing and using a connection with the unconscious that is extremely susceptible to power concerns. Educators need to be patient and wait for the affective atmosphere to settle before taking the students on their literate journeys (see Chapter Six). Elsewhere, I have termed this type of pedagogy 'affective literacy' (Cole, 2009, 2007a). Teachers should be aware of the language that they use in the pedagogic context, and how this language translates into the affective environment. The two-role model of affect in this chapter has been designed to deal with language and power, and to explain educative reciprocation in literacy.

The two-role model of affect and literacy

Gilles Deleuze ties up the ways in which power works through and in language with affect. The problems that confront this chapter are therefore 'what is affect?' and 'how does affect relate to building literate relationships in education?' Deleuze (1995) suggests that we get different answers to these questions depending upon whom we ask, and as such resists a clear definition of affect in his oeuvre. I have constructed the two ways in which affect is approached in the writing of Deleuze in terms of a model to aid comprehension of the idea, though this does not represent a unified theory of affect. Spinoza (1955) used affect in a combinatory manner in his system of ethics to connect desire with reason; language therefore takes on a powerful ethical and joyful cadence to communicate deeply felt emotions along with rational directives. Such combinatory desire, i.e. affecting and being affected, is the way in which one may deploy Spinozist affect to build literate relationships in education. Nietzsche (1968) used affect as a basis for sensation in his understanding of the will to power and the eternal return; language assumes power as it is combined with the ways in which the repetitions of time and the will drive one's life. The Nietzschean approach to building literate relationships in education works by locating the educative drives and making the 'taught moment' happen for teachers and learners (epiphanies). Bergson (1994) made affect part of his conception of *durée* and the *élan vital*, so that language is imbued with the subtle nuances of the continuities in time, memory and creativity, and these constitute vitalist power. The Bergsonian approach to building literate relationships in education depends on vitalizing knowledge in time, and making the energy of this encounter endure between lessons. The point of the Deleuzian scholarly synthesis and reinvention of these thinkers through his philosophical apprenticeship (Hardt, 1993) is not to become confused by the ways in which affect has been deployed to support different philosophical systems, but to realize that affect is a philosophical tool to build perspectives. In terms of education, one should not teach the truth of affect, nor rationalize it into a unified 'affect theory', but use affect to develop theory that will sustain and modify one's views with empirical evidence and the fluctuations contained in such evidence. Literate relationship building in education through Deleuzian practice is an amalgam of Spinoza–Nietzsche–Bergson philosophical elements that join together in literate acts.

In contrast to Deleuze's individual studies, his joint publications with Félix Guattari on *Capitalism and Schizophrenia* (1984, 1988) do not bear down on specific philosophical systems. This writing is populated by conceptual figures such as rhizomes that synthesize and distribute the arguments as they occur. Affect appears as a connective element in this argumentation that takes particular ideas and makes them open to reabsorption and usage in novel ways. For example, Deleuze and Guattari (1984, 1988) are concerned with the pre-figuration of conflict and power in primitive communities that has given rise to war machines and the modern state. The historical lineage and analysis of this situation is dispensed with in favour of a moving confrontation with pre-figuration. The analyses are nomadic; affect is used as a conceptual weapon and organizing principle that links players and moments in history with their realization in today's society. Deleuze and Guattari's (1988) writing provides a connection between the creative unconscious, where the ideas are synthesized, and the plane of becoming that impinges immanently on everything that we do (see Cole and Throssell, 2008) in practice. In terms of the power of language in literacy, affect sits in the unconscious in systematic and organized ways, for example in the libido, which may be realized in advertising campaigns or the scripted speeches of politicians. Our society has made a huge investment in education, and this point is imbued and distributed with affect through teacher-talk and educational research. There is an enormous interconnected field here, through which educational affect makes things happen in the lives of teachers, academics and students, who may develop responses to power and language in unconscious and sentient ways. Figure 3.1 represents a two-role model of affect that I have designed to show how power works through language in education.

The two-role model of affect as depicted in Figure 3.1 is a helpful way to understand the actions of affect in Deleuze for the purposes of literacy. The first role of affect often involves the word of the teacher and the truth of his or her educative discourses in the classroom. Clearly, this role of affect may take many shapes and forms, and will critically depend on the teacher's use of language, knowledge and ease when talking about the subject matter. The first role includes the instructional and organizational modes of education, which educators can fall back into, and these constitute regressive, one-dimensional affects. The first role of affect includes the character development and shaping by identity resources of the teacher, and therefore is co-determined by the specific personality of the teacher (see Chapter Six). The second role of affect involves the social and cultural consequences of language in the classroom. This role is open to anyone talking and playing with power relationships in the collective environment. For example, the class clown or highly disruptive student may take on the second role of affect if they dominate the teacher as a source of entertainment or attention for the group. The first role of affect is not the sole prerogative of the teacher, as students may also take on the role of expert. Likewise, the teacher should be conversant with the social and cultural consequences of their language in order to manipulate the second role of affect. This adaptive cognition points to the fact that it can be more difficult for student teachers or teachers from overseas to settle into new class environments to build literacy, as they would have no previous understanding of particular social affects. However, once the new teacher has

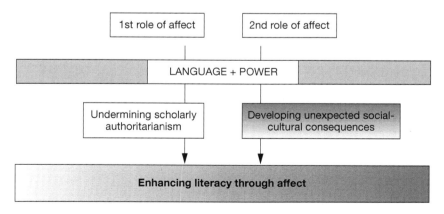

Figure 3.1 The two-role model of affect. I have designed this model to aid comprehension of the ideas that will be explained in this chapter. Deleuze does not name such a model in his work.

made the transition into the new class, they should be effective at using the two-role model of affect, as they will be conscious of the consequences of their language in an educative context (see Cole, 2008).

Making literate relationships with unconscious-affect

When Freud (1953) discussed affect in the interpretation of dreams, he was talking about a 'mood or tendency that is a determining influence on the dream,' (p. 627). Freud analysed various dreams that patients related to him, examining the symbolic and metonymic figures that these dreams represented. Affect appears in these dreams, not as constituent parts or as a comprehensible whole, but as a means to join the expression of the patients with particular emotional states. As such, anxiety, pain and paranoia permeate the dreams as affect without being named by the patients. In the role of the analyst, and in terms of the first role of affect in this multiple literacies chapter, Freud took it on himself to name the affect in the dreams, and to discuss the ways in which patients have articulated affect in their monologues. This situation could be designated as a parallel case to the analysis of building literate relationships through education. There are potential blockages, neuroses and misunderstandings with respect to articulating literate relationships through the power of language in education. This is because education, subjectivity and power in language are not unified or indeed cohesive units of analysis. When one speaks about building literate relationships in education, there is a type of displacement effect whereby the truth of the matter shifts and buckles through language, affect and power. This displacement was why Freud (1953) introduced the Id, Ego and Super-Ego as a distinctive layering in the analysis of the self. These subjective factors are representative of disunity and modes of abundance that exceed discourses of control or limitation. One must therefore expand the range of unconscious-affect from a device that makes the subconscious analyzable to include the social plane on which contemporary educational practices work. This social plane includes literate relationship building and the two-role model role of affect.

To find a strategic deployment of affect, one needs to turn to the second role of affect, and the ways in which affect has been taken up in, for example, contemporary feminism. Post-structural thinkers such as Elizabeth Grosz (1994) and Elspeth Probyn (2004) have worked to disavow the psychological and psychoanalytic basis of affect, and endeavoured to make affect mobile and without the dualism of the analyzed-analyst (see Cole, 2009) in their writing. Deleuze and Guattari (1984) strategically removed the Oedipus and Elektra interpretive templates from the dreams of the analyzed subject, in contrast to the power of the analyst. This action is parallel to when one looks for affect in literate relationships, as one cannot determine affective moods for students, cohorts or institutional discourses.

Rather, one should first examine one's emotional proclivities, and articulate the ways in which they are factors in the analysis. So, for example, if one observes a grade nine painting class with students disengaged and using the colours and brushes to make random splodges of colour and graffiti, what is one expressing, taking into account unconscious language-affect, when one writes up the report? The affect of rebellion, expressed through the creativity of the group action, should be included as a 'voice' in the discussion, as should the dissonance and factors of control that are present in the school. The discursive mode of the report must take into account the peer relationships and power games that would be shaping the affect of the class. There should be room in the writing for dynamic and changing experiences of the subjects, such as home-life influences and the power of the media. The report would include the writer's understandings of their reception and relationships in the research context, and the ways in which the group have reacted to the extra presence. All of these factors will contribute to the way literate relationships may be built. In summation, the report should not be a diagnosis of 'a lack of fulfilment of curriculum goals' caused by behaviour management problems or maladjusted students, but, according to the two-role model of affect, an attempt to understand the complicated ways affect populates this situation through becoming:

> Becoming [while happening in a gap], is [none the less] an extreme contiguity within a coupling of two sensations without resemblance, or, [it is] in the distance of a light that captures both [of the resemblances] in a single reflection ... It is a zone of indetermination, as if things, beasts, and persons endlessly reach that point that immediately precedes their natural differentiation. This is what is called an affect. (Deleuze and Guattari, 1994: p. 173)

The point is that becoming is not only about the ways in which changes emerge in the educational context, or the outcomes that education can be reduced to. The two-role model of affect is about the hidden processes included in becoming, and these are pivotal in terms of understanding how to build literate relationships. In a similar way to that described by Peter Clough (2002), who understands affect as constitutive of the social context of learning through the writing of educational narratives, the aspect of becoming that one may take from the two-role model of affect includes fictional elements and the narrative re-creation of life. In other words, the two-role model of affect does not determine becoming as a wholly factual or psychological account of events that aims towards teleology. The two-role model of affect presents events as processes of material unpickings and entangled situations. Literate relationships cannot be reduced to inter-subjectivity through the application of affect theory. In contrast, what emerges is a minor philosophy of education (Gregoriou, 2004) that attends to the movements of desire in language and power, and through literate relationships in a materialist frame. Whenever one speaks in an educational context, new connective apparatuses appear that communicate unconscious affect, that depend on the learning and power relationships that occur. One must therefore analyse the teaching and learning educational plane in order to make sense of the two-role model of affect in terms of literate relationships and the language of pedagogy.

Teaching and learning literacy with language-affect

The educational complex opened up by attending to the philosophy of Gilles Deleuze involves context and practice. Context is important, as affect is grounded in the situational and relational points of intensity under scrutiny in literate acts. Practice is thoroughly connected to language by the affect that one may produce due to the synthesis, analysis and representation of any repetition of an action (see Albrecht-Crane and Slack, 2007). The Deleuzian analysis at this point relies heavily on the work of socio-linguists such as William Labov (1971), who discovered that some of the rules of language, that he called 'variable rules', can generate systematic, endogenous or 'grown from within' variation (1971: p. 21). For example, in small urban communities, social networks develop that use language as a 'badge of identity' (De Landa, 1993: p. 14). These identities circulate around the community and define power relationships, allegiances and structures that can maintain or transform the local dialect. In effect, Labov's (1971) research findings give us a bridge or undifferentiated plane whereupon power relationships that could potentially undermine the circulation of social meaning in a system are stabilized. This moveable bridge provides a means for understanding literate relationship building in education. The lively endogenous variation of language in the student population sits in contrast to professional teaching manuals and the formal language production of textbooks. The teacher needs to find a balance between both spheres through educational practice that includes endogenous variation as affect and formal language study where appropriate. This is putting the two-role mode of affect to work in education by allowing new language to ripple through the interlocking surfaces of education, society and power.

Teaching and learning critically involves a combination of the two roles of affect. The word of the teacher is principally about the first role of affect. The teacher's language will transmit power, according to Deleuze (1992), as a function of its affect. If the teacher has researched his or her subject well, and speaks with passion and sincerity, these affects will permeate the atmosphere of the class, the learning context and the subsequent educational practice. The literate relationships that shall be built in this environment will rest on such affects. However, this building process is not a unidirectional or intentional relationship, according to Deleuze

(1992). This is because the second role of affect is thoroughly connected to teaching and learning due to the ways in which the socio-cultural context of the classroom funnels and plays with language, power and meaning through relationships. There is an undifferentiated plane in the educational context between the students and their culture that will draw on their social lives and not actively involve the teacher. This plane will define power relationships, literacy, language and affect (see Cole and Yang, 2008) from the cohort's perspective. The teacher cannot step into this plane from the outside, but must actively look for ways in which to connect with this plane through understanding the socio-cultural systems that are present in the cohort, but without trying to ape or become involved in them artificially. For example, including elements of the socio-cultural plane in knowledge building, acknowledging the students as experts, and taking the group on a literate journey whereby their contextual understandings can be seen to be important in the world and beyond a particular context. These examples are ways of working with the two-role model of affect in literacy.

Another example to illustrate the two-role model of affect in teaching and learning is that of a teacher who is investing time and energy writing up his or her classroom practice, and sending off the account to an educational academic. The first role of affect is important in terms of the validity of the account and the power of the language used by the teacher, the second role of affect takes place in the description of the teaching and learning context as an understanding of systematic endogenous variation. In other words, the teacher will not only have to think about the formal impact of his or her writing style, and the suitability for academic consumption, but the ways in which the writing deals with the specific desires and power relationships as constituted by the body of the class, and how these may be transformed from within (e.g. Boler, 1999 ; Bourdieu and Passeron, 1977). This teacher needs to explain the collective practices of teaching in his or her school, and the ways in which they relate to this particular instance of teaching and learning. He or she must construct the manner in which the students have learnt according to the specific pedagogic approach under analysis and the responses and understandings of the students to that pedagogy. The meaning of the report of best practice and the way this pedagogy builds literate relationships, therefore comes about due to the two roles of affect and the processes that are inherent within the language of the collective teaching context, or as Deleuze and Guattari (1988) have put it:

> … there is no simple identity between the statement and the act. If we wish to move to a real definition of the collective assemblage, we must ask of what [do] these acts [consist of] immanent to language [and] that are in redundancy with statements or that constitute *order-words* . (p. 80, my emphasis).

This movement towards a definition of the collective assemblage takes us further in understanding the two-role model of affect. According to the definition of the collective assemblage of Deleuze and Guattari (1988) the problem that causes educational systems to buckle and misfire is the production of order-words, or redundant instructions and directives that sit between the act and the statement. These order-words are incorporeal transformations (pp. 108-9) that take on board power and life, and circulate around places of education like the routing of electricity in plasterboard walls. The most obvious example of an order-word is the language involved with behaviour management. Teachers may spend their time repeating instructions or telling students off, when the real problem is a basic lack of engagement with the teaching and learning activities (cf. Woolfolk and Margetts, 2007) . The first role of affect is present through the voice of the teacher, and the stress that this sound might transmit. The second role of affect is constituted by the reactions of the students, in mimicry or laughter, in off task conversations, or cynical reactions to being reprimanded. The collective experience of such classrooms may be fragmentary and hostile. The example of the language used with behaviour management, that Deleuze and Guattari (1988) term as the order-words, shows how literate relationships may be damaged through schooling. Children will still behave badly in and through Deleuzian literacy studies, the difference that this practice brings out through the two roles of affect, is that the teachers should not misconstrue and add to this behaviour via barked or reactive instructions.

Collectivity involves the transmission of modes of working between different parties involved with educational action. This transmission is itself a practice of communication that is open to the two-role model of affect and the building of literate relationships. Any transformed practice will have to be represented and understood through language and the relational context of learning. Here Schatzki's account of practice is useful to supplement the two-role model of affect and building literate relationships in education. According to Schatzki (1996, 2001, 2002) in an important sense, practices prefigure individual actions. In other words, for him, practices precede actors and actions, and work to shape their performance as well as supplying meaning and significance in the context. So while any transformed practice is no doubt novel, it remains bounded by the relationships that the practice may develop between itself and the representation of other practices that are according to Deleuze structured and figured through affect. Schatzki (2002) views social activity as 'composed of a mesh of orders and practices', where orders are 'arrangements of entities, e.g. people, artefacts, things' and practices are 'organized activities' (p. 27), and both of these are present in Deleuze and Guattari's (1988) conception of 'order-words'. As such, the order-words rely heavily on the first role of affect that is determined by the power, tone and presence of the teacher's voice, and subsidiary factors such as body language and institutional representation of pedagogy. The second role of affect is implicated in practice as the social relations that are developed through teaching and learning are subject to constant variations in immanence and redundancy. For example, any indiscreet or throw-away lines of the teachers or students may be picked up and recycled in different contexts; strange and unlikely relationships or jokes that may be intuited by the students from the teacher's choice of content to illustrate a point (cf. Brown, McEvoy, and Bishop, 1991) . The control and discipline of the teacher and institute may be re-enacted due to the second role of affect in ways such as the acting out of scenes with exaggerated or cruel punishment, inter-personal violence or sexuality; in these instances the order-words are transformed through practice and the ways in which affectivity is contagious. Deleuze does not give us a neat solution to the free movement of desires, but asks us to follow them, and in particular through the use of figures such as the rhizome that may help us to understand how desire flows.

Literacy and erotic language-affects

The rhizome is a useful figure that one can take from Deleuze and Guattari (1988) and apply to the routing of desire through relationships, power and literacy in education. However, the rhizome does not deal with the potential intensification and feedback loops that the processes of multiple literacies imply. In terms of the example of the language of the classroom practitioner, or the writing up of 'best practice', the rhizome is akin to a Chinese box that one may feed these processes through to understand how power may evolve in language and out of these situations in, for example, literacy. Yet the rhizome is not a completely mobile system as is necessary for multiple literacies. What drives the rhizome? The two-role model of affect requires an extra level of impulse to enable a flexible mode of application when mapping literate pedagogy with affect, which is the aim of this chapter. Following on from the positioning of unconscious-affect, erotic language-affects are a potential means to create a plane of becoming for the two-role model of affect in literate (combinatory) relationships. These affects are plural as they imply multiple becomings. Two of the most vital factors to make education work that we derive from the investigation into affect are time and the force of the practice (cf. Fiumara, 2001). This is true in an intensive as well as an extensive sense, as the subjective time of the imagination needs to be dealt with as well as the objective time of the learning experience. If one uses the example of a teacher who is achieving great advances with their students using expressive, transactional and poetic language in a complex way (Britton, 1970), this says something profound about the intimacy and subjective sense of time (see Martindale, 1990) that the teacher has produced with this group, as well as the subsequent group relations. This type of behaviour may be apparent when the teacher has the students for long periods of learning-time, and the projects that the group set out to achieve are messy with respect to a clockwork appreciation of time, the group consensus and assessment. What one needs in terms of the two-role model of affect working in education to build literate relationships, are strong bonds between participants in the learning process in order to keep creativity and collective enunciation fluid, vital and alive.

These bonds might be created, preserved and moulded through use of erotic language-affects. One flinches when mentioning such an idea, as erotic language-affects have rarely figured on the educationalist's horizons, as there are moral and social taboos around discussing such a topic. Yet erotic language-affects fit into this chapter and exposition of the two-role model of affect and building literate relations in terms of:

- First, the philosophy of education that one may derive from the two-role model of affect. Erotic language-affects locate and strengthen the central, bonding elements of the thesis by creating the conditions whereby contiguity (cf. Irigaray, 1985) may be achieved and the will to resist interference from instrumental reason is heightened. This is important for the two-role model of affect as power may be drained through attention to the minute detail of theoretical construction of an argument for affect in education, or its exact consequences in terms of operation. Deleuze (e.g. 1994a, 2001) suggests that one enacts a concept in terms of putting philosophy to work, and erotic language-affects are one way of doing this. Furthermore, it should be noted that erotic language-affects are not a move in the direction of educational humanism (e.g. Maslow, 1970; Suler, 1980) or of completing a sense of the whole or unified self in education, as these affects indicate the subjective yet expansive principles associated with pleasure that build upon the closeness imbued by using language with power and the sense of time that one may derive from developing multiple literacies.

- Second, erotic language-affects work on the level of viewing, understanding and deciding what to do with the power of language once it has been recognized. In terms of language analysis, systemic functional linguistics has used this idea as an appraisal system (see Martin and White, 2005). This system offers a typology of the lexico-grammatical resources available to both construe and realize interpersonal dimensions of experience at the level of discourse semantics. This leads to a type of prosodic realization that can be saturating, intensifying or dominating. It also fits in well with the intention and direction of applying the two-role model of affect in literacy and making desire work through relation building and to the benefit of students, teachers and places of learning.

- The third meaning of erotic language-affects in this context refers specifically to the Deleuzian philosophical notion of affect as it has been derived from Spinoza. Philosophers such as Lloyd (1989) and Gatens (1996), have taken affect to infuse the mind with sexuality, as the Spinozist positioning of affectus with power leads one away from desexed, disembodied ideas. In fact, everything that the mind can think is henceforth tied to the body in the erotic language-affect of bodily ideation; so, for example, Deleuze and Guattari's (1984) body-without-organs reflects a body locked up and self-replicating in terms of producing streams of internal thoughts and language without external release. In education, this body may be conceived through closed systems, punishment and the walls of the isolated classroom. The coded language of teaching manuals and professional practice textbooks reproduce the body-without-organs because they drain the sprightly sexual body of emergent life through internalization and the subjectification of inflexible regulation (see Cole, 2007b). Erotic language-affects give us a way of talking about these connections, and applying the two-role model of affect to the transformations of the body that the education system enables and maintains. These changes in form may be sexual or power driven, or a subtle mixture of tacit learning tendencies that are continually present in relationships. This aspect of building relationships in education has been discussed with reference to ethology and pedagogy (e.g. Gaten, 1996). Deleuze's reading of Spinoza enables the understanding that bodies are made up of mixes of relationships that entangle and puncture as bodies come together and separate. In education, the two-role model of affect helps to analyze and mobilize this ethology and shows how erotic language-affects might be a way forward in terms of making multiple literacies work in combined relationships.

It should be possible to draw a line through the ways in which erotic language-affects take us towards an understanding of developing literacy. Yet the unification of the three strata of erotic language-affects is an analytic and synthetic process that shows how Deleuze's ideas are often resistant to summary and simplification. In many ways, this is the first role of affect working and playing with the meaning that one might get from the three aspects of erotic language-affects. The plane of becoming for literacy education that these affects sit upon is therefore not a surface-effect (see Colebrook, 2004), but part of the diagrammatical understanding that one may achieve with regard to relating in pedagogy through language and power from the philosophy of Deleuze (the social cartography). Speaking with the affects that are connected with eroticism creates a tone and atmosphere whereby power flows freely, yet could be misunderstood in the act of building literate relationships. This is in line with Deleuze's preoccupation with the nature of desire and examples of language production that he uses to illustrate his ideas such as 'stuttering' (Deleuze, 1994b). A teacher using erotic language-affects is closing the gap between him or herself, the knowledge and concepts under scrutiny, and the learner-subjects or the collective. Yet he or she is also taking a risk and leaving themselves open to potential moral inquiry by projecting the erotic element of this pedagogy, which is a clear breach of power and not using language to make desire flow through education by building literate relationships. The teacher should therefore carefully broach erotic language-affects through the two-role model of affect. Using affect in literacy teaching and learning denotes an increase in power for the educator that includes all the affective becomings that are present in the social and cultural context in which they operate. One means to achieve this is through the practice of affective literacy.

Affective literacy for teaching literature

Affective literacy in this chapter is a practice for teachers who use the two-role model of affect. The conscious search for affective and relational content in literature leads to improved engagement in language, characters and the plot of the story. There are elements of what happens when a teacher looks for affective content and uses this content to construct classes in reader response theory (e.g. Holland, 1968), in that these lessons narrow down on the affects that are present in texts, and they make them live through the work that the teachers and students share. The affects that motivate and excite the class into increased levels of sustained reading and analysis with respect to texts are also connected to the social and cultural aspects that were under scrutiny through study (i.e. the two-role model of affect). This resonates with much of the recent discussion about English teaching in Australia and critical literacy (see Luke, 2000). The study of literature should be relevant to students' lives, in that it should concern social and cultural issues in contemporary society. The practice of affective literacy as put forward in this chapter and as a development from the two-role model of affect combines social and cultural interest with affective stimulation. English and literacy teaching and learning in this context deal with the forces of power that are present in the lives of the participants and that construct and reconstruct subjectivities on the inside and from the outside.

Affective literacy

The historian Mark Amsler (2004) has used the term 'affective literacy' to describe the ways in which medieval texts were read. This reading constituted an acting-out of the action. The major players, the dialogues and the plot had to be understood in a bodily manner, one that leads to reliving the story through reading. This action may be in contrast to present understandings of literacy that focus on subjective linguistic comprehension abilities. Using affective literacy as a means to enhance English pedagogy by making text come alive, shifts the focus to influence decisions in terms of textual choice and practice, and with the unified aim of raising the affective engagement of the students. First, English teachers must develop an affective relationship with the text that they wish to teach (see Misson and Morgan, 2005). This means engaging with the work in a way that would move them deeply, i.e. the first role of affect. Stories about characters that teachers feel nothing about do not translate into affective sessions with the students. Once the teacher has established their connection with the text, they may go about differentiating it into affective themes. These themes will relate to the social and cultural context in which they are teaching, i.e. the second role of affect. Affective literacy sessions that are based on affect are interactive and include opportunities for negotiation and evaluation of tasks, especially with respect to assessment. Repetitive pedagogic choices may destroy affectivity, in that students will not participate in sessions if they always know what will happen next. In effect, the teacher applying affective literacy pedagogy in an unresponsive manner may unwittingly form an affective barrier to engagement through the repetition of the same (see Irigaray, 1985). The teachers and students using affective literacy pedagogy need to keep alive the imagination of everyone concerned with the activity (Greene, 1995), and through this process challenge the students and themselves to think otherwise about text and society.

1. Frankenstein

The first text that I have chosen to demonstrate how to use affective literacy and the two-role model of affect is the classic horror story by Mary Shelley (1818). The affective literacy approach is an appropriate English pedagogy for *Frankenstein*, as the themes that Shelley has incorporated into the story are affective and powerful, enabling the teacher to take these themes out of the story, and prepare individual lessons or units of work around them. This helps to alleviate the common problem that students have when they read *Frankenstein*, in that the density of the language that Shelley used can obscure the story and the consequent enjoyment in reading. Affective literacy in this context allows the student to analyse dramatic sections of the text and to take away the most salient issues through dynamic exercises.

1.1. Lesson Plan One – The Monster

Target group: Grade 10

Lesson objectives:
To analyze the creation of the monster in *Frankenstein*
To relate the monster to the idea of 'the other' in human society
To understand how the character of the monster functions in *Frankenstein*

Lesson procedures/materials:
This lesson can work as a standalone session, or be embedded in a series of lessons that focus on the idea of the monstrous in *Frankenstein* and society. The teacher will begin by asking the question: What is a monster? The class will construct a spider-diagram to represent the responses around the idea of the monster: e.g. ugly, strange, frightening, etc. The teacher will distribute three sections of the story that describe the monster to different groups. Each group will read their particular section and answer the questions:

1.b   What language does Shelley use to describe the monster?
2.   How do the monster and/or Victor Frankenstein feel at this point in the story?
3.   What is the relationship between the monster and his creator Victor Frankenstein in your section?
Each group will feed back their responses to the rest of the class. This whole-class discussion will be guided by the question: How does Shelley create otherness through writing about the monster?
Follow-up work can include analysis of the monster as portrayed in films and the media.

Curriculum links:
This English literature session will connect with the social sciences in that discriminated-against groups become 'the other' to the mainstream through the processes that Shelley describes in *Frankenstein*.

Assessment of session:
This lesson is based upon reading about and responding to the monster in *Frankenstein*. Teachers should be aware of the level of engagement and articulation of the ideas by the students. A formal oral presentation or written piece regarding the idea of the monstrous in *Frankenstein* and society would be developed.

This example introduces an important idea that runs through affective literacy practices, the analysis of 'the other'. This term resonates with psychological and sociological aspects of power. Mainstream society has tended to single out and discriminate against what are perceived as 'others'. The monster in Shelley is the classic construction of otherness. He/It is not human, and he/it is not part of nature. This worrying thought empha-sizes the affective nature of the idea. Is the monster Victor Frankenstein's alter ego? What do we sacrifice when we ruthlessly pursue our goals? The otherness of the monster resonates with the ways in which physical deformity, disease, obesity and disabilities are treated and categorized as other by mainstream society.

1.2. Lesson Plan Two – Horror

Target group: Grade 9

Lesson objectives:
To examine the idea of horror in *Frankenstein*
To act out scary scenes from *Frankenstein*
To make connections between the Gothicism of *Frankenstein* and everyday life.

Lesson procedures/materials:
This lesson will concentrate on the aspect of horror in *Frankenstein*. As one of the prime examples of Gothic literature, this lesson may be embedded in other lessons that focus on horror in *Dracula* or in popular films such as *Nightmare on Elm Street*. The teacher will start the session by trying to surprise the students for dramatic effect. They could wear a mask or speak in a scary voice, or tell them a short scary story with the lights in the classroom off. Focus question for class discussion after this experience: How does this make me feel?
The lesson will progress into the enactment of three horrifying scenes from *Frankenstein* in groups. The preparation and performance of these plays should also be a formative English literary experience in that students would consider the style and form of each scene. They will write dialogue and prepare a stage to enhance the horror of the moment:

1. The birth of the monster. One group will re-enact the moment that the monster is born. This critical point in the novel is filled with suspense.
2. The passage of action where the monster learns language and values from the people in the cottage, and subsequently wants to be accepted by them. Once the monster comes out of hiding, they see his deformities and react with revulsion.
3. The meeting between Victor Frankenstein and his monster in the ice cave. This pivotal scene of the story between the creator and the created is rife with horror. The lesson ends with a discussion about the three plays and how these aspects of fear might be present in everyday life: e.g. behaviours getting out of control (such as addictions or obsessions), being rejected or discarded by groups, or meeting your own worst nightmare!

Curriculum links:
This lesson based on a literary text uses drama techniques to explore horror. It could also be connected with the arts in terms of representing feelings of horror through painting and music in follow-up lessons.

Assessment of session:
The plays may be assessed using class generated criteria such as audience impact, quality of dialogue, meaning and relevance, pace and dramatic structure.

This second lesson draws on the affective power of fear. This is not in order to make the students fearful, but to use fear to engage with the creation of horror in the text. The teacher could cue up video snippets and show them to each group so that students get a better idea about particular scenes. The teacher could also prepare summaries of the action at each point in the story for the students to read. This lesson should be fun and interactive, and shows how affective literacy prioritizes the connection between language and the acting out and experiencing of this language. This lesson could be extended over several periods so that students have time to practise their drama pieces and use the arts, such as music and dance, to explore the creative possibilities of the scenes.

1.3. Lesson Plan Three – Passion

Target group: Grade 11/12

Lesson objectives:
To read a section of Frankenstein and analyze it for emotional content
To understand some of the complex passions of Mary Shelley
To make connections between Romanticism and *Frankenstein*

Lesson procedures/materials:
This lesson focuses on the ways in which Victor Frankenstein is guided and dictated by Shelley's underlying passions. It could be embedded within a complete novel study of the text, or the study of key romantic authors such as Byron or Goethe. The teacher starts the session by emphasizing the links with Romanticism in *Frankenstein*. Key terms of reference to introduce the ideas of this lesson include: the idealization of nature, moral inquiry and the science of emotions.
Students will read an on-line article about *Frankenstein* at: http://www. watershedonline.ca/literature/frankenstein/prometheus.html

Discussion questions:
What are the passions of Prometheus as portrayed by this critic?
How did Shelly succeed in portraying heightened passion through the writing of *Frankenstein*?
What is the significance of the male–female distribution of attributes in the story of *Frankenstein*?

Groups can choose one question to work on and feed back to the rest of the class at the end of the session with their findings. They will find textual references from *Frankenstein* to back up their assertions. This feedback should include a discussion about the ways in which Shelley has used affective intensity to add meaning and power to her story. The protagonist follows his passion to its logical conclusion without regard for the consequences. This resonates, for example, with the contemporary tension between scientific exploration and environmental effects. Shelley pointed this out in 1818 through the writing of *Frankenstein*.

Curriculum links:
This English lesson requires deep engagement with the text and an essay on the passions in *Frankenstein*. Students should be able to make links from this session with psychology and philosophy.

Assessment of session:
This lesson could lead to the completion of an essay that relates to one of the discussion titles.

2. *Wide Sargasso Sea*

The second text that I will use to show how affective literacy and the two-role model of affect works in the classroom context is Jean Rhys's (2000) novel, *Wide Sargasso Sea*. This book may be studied at pre-tertiary level as part of an English Literature course. Furthermore, the themes that I have drawn out from this novel could be taught in any grade, as they demonstrate topics that would engage students in affective literacy sessions. Teachers may therefore take these lesson plans and adapt and convert them into their context by taking texts from colonial history. In so doing, teachers would apply the principles of affective literacy to literature study throughout the high school curriculum.

2.1. Lesson Plan One – Racism

Target group: Grade 11/12

Lesson objectives:
To understand the issue of racism as presented in *Wide Sargasso Sea*
To examine sections of text that deal with racism
To make connections between colonial and contemporary society

Lesson procedures/materials:
This lesson provokes the students to think about racism and its context in the British Empire. The teacher starts the lesson by handing out pieces of paper of different tones, ranging from pure black to pure white. The students will be asked to categorize the tones from the most black to the most white, and to think of suitable names for each. The teacher will guide the students to understand that this process was prevalent in the British Empire and was applied to people. In the next section of the lesson, the class breaks into groups and finds descriptions of characters that appear in the text. Half of the class should concentrate on section 1, the other on section 2. Each group answers the questions:

1. What language does Jean Rhys use to describe the characters?
2. What are the racial overtones of this language in terms of the construction of characters?

The groups give feedback to the rest of the class with their findings. Discussion of racial issues in *Wide Sargasso Sea* should be extended to make connections with recent occurrences in Australian society. How does colonialism still play a role in Australia?

Curriculum links:
There are clear links in this session with geography and history. Yet the teacher should emphasize the personal qualities of the lesson as it is also about language and meaning.

Racism still generates interest and controversy in education, despite the influence of egalitarian pedagogy and the values of multiculturalism in a democratic society. Rhys beautifully portrays the reality of racist colonial language that permeated the whole of Jamaican society. She also shows how the use of English carried with it factors of discrimination in colonial society, such as the owner–slave values of the plantation owners. Students may be stimulated to explore these influences in colonial history, as well as the powerful facts of slavery. All these topics could become the focus of extended investigation, which shows how affective literacy may branch out into the discovery of related facts and histories that add value to the text.

2.2. Lesson Plan Two – Men and Women

Target group: Grade 11/12

Lesson objectives:
To understand the gendered writing of *Wide Sargasso Sea*
To analyze sections of *Wide Sargasso Sea* for language that carries gender bias
To examine the difference between male and female perspectives on the world

Lesson procedure/materials:
The teacher asks students to write down a short description (50 words) of an event that they all have experienced. Individual students will read their descriptions and the whole class will analyze how the boys have picked out different aspects of the event, and used varying language from the girls. The boys will be handed a section of part one of *Wide Sargasso Sea* and the girls will analyze a section of part two. They will look at:

1. Use of adjectives
2. The detail of characterization
3. How the narrators connect themselves with nature and other people.

The students should find that part one uses a rich array of adjectives, goes into more depth when describing character, and that the narrator makes subtle and nuanced connections with everything around her. In contrast, the narrator of part two uses more literal adjectives, lacks understanding about others, and places an 'apartness' between himself and the outside world. Class discussion: Is this true of gender divisions in contemporary society? What evidence do they have for their assertions?

One of the great joys of *Wide Sargasso Sea* is the way in which Rhys contrasts the narrative perspectives in part one and part two. Rhys's heroine, Antoinette, narrates part one and it is clear that this is where Rhys's sympathies lie. Antoinette is the 'mad woman in the attic' in *Jane Eyre* (Brontë, 2003), the classic 'other' of English literature. Not only was she Rochester's first wife, she was also a Creole, which made her a figure of mystery and intrigue. Rhys attempts to unpack this character by writing her pre-history before she went to England, and before she married Rochester. She is an extraordinarily sensitive and aware young woman, sensual and profound, responsive and impulsive, and the witness to the ruins of colonial enterprise in Jamaica. In contrast, Rochester is cold and calculating, disconnected from nature and Jamaican society. This gendered difference and consequently entwined story would be used by the teacher as an affective impulse to study the text. Furthermore, this lesson would give students the tools to investigate other texts that show gender divisions.

2.3. Lesson Plan Three – Madness

Target group: Grade 11/12

Lesson objectives:
To understand the madness of Antoinette
To analyze how Jean Rhys uses language to demonstrate madness
To make connections between madness and otherness

Lesson procedure/materials:
The teacher should state at the beginning of this lesson that madness is no joke. They could do this by discussing data about mental disease, available at: http://www.aihw.gov.au/mentalhealth/index.cfm. This discussion should provide a chance for students to express any anxieties that they have about this topic. Students will analyze three sections of *Wide Sargasso Sea* in groups, and answer the questions:

1. What is Antoinette's state of mind at this juncture?
2. What language does Rhys use to indicate madness?
3. What are Antoinette's major relationships at this point in the text?

The groups will feed back their findings and a picture of Antoinette's mental state should emerge. In part one she is extremely sensitive and open to every sensation around her. Students will pick up that this openness could lead to not being able to cope with reality, especially in the context of Antoinette's life. In part two, Antoinette's madness is constructed by Rochester. The group with this section of text would pick up how he positions her behaviour as mad. In part three, madness is fully apparent, and students will have no trouble in identifying the mad language and intense emotional states of Antoinette. This lesson concludes with a broader discussion about madness and otherness. This is the process by which people experiencing mental difficulties are excluded from the mainstream.

Curriculum links:
This is an English literature session that enables students to speak in a focused manner about madness. It therefore connects strongly with the health curriculum.

The issue of mental health can be a difficult topic to approach at any stage of education. In *Jane Eyre* the way in which Rochester locks Antoinette up in his attic is an analogy for how mental disease has been dealt with by 'respectable' society via isolation, seclusion and misunderstanding. This is an extremely affective theme, which can be purposefully taught through literature. Jean Rhys deals with madness in an insightful manner. Her representation of Antoinette's plight may teach students to shy away from labelling madness, and to explore the factors that go into creating mental illness, both social and psychological. This lesson takes the affective topic of madness and situates it by understanding how an author has used language to unpack a character that has been universally labelled as being mad.

Applications of affective literacy

Affective literacy is transformative in that the deliberate use of affective issues enlivens lesson planning and the subsequent lessons. Affective content guides the pedagogic choices of the teachers and the focus of the students. The intention behind this strategy is to increase engagement in literacy and to work on the attitudinal and creative aspects in the multiple literacies classroom. This is complementary to using the pleasure of reading (see Clark and Rumbold, 2006) in that the enjoyable, interactive and gripping content of texts is focused upon, explored and used to push pedagogy. Whilst these choices necessitate a positive subjective proclivity on the part of the teacher, the decisions of the teacher are also embedded in social and cultural values, as students must make connections between the teacher's choices and their own lives, as has been stated in the two-role model of affect. This affective pedagogy for using text can be applied to other curriculum discipline areas such the humanities, drama, psychology, sociology and philosophy, as multiple literacy encounters in these subjects require a thorough understanding and grounding in affect, the workings of power and the multiplicity of literacies.

Conclusion

The two-role model of affect enables understanding of how affect works through language and in education. Affective literacy designates a requisite practice within Multiple Literacies Theory to manipulate affect. The statement of the two-role model of affect and the construction of affective literacy provide the educator with powerful tools to open up their work. However, the use of Deleuzian literacy studies also warns against any practice becoming fixed or stratified in terms of a mandated way of teaching and learning. The affect that one wants to incorporate into classroom action is mobile, interconnected, pre-personal and singular. Thus, multiple literacies practice has to follow the movement of affect to counteract power concerns that might isolate or expose affect to normative forces of control. This action is in part due to understanding and working with the consequences of the two-role model of affect in education and making them a part of affective literacy practice.

References

Albrecht-Crane, C. and Slack, J. D. (2007). Toward a Pedagogy of Affect. In A. Hickey-Moody and P. Malins (eds), *Deleuzian Encounters: Studies in contemporary social issues* (pp. 191–216). London: Palgrave Macmillan.

Amsler, M. (2004). Affective Literacy: Gestures of Reading in the Later Middle Ages. University of Wisconsin-Milwaukee: *Essays in Medieval Studies*. Available online at http://muse.jhu.edu/journals/essays_in_medieval_studies/v018/18.1amsler.html (accessed 8 November 2005).

Britton, J. (1970). *Language and Learning*. Harmondsworth: Penguin Books.

Brontë, C. (2003). *Jane Eyre*. New York: Dover Thrift Editions.

Brown, W. H., McEvoy, M. A. and Bishop, N. (1991). Incidental Teaching of Social Behaviour. *Teaching Exceptional Children*, 24:1, 35–8.

Boler, M. (1999). *Feeling Power: Emotions and education*. New York: Routledge.

Bourdieu, P. and Passeron, J.-C. (1977). *Reproduction in Education, Society and Culture*. London: Sage.

Clark, C. and Rumbold, K. (2006). Reading for pleasure: A research overview. *National Literacy Trust*. Available online at http://www.literacytrust.org.uk/assets/0000/0562/Reading_pleasure_2006.pdf (accessed 20 January 2012).

Clough, P. (2002). *Narratives and Fictions in Educational Research*. New York: McGraw-Hill Education.

Cole, D. R. (2005). Learning Through the Virtual. *CTHEORY*, 1. Available online at http://www.ctheory.net/articles.aspx?id=445 (accessed 20 January 2012).

—(2007a). Teaching Frankenstein and Wide Sargasso Sea Using Affective Literacy. *English in Australia*, 42:2, 69–75.

—(2007b). Virtual Terrorism and the Internet E-Learning Options. *E-Learning*, 4:2, 116–27.

—(2008). Deleuze and the narrative forms of educational otherness. In I. Semetsky ed. *Nomadic Education: Variations on a Theme by Deleuze & Guattari* (pp. 17–35). Rotterdam: Sense Publishers.

—(2009). Deleuzian Affective Literacy for Teaching Literature: A Literary Perspective on Multiple Literacies Theory. In D. Masny and D. R. Cole (eds), *Multiple Literacies Theory: A Deleuzian Perspective* (pp. 63–79). Rotterdam: Sense Publishers.

Cole, D. R. and Yang, G. Y. (2008). Affective Literacy for TESOL Teachers in China. *Prospect*, 23:1, 37–45.

Cole, D. R. and Throssell, P. (2008). Epiphanies in Action: Teaching and learning in synchronous harmony. *The International Journal of Learning*, 15:7, 175–84.

Colebrook, C. (2004). The Sense of Space: On the specificity of affect in Deleuze and Guattari. *Postmodern Culture*, 15:1. Available online at http://pmc.iath.virginia.edu/text-only/issue.904/15.1colebrook.txt (accessed 20 January 2012).

Damasio, A. (2003). *Looking for Spinoza: Joy, Sorrow, and the Feeling Brain*. Orlando: Harcourt.

David, K. and Charlton, T. (eds) (1996). *Pastoral care matters in primary and middle schools*. London: Routledge.

De Landa, M. (1993). Virtual environments and the emergence of synthetic reason. Available online at http://www.t0.or.at/delanda/delanda.htm (accessed 20 January 2012).

Deleuze, G. (1983). *Nietzsche and Philosophy* (H. Tomlinson, trans.). New York: Columbia University Press.

—(1991). *Bergsonism* (H. Tomlinson and B. Habberjam, trans.). New York: Zone Books.

—(1992). *Expressionism in Philosophy: Spinoza* (M. Joughin, trans.). New York: Zone Books.

—(1994a). *Difference and Repetition* (P. Patton, trans.). London: The Athlone Press.

—(1994b). He Stuttered. In C. V. Boundas and D. Olkowsky (eds), *Gilles Deleuze and the Theatre of Philosophy* (pp. 22–33). London: Routledge.

—(1995). *Negotiations* (M. Joughin, trans.). New York: Columbia University Press.

—(2001). Dualism, Monism and Multiplicities (Desire–Pleasure–Jouissance), Seminar of 26 March 1973 (D. W. Smith, trans.). *Contretemps*, 2: May, 92–108.

Deleuze, G. and Guattari, F. (1984). *Anti-Oedipus: Capitalism and schizophrenia* (R. Hurley, M. Steem and H. R. Lane, trans.). London: The Athlone Press.

—(1988). *A Thousand Plateaus: Capitalism and schizophrenia II*, (B. Massumi, trans.). London: The Athlone Press.

—(1994). *What is Philosophy?* (H. Tomlinson and G. Burchill, trans.). London: Verso.

Fiumara, G. C. (2001). *The Mind's Affective Life; A psychoanalytic and philosophical inquiry*. Hove: Brunner-Routledge.

Foucault, M. (1980). *Power/Knowledge: Selected interviews/other writings*. Brighton: Harvester Press.

Freud, S. (1953) The Interpretation of Dreams (J. Strachey, trans.). In J. Strachey ed. *The Pelican Freud Library* Volume 4. Harmondsworth: Penguin Books.

Gatens, M. (1996). Through a Spinozist lens: ethology, difference, power. In P. Patton ed., *Deleuze: a critical reader* (pp. 162–87). Oxford: Blackwell.

Greene, M. (1995). *Releasing the imagination: essays on Education, the Arts and Social Change*. San Francisco: Jossey-Bass.

Gregg, M. and Seigworth, G. J. (eds) (2010). *The Affect Theory Reader*. Durham, NC, and London: Duke University Press.

Gregoriou, Z. (2004). Commencing the Rhizome: Towards a minor philosophy of education. *Educational Philosophy and Theory*, 36:3, 233–51.

Grosz, E. (1994). *Volatile Bodies: Toward a corporeal feminism*. Bloomington and Indianapolis, IN: Indiana University Press.

Hardt, M. (1993). *Gilles Deleuze: An apprenticeship in philosophy*. London: UCL Press.

Holland, N. N. (1968). *The Dynamics of Literary Response*. New York: Columbia University Press.

Irigaray, L. (1985). *Speculum of the Other Woman*. Ithaca, NY: Cornell University Press.

Labov, W. (1971). *Sociolinguistic Patterns*. Philadelphia: University of Pennsylvania Press.

Lloyd, G. (1989). Woman as Other: Sex, Gender and Subjectivity. *Australian Feminist Studies*, 10, 13–22.

Luke, A. (2000). Critical literacy in Australia. *Journal of adolescent and adult literacy*, 43, 448–61.

Martin, J. R. and White, P. R. R. (2005). *The Language of Evaluation: Appraisal in English*. Basingstoke: Palgrave Macmillan.

Martindale, C. (1990). *The Clockwork Muse: The predictability of artistic styles*. New York: Basic Books.

Maslow, A. H. (1970). *Motivation and Personality*, 2nd edn. New York: Harper and Row.

McWilliam, E. (1996). Pedagogies, technologies, bodies. In E. McWilliam and P. G. Taylor (eds), *Pedagogy, Technology and the Body* (pp. 79–87). New York: Peter Lang.

Misson, R. and Morgan, W. (2005). Beyond the Pleasure principle? Confessions of a Critical Literacy Teacher. *English in Australia*, 144: Summer, 17–25.

Nietzsche, F. (1968). *The Will to Power* (R. J. Hollingdale and W. Kaufmann, trans). New York: Random House.

Probyn, E. (2004). Teaching Bodies: Affects in the classroom. *Body and Society*, 10:4, 21–43.

Rhys, J. (2000). *Wide Sargasso Sea*. London: Penguin Books.

Schatzki, T. R. (1996). *Social Practices: A Wittgensteinian approach to human activity and the social*. Cambridge: Cambridge University Press.

—(2001). Introduction: Practice theory. In T. R. Schatzki, K. Knorr Cetina and E. von Savigny (eds), *The Practice Turn in Contemporary Theory* (pp. 1–15). London and New York: Routledge.

—(2002). *The Site of the Social: A philosophical account of the constitution of social life and change*. University Park, PA: Pennsylvania State University Press.

Semetsky, I. (2006). *Deleuze, Education and Becoming*. Rotterdam: Sense Publishers.

Shelley, M. (1818). *Frankenstein or, The Modern Prometheus*, Henry Colburn and Richards Bentley, London.

Spinoza, B. (1955). *The Ethics* (R. H. M. Elwes, trans.). New York: Dover Press.

Suler, J. R. (1980). Primary Process Thinking and Creativity. *Psychological Bulletin*, 88, 144–65.

Woolfolk, A. and Margetts, K. (2007). *Educational Psychology*. Sydney: Pearson Education Australia.

Youngblood, A. J. (2010). Deleuze and the girl. *International Journal of Qualitative Studies in Education*, 23:5, 579–87.

CHAPTER FOUR

What is reading? A cartography of reading

Diana Masny

Introduction

The topic of reading is vast. Where and how do you enter the domain that is reading? Reading is a very important concept in society broadly, although reading has been associated almost exclusively with literacy. Literacy, what I consider to be the received view, comprises reading, writing, and processing information[1] (UNESCO, 2008). In modern times, literacy has come to be associated with the printed word/text legitimated through institutions, often referred to as school-based literacy. It was not always the case. In the eighteenth century, many forms of printed text were valued (Cook-Gumperz, 1986). In fact, according to Cook-Gumperz, literacies, that is, forms of writing other than those used by institutions, were just as valued. Political, economic and social forces eclipsed all forms of literacy and foregrounded school-based literacy.[2] Another aspect that has been eclipsed is oral literacy. While still valued in many societies today, these aspects' role has been diminished considerably.

In keeping with the theme of this book, this chapter aims to take a different perspective by mapping a cartography of reading. The chapter produces the structure of a map/rhizome, with each section considered an entry. The cartography of reading entry is presented. To this end we will review what reading is in the received/conventional view. In psychological terms, for example, reading is viewed as a cognitive process (Prior *et al.*, 2011). In education, in particular in Language Arts, reading quite often refers to what a text means. Reading is also considered functional and a skill (Wang *et al.*, 2009). With Multiple Literacies Theory (MLT) (Masny, 2009a), reading is a rhizome. Reading, reading the world and reading self are considered as texts. When reading is reading text, it is not about what a text means. Rather, it is how reading text functions and what reading text produces. Moreover, reading is conceptualized as immanent. In addition, reading is disruptive and takes place in interested ways. Since reading is a process, it is related to the concept of becoming (TP). What makes this conceptualization of reading different is its antihumanist and anti-Cartesian stance. Reading is understood in relation to an assemblage, the combination of elements and the relation of the elements to each other in an assemblage is effected through the power to affect and be affected. Affect disrupts and deterritorializes reading the world and self in this process, becoming.

The reading, reading the world and self entry conceptualizes each of these components separately. They nevertheless intertwine. These conceptualiza-tions are effected in connection with a study of five multilingual children and how they perceive acquiring different writing systems simultaneously and the impact of perceptions on reading, reading the world and self. Accordingly, the following concepts created within MLT and accompanied with a vignette will be presented: reading as disruptive and immanent, reading the world and reading self as well as the intertwining of reading, reading the world and self (RRWS). In addition, conceptualizations of sense and text are addressed. It is important to note that, while each concept is presented in a distinct manner, they nevertheless have relationships to each other:

> A concept has a becoming that involves its relationship with concepts situated on the same plane. Here concepts link up with each other, support one another, coordinate their contours, articulate their respective problems, and belong to the same philosophy, even they have different histories. (WP: p. 18)

The exit from this chapter takes up concept creation with regard to reading, reading the world and self in relation to learning and teaching, assessment and curriculum. These are just some elements that exit in untimely ways as lines of flight that can happen in an 'aha' moment (Lines, 2008) as well as the parenthetical remark (Daignault, 2011) that creates a moment in both cases for lines of becoming that disrupt overcoded literacy practices.

What is reading (conventional view)?

While there are many studies that focus on the social aspects of reading, reading and learning to read is most often taken up as cognitive processes/

skills. What characterizes these studies is that they constitute the received view, that is, a modern stance which can be characterized in many ways. I will focus on five: the centreed subject, developmental stages, individual differences, representation and closed systems. These characteristics are highlighted in studies in psychology/psycholinguistics and applied linguistics selected for this entry.

Reading in the received view is characteristic of studies in applied linguistics. Such studies focus on how children acquire reading skills measured in terms of cognitive abilities, phonological awareness, orthography, and vocabulary skills. There are studies that examine children's reading skills development in many different languages, for example, African languages (Asfaha *et al.*, 2009), Arabic (Levin *et al.*, 2008), and Spanish (Cuetos and Suarez-Coalla, 2009). In addition, the field of applied linguistics has turned its attention to children learning to read simultaneously in different writing systems, as in the case of Chinese–English biliterate children (Luk and Bialystok, 2008; Wang *et al.*, 2009).

While most of the above studies are quantitative in nature and postpositivist, the field of applied linguistics has produced qualitative studies. One such example is Trudell (2006), who examines the emergence of literacy in the mother tongue of a minority language community in Cameroon. The alternatives to English for learning and communication are important to the community. The language of formal education is English. However, the author claims that the uses of the minority language are shaped by existing literacy practices in English. These findings are based on qualitative case study research. The title of the study is *Language Development and Social Uses of Literacy*. 'Language development' in the title of the study refers to the creation of a written form for languages which do not have one and the production of a body of print literature in that language. Literacies are viewed in New Literacy Studies in terms of 'social practices' with a focus on the centreed subject who selects/chooses certain practices (and not others). The proposed 'silo model of literacy use' (Trudell, 2006: p. 638) suggests a closed arborescent (root-like) system: 'At present the majority of instances of written text use centre around two particular social contexts: the school and the church. These two contexts might be called silos of literacy practice (in analogy to the unitary, self-contained structures called "silos"' (p. 638). Literacy practices in different languages are also linked to identity and thus to representation of an identity. 'The language of literacy is implicated in the forging of local and national identity' (p. 625) in (post)colonial contexts in Africa.

Other examples stem from second language research such as Cho *et al.* (2010) in which researchers' concern regarding English language learners' (ELLs) reading achievement led them to conduct a study exploring issues related to reading intervention. The study draws upon interviews and focus groups with instructors and students in order to shed light on the role of motivation and engagement in reading activities. They found that the combination of participants' high interest, the quality of instruction and the learning environment were critical for student engagement in reading. The focus of the study is on individual differences in student achievement in reading on the basis of a reading intervention program that attends to both cognitive and affective processing. In addition, looking at emotional factors and motivation (e.g. in terms of self-efficacy, social interactions, etc.) and references to 'scaffolding' based on students' prior experiences and knowledge places the subject at the centre of the process.

Pang (2008) performs a meta-analysis on studies in applied linguistics and cognitive and educational psychology that characterize good and poor readers. This paper synthesizes findings along three dimensions: language knowledge and processing ability, cognitive ability, and metacognitive strategic competence.

The influence of psychological perspectives and the received view of reading focus on reading comprehension studies, for instance, with both young children (in Grade 1; Wang et al., 2011) and older children (7–11-year-olds; Pike et al., 2010). In these studies, the subject is at the centre when reading is perceived as individual cognitive skills. In addition, recent studies in psychological and psycholinguistic perspectives continue to place a particular emphasis on the role of phonological awareness in determining success in learning to read; for example, Cardoso-Martins et al.'s (2011) study of emergent literacy with pre-school-age children in Brazil. There is also Saiegh-Haddad et al.'s (2011) study of phonemic recognition with 5-year-old Arabic children and Prior et al.'s (2011) research with 5–6-year-olds in Australia learning to read in English. In most cases, developmental stages of acquisition are posited rendering the notion that they may be guiding principles for acquisition but they are nevertheless fixed stages.

Moreover, the received views of literacy often translate into school-based ways of reading and becoming literate. These studies operate within a closed system, that is, they are interested in the determinacy of an outcome related to psychological predictors and measures of reading success and school-readiness (Prior et al., 2011; Romano et al., 2010). In addition, these psychological studies also become powerful arguments in the name of 'evidence-based practice', influencing the development of school programming and a literacy curriculum focusing on phonological, morphological, and orthographic awareness (Berninger et al., 2010).

If an individual is unsuccessful at reading and writing, he or she is considered illiterate. In one study (Eme et al., 2010), functional illiteracy was defined as 'the absence of written language skills in adolescents and adults despite the fact that they have attended school ... It also describes individuals who can use written language to only a very limited extent ...' Functional illiteracy refers to 'a lack of success in the functional acquisition of written language' (Eme et al., 2010: p. 1349). The authors posit that individual differences are related to 'sociocultural disadvantage' and 'individual cognitive abilities'. There is a sense that ILL-literates (low literates) are lacking (deficit models) and need to be (can be) 'fixed' through various interventions.

A final area in which psychological studies of reading in the received view tend to dominate is in research aimed at addressing the particular challenges faced by children learning to read who have diverse linguistic backgrounds and abilities. In the following studies I note that individuals and their abilities at particular skills are referred to in terms of disadvantages (emergent readers with less developed auditory processing abilities are considered to be at a significant disadvantage since auditory processing is key to phonological awareness; Corriveau *et al.*, 2010), and deficits in oral language skills. In a study with young Chinese children, deficits in oral languages skills were considered to be 'at risk' factors in becoming 'poor readers' (Liu *et al.*, 2010). Collectively these studies are premised on deficit models of literacy with a view to minimizing perceived achievement gaps in reading among children.

In sum, research, operationalized within a humanist, Cartesian and closed determinate system, places at the centre the autonomous thinking subject. In addition, the findings of a study, in other words, what is being found/discovered, ground the data empirically. Discussions of the findings tend to revolve around what they mean and represent. When researchers focus on the ways in which the data can predict results (predictors of reading readiness), then such studies contribute to fixing (determinacy) outcomes of literacy practices and interventions. MLT proposes a different view of reading and literacy as untimely, indeterminate and nonrepresentational operating as open systems. Because MLT is closely linked to transcendental empiricism (see Chapter One), the manner of conducting research on literacies also involves indeterminacy, non-representation and the decentreed subject. These aspects of research will unfold in the presentation of vignettes in the following entries.

What is reading?

To respond to this, perhaps Deleuze (NG) might have us back that question up a bit and ask what is a book? It seems a straightforward question, but it has a bearing on the conceptualization of text and the conceptualization of reading. For Deleuze, a text does not represent and therefore reading is not about interpretation. Instead, reading is about sense that emerges as an event (LS). In NG, Deleuze distinguishes his particular conceptualization of a book (in this case *Anti-Oedipus*) as a 'little non-signifying machine' from semiotic approaches, as follows:

> You either see it as a box with something inside and start looking for
> what it signifies, and then if you're even more perverse and depraved you

set off after signifiers. And you treat the next book like a box contained in the first or containing it. And you annotate and interpret and question, and write a book about the book, and so on and on. Or there's another way: you see the book as a little non-signifying machine, and the only question is "Does it work, and how does it work?" How does it work for you? ... This second way of reading's *intensive* [emphasis added]: something comes through or it doesn't. There's nothing to explain, nothing to understand, nothing to interpret. It's like plugging in to an electric circuit ... It relates a book directly to what's Outside ... one flow among others, with no special place in relation to the others, that comes into relations of current, countercurrent, and eddy with other flows – flows of shit, sperm, words, action, eroticism, money, politics, and so on. (NG: pp. 7–8)

A particular kind of reading, that is reading intensively and immanently where sense is an event that happens, is an entry to MLT.

Rhizomatic cartography of reading

In this entry, I am interested in mapping out a rhizomatic cartography of reading, that is, reading, reading the world and reading self. What does reading do? How does it function? What does it produce? The concept of reading presented in this chapter has been conceptualized within MLT. Multiple Literacies Theory is a concept created as a theoretical-practical approach to reading (Masny, 2009a, 2011). Concepts are created in response to problems in life locally and globally. What might these problems be in relation to reading? For one, viewing the subject at the centre places considerable weight for reading as an individual responsibility despite the supportive role of institutions. Moreover, there is the perspective of reading as a human activity because humans have the capacity to retain and manipulate symbols. Finally the notion that reading, while defined to include more than the ability to read and write, is an end point, a result.

MLT focuses on reading, reading the world and self as texts. MLT posits reading as intensive and immanent. Reading is in a process of deterritorialization and becoming. As we explore the different concepts related to reading, each one will be accompanied by a vignette taken from a study involving five multilingual children aged 5 to 7 years old and learning different writing systems simultaneously (Masny, 2009b). The inserted vignettes are not empirical data that are representative of what reading is; rather, as part of the assemblage (e.g. this chapter, book, writer, reader, etc.), they effectuate the power to affect and be affected and transform the assemblage including reading, reading the world and self.

How is reading a rhizomatic cartography? Linking up with the chapter on cartography of multiple literacies, this entry looks at reading and its rhizomatic pathways, that is, reading as intensive and immanent. Accordingly, lines of flight shoot through segmentary lines associated with a territory to disrupt/deterritorialize and reterritorialize. This repetition happens and each time it is different.

Reading is intensive

In the virtual, reading consists of pre-personal asignifying machines in an assemblage. When reading happens in the actual, signifying machines actualize *in situ*. To read is intensive. It is a process that involves reading critically and disruptively. To read critically is to disrupt the machinic relations within an assemblage or across assemblages. To read intensively signals that cognitive, social, cultural, and political forces are at work in reading critically. Deleuze proposes an intensive way of reading: 'something comes through or it does not. There is nothing to explain, nothing to understand, nothing to interpret' (NG: pp. 8–9). In MLT, reading disrupts in an interested way in relation to the power to affect and be affected.

In the following vignette the teacher, Madame Matisse, views a videotape made by the researcher of one classroom observation focusing on the child called Hello Kitty. Hello Kitty (a pseudonym selected by the child) is 7–8 years old during the study. Her mother is Francophone and speaks English as well. Her father is a unilingual English speaker. The family lives in Ottawa and the children attend school where French is the sole language of instruction. Since the family resides in a majority English-speaking province and their mother attended a French-language school, minority language rights of the children to attend French language schools are guaranteed under the Canadian Charter of Rights and Freedom (Government of Canada, 1982).

> *Researcher:* Hello Kitty is making horizontal lines? (as if wanting to create lines in order to write between the lines).
> *Madame Matisse:* Yes but in her notebook, there are no lines and she does not make any lines.
> *R:* No
> *MM:* One is not allowed to talk. One is not allowed to write. The young children before napping will sing or swing to and fro … that's the way it is.
> *MM:* The reading of what has been written. Hello Kitty verifies to see how it is written. It allows for Hello Kitty to see what she is writing, what she is producing.
> *R:* Yes.
> *MM:* What is produced is not always appropriate in terms of what should be produced. I don't remember how she wrote squirrel (*écureuil*).

MM: The glare from the camera.

R: Yes. There, not only the sheet there, you also have the manuscript.

MM: Why is there no colour in the little stories?

MM: Well, we wrote to the editor to ask him why there were no colours in the little stories, in the first level stories. And as a matter of fact, I brought the book to the book fair in Montréal. The editor wrote back to say that it was too expensive to print in/with colours. But it really was a very important question.

R: For Hello Kitty?

MM: Yes of course, they come out of reading the little story books. Little novels, even if there are only three minuscule chapters.

MM: The title in colour perhaps? Inside there are drawings/illustrations but there is no colour. Then it was decided that if the book belongs to you, then you can colour inside.

R: Did she [HK] do it?

MM: No.

In this vignette, Hello Kitty is drawing lines in her notebook that does not have any already. She is creating a story. The conversation moves on to little stories produced in books for children in grade 1 (6–7 years old). When the child Hello Kitty (a text, a desiring machine) enters into a relationship with the little story book (a text, an asignifying machine), a complex assemblage is formed; however, what the virtual potential of this assemblage will produce cannot be predicted. What comes through? What is produced? Reading critically, that is disruptively, actualizes and produces a signifying machine; one that raises questions for Hello Kitty about how it is that the little story books have no colour. This is the effect of reading going on in an interested way. It suggests how power to affect and be affected, life's power to disrupt, contributes to the complexity of proliferating rhizomatic, machinic relations. Reading brought on a deterritorialization unpredictably which became a moment to then reterritorialize in the manner of writing a letter to the publisher and Hello Kitty wanting to create her own book with colour in it (even though the teacher says she doesn't actually do this). Her teacher writes to the book's publisher; desiring machines encounter the abstract machines of economics at work that make adding colour to the little books financially unviable. The book is an asignifying machine in the virtual whose actualizations far exceed what can be accounted for by reading as interpretation and a search for a given meaning.

Reading is immanent

Reading in untimely ways suggests that there is no way of predicting when, where and how the disruption happens. To read immanently refers to the *thought of …* in reading. An example: you are walking down the corridor at work. The reading of the smell of coffee has disrupted an assemblage (you, office, hallway, other co-workers, etc. ...). What could happen next? You might look at your watch and see it is 4 o'clock: a visual and printed reading. This rhizomatic rupture might lead to the thought of a break, possibly going home or possibly the thought of a next vacation: reading as immanent. Reading is a process with the power to affect and be affected (Masny, 2006).

In the next vignette, the researcher is having a conversation with Anne and Cristelle at the daycare centre (year 1 of the study).

> *Researcher:* And tell me what gives you ideas, Anne?
> *Anne:* The computer in my head.
> *R:* The computer in your head?
> *A:* Yes, I have a computer in my head and then I have a shop of little chips. And then I can put them in my computer and I can memorize what I want in the chip.
> *R:* Ok.
> *A:* Chip, but there is a little chip with something in it and I always have to put that chip in combination with another chip that I want.
> *R:* Do you also have a head-computer (computer for a head)?
> *A:* No.
> *R:* Is there anything else that gives you ideas?
> *Cristelle:* I have little secret people/men in my head and jump on top of my trampoline in my house.
> *Cr:* There is a little house and everything inside is a mess.
> *R:* In your head?
> *Cr:* It is the opposite.
> *A: (interrupting)* I write, I write and I want to see what I have written.
> *Cr:* It is always the opposite. They do it and the when you tell them to do it, they won't.
> *R:* In your head?
> *Cr:* Yes. I say 'do little boy' and they do 'not do little boy'.
> *R:* And so what do you do with that when it comes time to write?
> *Cr:* Yes, it gives me ideas!

Immanence refers to the *thought of* ... It emphasizes the pre-personal and untimely aspect of reading; that which cannot be controlled or predicted by what has been actualized before. As Colebrook (2002a) says, 'thinking happens to us, from without. There is a necessity to thinking, for the event of thought lies beyond the autonomy of choice. Thinking happens' (p. 38). In MLT, reading is an event that goes on even when what appears to be happening, at least in conventional terms, is writing. In this vignette, it would seem that there are pre-personal ideas in both minds. They are pre-personal asignifying machines in that ideas are not created by Cristelle and Anne. Rather, they are encased in chips and in secret men and these ideas actualize once they are put to writing in a particular place and space, this time operating within an assemblage (Anne, Cristelle, daycare centre, research, room, social machine, etc. ...). The particular time and space is reflected in that in one situation, ideas are in chips while in the other situation ideas are encased in little men that jump on a trampoline and where the house is a mess. When asked if the messy house with the trampoline is in Cristelle's head, Anne interrupts. When Cristelle speaks again, might there be in her head encounters with different parts of the assemblage and how they relate to each other? The little secret men seem to be acting against her wishes. In other words, as Cristelle says, they do the opposite of what they are intended to be doing. Are these little secret men part of an assemblage that deterritorializes asignifying machines and actualizes signifying ideas when Cristelle finally exclaims: it gives me ideas? What immanent reading is happening? For Anne, the thought of ideas in chips and what these ideas look like will become visible once pen is put to paper or the computer. For Cristelle, she exclaims that the little men give her ideas. What these ideas will say and how they will say it is also unpredictable. Might the children's descriptions of the processes going on in their heads as they prepare to write suggest the immanent character of reading? How is Anne surprised by her own writing? She wants 'to see what she has written'. How is Cristelle a part of the reading event as an assemblage, rather than an actively controlling subject? Immanence cannot be represented and apprehended, but here we might palpate (May, 2005) the operation of immanence in reading.

In sum, reading is about mapping events of experiences on different planes: reading immanently, intensively and in interested ways (foregrounding certain thoughts and experiences that disrupt). To read intensively and immanently extends the power to read differently and to think differently, to go beyond what is to what could be, the virtual–actual interaction: difference and becoming.

Reading the world

How does reading the world function? Reading the world is virtual and actual. In the virtual, reading the world consists in an asignifying machinic assemblage that includes asignifying worldview (Masny, 2012). Reading the world actualizes *in situ*, in a specific time and space, in relation to an assemblage that includes worldview actualized as beliefs in an open system. Reading the world connects with the assemblage. It flows/circulates through the assemblage. The assemblage could deterritorialize because reading immanently and intensively as well as reading the world is an event and a different assemblage reterritorializes. Moreover, a deterritorialization of the assemblage can reterritorialize reading the world.

This interview was conducted in Spanish at home with Estrella, her mother and a research assistant who spoke Spanish (year 2 of the study)

Estrella: I like to read in French because in Spanish it feels more difficult I do not know why. I only like to read what I have written in Spanish, but in French I write and read all the things.

Research assistant: What kind of stories do you like to read?

E: Well, what I like to read are not stories but things about real life. About animals I like. I do not like the experiments. I want to know what is happening to them, why they are becoming extinct, or why they are coming to an end. Also, all kinds of things. The marmots. Everything. But what interest me the most is the snow leopards.

Mother: Don't you like adventure stories and fairy tales? Don't you like those?

E: I like those more or less.

M: But I thought that you love them like Harry Potter and all of that.

E: Those are of real human beings.

M: No those are fantasy stories.

E: But those are humans!

M: The characters are human, but the stories are fantasy stories. There is not Hogwarts.

E: I don't care. What I care about is that they are of real people.

Reading the world involves asignifying texts and worldviews in the virtual. How do they actualize in this vignette, in this particular assemblage where the human and the nonhuman come into a relation? In the actual, worldviews reterritorialize as beliefs that fuel the discourse created with Estrella and her mother (Masny, 2012). Estrella loves to write, and during the study she produced a lengthy story in Spanish about a princess called Oceano. However, she does not like to read anything but her own texts in Spanish. In French, reading is about animals, not animal characters in a story. Reading the world happens in different ways in different contexts. Could it be that writing is for fairy tales and adventure stories such as Harry Potter about 'things in real life'? Reading the world as an open system brings in snow leopards and Harry Potter. Estrella talks about enjoying reading 'real life' stories giving the example of endangered animals. The virtual dimension of sense actualizes as a signifying machine and the effect of reading the world is a belief system (actual) in which snow leopards are part of 'real life'. Then the mother introduces the world-famous Harry Potter series, describing it as a 'fantasy story' (i.e. not 'real life'). A different belief system enters the assemblage, the open system, in this event of reading the world. How does the introduction of difference reconfigure and deterritorialize the assemblage (virtual), thereby opening the potential for the transformation of a belief system (actual)? The mother's utterance expresses a belief system in the actual (apparently contrary to the child's) which becomes virtual again. How does virtual sense actualize in the case of the child? How might a reterritorialization take place? Estrella seems to refuse her mother's assertions about the status of the Harry Potter stories and the people in them, finally reaffirming that they are 'real people'. The processes of de/reterritorialization when reading the world are the productive power of difference.

In sum, reading the world is virtual and actual. In the virtual there are pre-personal asignifying worldviews that when actualized emerge as beliefs. In this vignette, worldviews and Estrella are part of an assemblage. Worldviews actualize into beliefs – in this case, a belief that, while Hogwarts may not be a real place, Hogwarts is about real people. Is the nonhuman like Harry Potter or Hermione deterritorialized and in the process of becoming reterritorialized as human? Is this reading the world when bodies meet and relationality happens effectuating a *becoming other*?

Reading self

The self is not defined by its identity but by a process of 'becoming'. (ECC: xxix)

Reading self, like reading and reading the world, is a process that flows/circulates in an assemblage. Reading self is both virtual and actual. In the virtual, reading self consists of (affects and percepts). This process is one of becoming that deterritorializes. Reading self is actualized and sense emerges as part of a signifying assemblage charged with affection and perception. It is the power to affect and be affected. Take the example of coffee once more. A particular assemblage in which reading self and reading the world (a desiring machine – the smell of coffee, the clock, the time of day, place, etc. happening in the mind – and a social machine, etc.) happens at that particular moment in the mind. This assemblage disturbs (deterritorializes) and creates a different reading, a becoming on a plane of immanence. Deterritorialization as becoming produces the *thought of* a coffee break perhaps. Transformations happen in the process of becoming. Then there is a reterritorialization of reading self and the world that flows through the assemblage and thereby the assemblage reconfigures. It is not a return to what was. It is a different assemblage.

The following vignette is based on an interview at home with Estrella and her mother. We were discussing the different-levelled books for young children (year 1 of the study)

> *Mother:* Ah ah see. So at first they would come let's say with a book. They would start with a book like that in French and they would increase the ... you know like a couple of lines. But also even with a couple of lines they would start with very easy easy language and then they would increase the level of complexity with the same amount of lines and so it has been a progress so now you know more contractions, more ee difficult longer words or it was a difficult passage with longer words they would try to repeat them all along

the book. So that real in the head so then they would start the difficult and like they have the level of difficulty and the kids could see oh! this is level 1, oh! this is baba babébé I don't know.

Estrella: Bébé fafa.

M: Bébé fafa. Or something eee so they would come and then she is very proud I am now in level 3. So between the kids here I think competition a little bit of competition oh! they can see oh! now I am level 3 so they show each other and so the next time she would show up with a 5. Sometimes she was a bit too ambitious, she would come with a 7 and then she would realize herself, realize it was too challenging she would go back lets say to 5 but within a week or two weeks she was she was already at that at the other level and now I'm really surprise she brought this.

Researcher: Yes yes.

M: I'm really surprised and I don't know if she actually, when she brings books like that it's very challenging for her so what I have to do is get a ruler and so she doesn't get overwhelmed because her body language, like she gets anxious. Like we're, if she starts reading like that she tends to move and then she's climbing all over me and she gets very anxious. So then what I start to do I go, I cover it and then I go one by one.

R: One line at a time.

M: One line at a time and then she feels not so anxious.

Reading self is a process. What does it do? How does it function? In a virtual assemblage, reading self is responsible for asignifying machines reading each other in terms of how they relate when encountering each other (relationality of encounters). There is the virtual resonance of sensa-tions (percepts and affects) that are actualized as signifying assemblages in the actual. What is produced? Reading self refers to reading the relation-ality of encounters within the assemblage. In this vignette, each machine in the assemblage (Estrella, Mother, book, social machine, reading the world, etc.) focuses on reading each other in relation to different levels of book. There is a reading self, the assemblage that includes level 3 books. Then a deterritorialization of the assemblage happens and the challenge is on for a level 5 book in the becoming-proficient reader. When the assemblage includes level 7 books, then once more the assemblage is reconfigured, and reconfigured differently. Reading self of the assemblage happens as different machines read each other. In addition, affect plays an important role as anxiety, in this instance, is part of the assemblage. Anxiety deterritorializes and the assemblage reconfigures. Mother as part of the assemblage creates a different relationship to Estrella. This assemblage produces another reading self. There is a reterritorialization happening. It is the operation of difference between these de/reterritorializations that drives reading self as a process of becoming. In the virtual, percepts and affects relate in an assemblage and create a transformation which becomes actualized when reading self. From investment in such literate practices how is Estrella *becoming other*? How is the child transformed in this process of becoming literate?

Reading and sense

Reading is about sense. Sense is not about interpretation. Deleuze was not interested in interpretation. Interpretation involves finding the meaning behind the text as if there is a truth to be discovered. In addition, when a text awaits interpretation, interpretation is grounded in transcendent empiricism. The reader seeks to rationalize his/her interpretation through essentialism, that is, what are the essential truths that justify this interpretation. The reader wants to explain the interpretation but also to provide justification of the interpretation. Finally, interpretation places the subject at the centre as the autonomous thinking subject. 'In truth, significance and interpretosis are the two diseases of the earth or the skin, in other words, humankind's fundamental neurosis' (TP: p. 144).

For Deleuze, sense is an event that emerges (Colebrook, 2002a). Sense is virtual. It is activated when words, notes and icons are actualized *in situ* and in interested ways. Sense expresses not what something is but its power to become. *Sense* is an event (LS: p. 176) – 'the event is sense itself'. Sense has virtual–actual components. Language, for instance, is the virtual dimension of sense because language is more than its actual element (Colebrook, 2002a). Perhaps sense as virtual becomes actualized, just as the event is actualized as an 'instantaneous production intrinsic to interactions between various kinds of forces' (that is, assemblage) (Stagoll, 2005: p. 87). This product (that is, sense-event) is not a state of affairs, but a transformation; a becoming.

In the next vignette, Dora is talking with the researcher about a video clip of a mini-lesson Dora taught her classmate. Dora is describing the process she undertakes to write the words, eyes (*yeux*) and puppet (*marionette*) (year 2 of the study). Dora was also born in Canada. Her family comes from Djibouti, a former French colony. In the home, the children are used to hearing French, Afar (the language of the region), Somali and Arabic. In addition, the children speak English in the neighborhood. Dora's mother is an early childhood educator while her father teaches French as a second language.

> *Researcher:* What did you write here? (researcher and Dora are viewing a piece of Dora's writing together)
> *Dora:* Here are the eyes of the puppet.
> *R:* Ok. I recall that when you wrote the word, 'here are the eyes', it seems that at that point you stopped writing for a moment. What was happening?

D: Because I could not remember how one writes 'eyes'.
R: What did you do to recall how to write the word? What did you
   do? I was hearing you say all sorts of things. What were you saying?
D: Hmm mm. I read the word, 'eyes'.
R: You read it where?
D: In my head.
R: In your head. And then what did you do? And then there is the
   word puppet. You seem to hesitate when writing this word. What
   was happening when you came to write this word?
R: Would you like to see the word (video clip) once more? (upon
   viewing) Does it look alright?
D: No.
R: What would you like to change?
D: Eyes and puppet.
R: You want to change both. Go ahead and then perhaps tell me more
   about this change.
(‡)
D: mistake. I wanted to make an 'e'.
R: Ok, that looks like an 'e'. Yes, let's continue.

Dora articulates the process of writing words when there is a spelling
mistake. Reading is conceptualized as reading intensively (disruptively)
and immanently (bringing on the thought of …) in connection with 'a life'
(the pre-personal) that bring 'inside' and 'outside' a text into a relation.
As such, reading is concerned with assemblages, with the reading event:
movement, a becoming. Reading then is not limited to the received view
as looking at and interpreting the meaning of a text. Instead, reading is an
event that involves a relationship between bodies (a text, a child, a brain, a
time of day, etc.) within an assemblage of life. The machinic assemblage of
life produces sense, that is, not what a text is or means, but how it might
become.

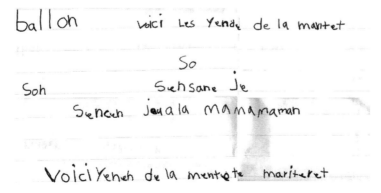

Figure 4.1 Dora's sentence: *Here are the puppet's eyes.*

Even writing involves reading, reading the world and reading self as literacies as processes happen intensively and immanently. In this vignette, Dora talks about how she writes her sentence, here are the puppet's eyes (*voici les yeux de la marionette*) and what happens when she cannot remember how to write eyes (*yeux*). She tells us she reads the word 'in her head'. The mind is a site of rhizomatic connections happening as an effect of reading, reading the world and self. What is produced?

Dora goes on to say that she would like to change eyes and puppet because she has made a mistake and she wants to add an 'e'. What is the process for the change to come about? What kind of assemblage produces this orthographic change? Might it involve connections happening in the mind with accepted, standard forms of orthography? With the words seen elsewhere (e.g. in a storybook)? With feedback from a teacher-body? With a dictionary? With a classmate? Might the change be connected to a becoming, that is, ways in which reading, reading the world and self transforms bodies: Dora, French orthography, the words eyes and puppet, etc.?

Reading as text

Deleuze (NG) offers a different way of reading texts as 'non-signifying machines' (p. 8), so that the question is no longer 'What do they [texts] *mean*?' but rather, 'How do they work?' and 'What do they produce?' (Masny, 2006). Each text in the actual and virtual is a machinic assemblage. In the virtual, text consists of pre-personal, *asignifiying* machines. Text actualizes through an assemblage of heterogeneous forces that come together in a particular time and place (actualization of a sense-event). Text is a sense event, an outcome of virtual events connecting with actual experiences (Masny, 2009a).

Text as a territory in the actual deterritorializes in the virtual through reading intensively (disruptive) and immanently. This process opens up possibilities for lines of flight and becoming to happen and reterritorialize in the actual into another discourse and transformation of the assemblage. Texts, in a broad sense, can refer to music, visual arts (painting, sculpting), physics, mathematics, and digital remixes, for example. In the virtual, they are asignifying texts. When machines connect, the encounter is textual. Machines, reading each other, reading the world both intensively and immanently, deterritorialize the abstract assemblage. A particular assemblage actualizes in a particular way because of the relation that each machine encounters with the other. It is an event from which sense actualizes.

In the following vignette, the daycare centre educator is in conversation with the researcher about Cristelle (Year 2 of the study).

Researcher: What does Cristelle read?

Educator: What does she read? Often she will read, she will take, she likes cartoons a lot. Often she will choose a cartoon book and she also likes adventure stories. Yes, she likes when something is going on in it.

R: Ok.

Ed: Yes. Once she told me that if I were her, I would not have done the drawings like that.

How might the educator's comments about Cristelle's response to reading texts – 'if I were her, I would not have done the drawings like that' – suggest how reading, reading the world and self effects a disruption (reading intensively) and brings on the thought of (reading immanently) difference? Throughout the two-year research project, the assemblage that includes Cristelle would often disrupt what a text should look like. As I got to know Cristelle, this kind of questioning, focusing on the artwork of a reading text (e.g. cartoon strips), was often part of our conversations, Cristelle's constant insistence, let's have pictures! How is such desire produced as the effect of the machinic assemblages of a reading event?

With Deleuze, the sense of art (not what it means but how it becomes) is effected through the actualization of virtual affects and percepts as affections and sensations (colour, texture, etc.). A disruption in the assemblage that was the educator, the book, Cristelle, etc. happened. Reading was critical and intensive. In the virtual, perhaps it was the *thought of* the illustrations in a book? The lines? The colours? Reading became immanent. The assemblage transformed in the process of becoming *other* (the illustrations would have been different). Becoming is central to MLT. Reading as text, in this context of deterritorialization, consists of virtual (impersonal) abstract machines in an assemblage (book, colours, lines, textures, etc. ...). When abstract machines actualize as concrete machines in an assemblage, the assemblage transforms and from this event in which a deterritorialization happened, *becoming other* is effectuated.

Reading, reading the world and self (RRWS)

RRWS are intricately intertwined but distinct and draw on the virtual and the actual. Reading is intensive and immanent. To read intensively is to read critically. To read intensively signals that cognitive, social, cultural, and political forces are at work in reading critically. In so doing, reading critically is reading disruptively, and in interested and untimely ways. Moreover, because reading happens in untimely ways, there is no prediction about how reading is taken up. This leads us to reading as immanence. Take the example of watching a movie. How often do you see a scene that may transport you to think of what might happen next? Another possibility might be creating connections with your life and the thought of this happening to you or your dog. Not only is reading untimely but it is also is the thought of what can happen. In this way, reading as sense emerges and a power to become happens (Masny, 2009b).

Reading the world is the point at which language (the human and the non-human) and the world meet and sense actualizes *in situ*. Reading self is an event both virtual and actual. In the virtual, reading self as stated earlier focuses on how the asignifying machines within an assemblage relate to each other and what happens in the encounters within the assemblage. Through this process, machines in the assemblage resonate to produce sensations (affects and percepts). This process is one of becoming that deterritorializes. An assemblage actualizes *in situ* and sense emerges as an effect of signifying assemblages that relate to each other (reading self) charged with affection and the perception: the relationality of encounters. Take the example of coffee once more. A territorialization consists of a particular assemblage of concrete social and desiring machines and reading the world. When these machines in the assemblage read each other (reading self), this assemblage disturbs (deterritorializes) and creates a different reading, a becoming on a plane of immanence (reading intensively and immanently). Deterritorialization produces the *thought of* a next vacation, perhaps. There has been a transformation. Then there is a reterritorialization of reading self and the world. It is not a return to what was. These are different assemblages. What constitute assemblages are events of life, 'creations that need to be selected and assessed according to their power to act and intervene in life' (Colebrook, 2002b: p. xliv) while reading intensively and immanently.

In the following vignette, the researcher is having a conversation with Cristelle about a writing activity she completed in a Language Arts class the day before.

My riddle. I am brown and one eats me at Easter. I am hidden while you look for me. I am delicious when you eat me. Who am I. Chocolate.

Researcher: What do you think of the activity you did, the riddle?
Cristelle: It was amusing.
R: What did you find amusing?
Cr: One can write anything at all.
R: Did that please you?
Cr: Yes!!!
R: What did you find that was pleasing?
Cr: One can write words one likes.
R: Do you have many words you like?
Cr: I used one.
R: Yes, which one?
Cr: Chocolate.

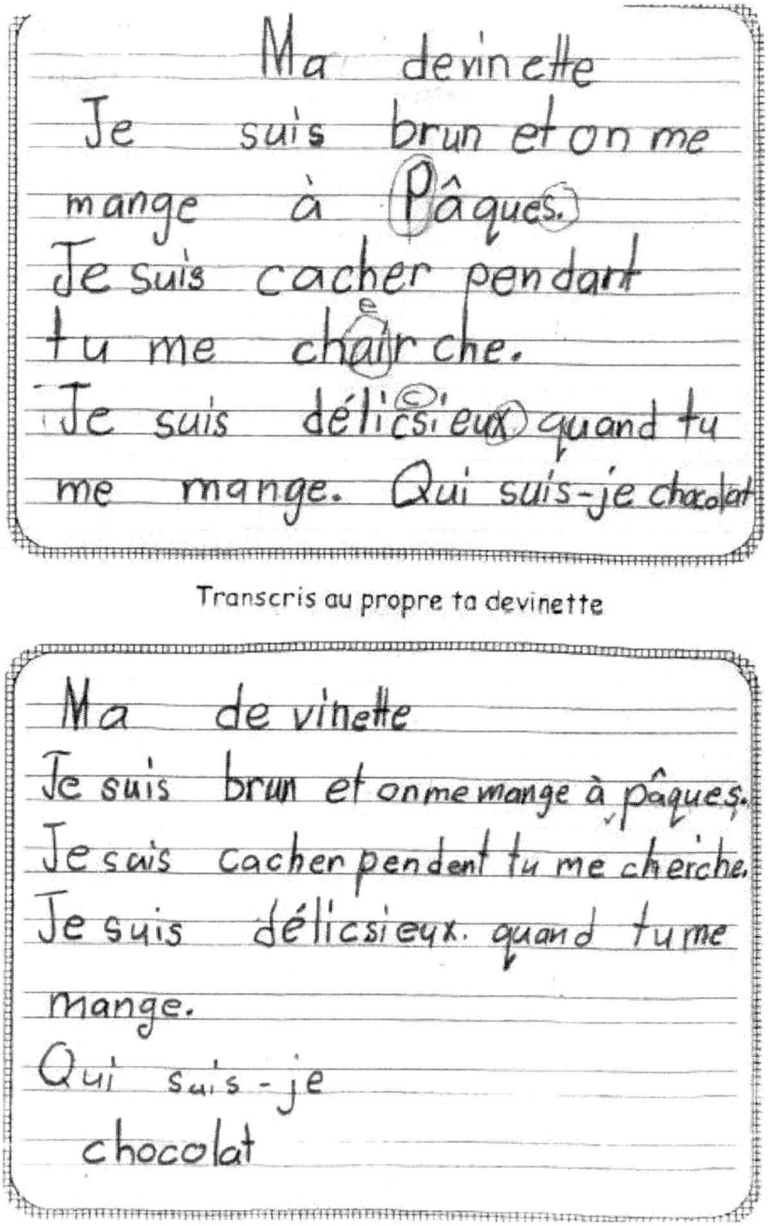

Ma devinette
Je suis brun et on me
mange à Pâques.
Je suis cacher pendant
tu me chairche.
Je suis délicsieux quand tu
me mange. Qui suis-je chocolat

Transcris au propre ta devinette

Ma de vinette
Je suis brun et on me mange à pâques.
Je suis cacher pendent tu me cherche.
Je suis délicsieux. quand tu me
mange.
Qui suis-je
chocolat

Figure 4.2 Cristelle's riddle.

R: Ah, ha, ok. Because you like chocolate? Is that it? Yes *(after Cristelle nods in the affirmative)*. Ok.
(Cristelle interrupts and interjects)
Cr: And we call my dad, Mister Chocolate.
R: You call your dad Mister Chocolate?
Cr: Sometimes.
R: Sometimes, yes.
(Cristelle interrupts and interjects)
Cr: Because he eats our chocolates.
R: He eats your chocolate?
(Cristelle laughs)
Cr: Yes, at Halloween, he takes my bag of candies *(laughs)*. He takes some of the chocolate and puts it in his drawer. After I try to find the pieces of chocolate I prefer but I looked in my dad's drawer and all the chocolate was in the drawer.

Would doing the riddle activity be an event read critically: the potential of taking this activity down a different path? Cristelle often expresses her displeasure at writing. Yet here the writing activity is amusing. The criteria for choosing words: those with the power to affect and be affected in an assemblage (activity, Cristelle, classroom, classmates, etc. ...). Affect brings on the *thought of* ... (reading as immanent) the word, chocolate. The activity does not end there. Chocolate was disrupted and reterritorialized as Mister Chocolate, Cristelle's father. Mister Chocolate was deterritorialized in another untimely event, the Halloween episode. These disruptions and different pathways are rhizomatic. This process involves reading intensively, immanently, reading the world and reading self (the different machines in relation to each other within the assemblage). While reading, reading the world and reading self are intertwined, they are nevertheless distinct.

Exit

Moving out of the chapter, the question of what is reading and how it happens is a story about mapping literacies through a rhizomatic cartography in which reading is intensive and immanent. Moreover, reading is a process that in the virtual consists of asignifying machines which deterritorialize and reterritorialize in an assemblage in the actual. In the actual, the assemblage has a particular combination that is unique to a particular context. Reading, reading the world and self circulate in the assemblage to reterritorialize until the assemblage deterritorializes once more. Becoming is central to MLT. Through deterritorialization, becoming *other* forms and transforms the human and the non-human from events. Semetsky writes: 'The event itself, the human experience per se, is to be considered as ... "the inventive potential" ... or becoming other than the present self' (Semetsky, 2003: p. 213). Reading is also virtual and actual. It circulates in an assemblage engaging in the virtual–actual of an assemblage. From the flow of continuous investment in reading, and reading the world on various intersecting planes (virtual plane of consistency and actual plane of composition) and in different contexts (school, home, community, etc.), becoming *other* happens.

What is the link between reading and rhizomatic cartography? How does it function?

What does it produce? When a deterritorialization occurs as an event, the direction of the line of flight is unpredictable. Take for instance the riddle activity – how one connection became linked to another in an untimely way, a rhizome with lines of flight shooting through segmentary lines with its overcoding literacy practices. This is what reading does. Reading disrupts overcoded literacy practices which then reterritorialize differently.

What then is the relationship of reading as a process to teaching, learning, pedagogy and assessment, and curriculum? The key is the rhizome, mapping literacies, reading how teaching, learning, pedagogy, assessment and curriculum happen. In teaching, Lines (2008) refers to an 'aha' moment. He describes it as the moment when the learning and teaching in a relational environment of the class resonates producing sensations, affects and percepts that actualize as affections and perceptions. 'This is the time when teachers and students resonate with the learning moment and intuitively concur with the particular configuration of the learning experience at hand' (Lines, 2008: p. 138). An 'aha' moment is an event when a deterritorialization unfolds and learning and teaching take off on rhizomatic pathways in the process of reading the world and self intensively and immanently. The overcoded teaching practices (tracings referred to in Chapter Two) as well as learning strategies are disrupted and desiring machines (machines produced in the assemblage) take over and this moment provides the potentiality for becoming *other* (than the previous teacher-practices and learner-strategies). This is the moment when the tracing is put back on the map. Reading critically and immanently also brings disruption to assessment and the way assessment is conducted as a territory of a supercoded practice. This calls for concept creation related to policy, curriculum and accountability. What do they do? How do they function? What do they produce?

In curriculum, this 'aha' moment can also refer to being on the lookout (*être aux aguets*) for a parenthetical remark, according to Daignault (2011). It is that moment of deterritorialization, disrupting an institutionalized curriculum and taking off on lines of flight through reading the world and self intensively and immanently. In the end, becoming *other* is important as a concept that creates change in the middle of territories that reterritorialize differently each time because transformations transform.

References

Asfaha, Y. M., Kurvers, J. and Kroon, S. (2009). Grain size in script and teaching: Literacy acquisition in Ge'ez and Latin. *Applied Psycholinguistics*, 30(4), 709–24.

Berninger, V. W., Abbott, R. D., Nagy, W. and Carlisle, J. (2010). Growth in phonological, orthographic, and morphological awareness in grades 1 to 6. *Journal of Psycholinguistic Research*, 39(2), 141–63.

Cardoso-Martins, C., Mesquita, T. C. L. and Ehri, L. (2011). Letter names and phonological awareness help children to learn letter-sound relations. *Journal of Experimental Child Psychology*, 109(1), 25–38.

Cho, S., Xu, Y. and Rhodes, J. A. (2010). Examining English language learners' motivation of and engagement in reading: A qualitative study. *The Reading Matrix: An International Online Journal*, 10(2), 205–21.

Colebrook, C. (2002a). *Gilles Deleuze*. New York: Routledge.

—(2002b). *Understanding Deleuze*. London: Unwin.

Cook-Gumperz, J. (1986). *The construction of literacy*. Cambridge: Cambridge University Press.

Corriveau, K. H., Goswami, U. and Thomson, J. M. (2010). Auditory processing and early literacy skills in a preschool and kindergarten population. *Journal of Learning Disabilities*, 43(4), 369–82.

Cuetos, F. and Suarez-Coalla, P. (2009). From grapheme to word in reading acquisition in Spanish. *Applied Psycholinguistics*, 30(4), 583–601.

Daignault, J. (2011). In conversation with Jacques Daignault and Diana Masny. *Policy Futures in Education*, 9(4), 528–39. Available online at http://dx.doi.org/10.2304/pfie.2011.9.4.528 (accessed 24 January 2012).

Eme, E., Lacroix. L. and Almecija, A. (2010). Oral narrative skills in French adults who are functionally illiterate: Linguistic features and discourse organization, *Journal of Speech, Language, and Hearing Research*, 53(5), 1349–71.

Government of Canada (1982). *Canadian Charter of Rights and Freedoms*. Ottawa: Department of Justice. Available online at http://laws-lois.justice.gc.ca/eng/charter (accessed 19 August 2011).

International Association for the Evaluation of Educational Achievement (2011). *Trends in international mathematics and science study 2011 (TIMSS 2011)*. Available online at http://www.iea.nl/timss_2011.html (accessed 24 January 2012).

International Association for the Evaluation of Educational Achievement (2011). *Progress in international reading literacy study 2011 (PIRLS 2011)*.Available online at http://www.iea.nl/pirls_2011.html (accessed 24 January 2012).

Levin, I., Saiegh-Haddad, E., Hende, N. and Ziv, M. (2008). Early literacy in Arabic: An intervention study among Israeli Palestinian kindergartners. *Applied Psycholinguistics*, 29(3), 413–36.

Lines, D. (2008). *Nomadic Education*. I. Semetsky ed. Rotterdam: Sense Publishing.

Liu, P. D., McBride-Chang, C., Wong, A. M., Tardif, T., Stokes, S. F., Fletcher, P. and Hua S. (2010). Early oral language markers of poor reading performance in Hong Kong Chinese children. *Journal of Learning Disabilities*, 43(4), 322–31.

Luk, G. and Bialystok, E. (2008). Common and distinct cognitive bases for reading in English–Cantonese bilinguals. *Applied Psycholinguistics*, 29(2), 269–89.

Masny, D. (2006). Learning and creative processes: A poststructural perspective on language and multiple literacies. *International Journal of Learning, 12*(5), 147–55.

—(2009a). *Bridging access, equity and quality: The case for multiple literacies.* Refereed paper presented at the National Conference of the Australian Association for the Teaching of English (AATE) for Teachers of English and Literacy, Wrest Point Conference Centre. Hobart, Tasmania. Available online at http://www.englishliteracyconference.com.au/files/documents/hobart/conferencePapers/refereed/MasnyDiana.pdf (accessed 17 January 2012).

—(2009b). Literacies as becoming: A child's conceptualizations of writing systems. In D. Masny and D. R. Cole, *Multiple literacies theory: A Deleuzian perspective* (pp. 13–30). Rotterdam: Sense Publishers.

—(2011). Multiple Literacies Theory: Exploring futures. *Policy Futures in Education, 9*(4), 494–504. Available online at http://dx.doi.org/10.2304/pfie.2011.9.4.494 (accessed 24 January 2012).

—(2012). Multiple Literacies Theory: Discourse, sensation, resonance and becoming. *Discourse* (pp. 113–28), 33(1).

May, T. (2005). *Gilles Deleuze: An introduction.* Cambridge: Cambridge University Press.

Pang, J. (2008). Research on good and poor reader characteristics: Implications for L2 reading research in China. *Reading in a Foreign Language*, 20(1), 1–18.

Pike, M. M., Barnes, M. A. and Barron, R. W. (2010). The role of illustrations in children's inferential comprehension. *Journal of Experimental Child Psychology*, 105(3), 243–55.

Prior, M., Bavin, E. and Ong, B. (2011). Predictors of school readiness in five- to six-year-old children from an Australian longitudinal community sample. *Educational Psychology*, 31(1), 3–16.

Romano, E., Babchishin, L., Pagani, L. S. and Kohen, D. (2010). School readiness and later achievement: Replication and extension using a nationwide Canadian survey. *Developmental Psychology*, 46(5), 995–1007.

Saiegh-Haddad, E., Levin, I., Hende, N. and Ziv, M.. (2011). The linguistic affiliation constraint and phoneme recognition in diglossic Arabic. *Journal of Child Language*, 38(2), 297–315.

Semetsky, I. (2003). The problematics of human subjectivity: Gilles Deleuze and the Deweyan legacy. *Studies in Philosophy and Education*, 22, 211–25.

Stagoll, C. (2005). Event. In A. Parr ed., *The Deleuze dictionary* (pp. 87–9). New York: Columbia University Press.

Trudell, B. (2006). Language development and social uses of literacy: A study of literacy practices in Cameroonian minority language communities. *International Journal of Bilingual Education and Bilingualism*, 9(5), 625–42.

UNESCO (2008). *The Global Literacy Challenge.* Paris: UNESCO. Available online at http://unesdoc.unesco.org/images/0016/001631/163170e.pdf (accessed 24 January 2012).

Wang, H.-C., Castles, A., Nickels, L. and Nation, K. (2011). Context effects on orthographic learning of regular and irregular words. *Journal of Experimental Child Psychology*, 109(1), 39–57.

Wang, M., Yang, C. and Cheng, C. (2009). The contributions of phonology, orthography, and morphology in Chinese–English biliteracy acquisition. *Applied Psycholinguistics*, 30(2), 291–314.

Notes

1 UNESCO's working definition of literacy from 2005 refers to the 'ability to identify, understand, interpret, create, communicate, and compute, using printed and written materials associated with varying contexts' (UNESCO, 2008: p. 21).

2 Conventional definitions of reading refer mainly to school-based literacy which is an indicator of the literacy rate of a country. It has become an important benchmark in the education, economics, and health of a nation. One might venture to say that literacy rates are important to a country's stature in the world. Note for example international tests continuously being conducted: Progress in International Reading Literacy Study (PIRLS) and the Programme for International Student Assessment (PISA), Trends in International Mathematics and Science Study (TIMSS) for school-age children. Testing has become a way for a country to be accountable to its citizens and the world!

CHAPTER FIVE

Cartographies of talking groups

Diana Masny

Introduction

In Lewis Carroll's *Alice in Wonderland*, Humpy Dumpty says: '... when I use a word, it means what I want it to, no more, no less ... the question is which is to be master ...'. Deleuze responds by stating that the subject is not master of the word it chooses to express its beliefs or desires (Lambert, 2002). 'What comes first is the collective assemblage of enunciation resulting in the assignations of individuality and their shifting distribution within discourse' (TP: p. 80).

There are undoubtedly many questions connected to the title of this chapter, collective enunciations. What are they? How are they related to literacy studies? What is the significance of collective enunciations for literacies? The structure of the chapter is as follows: the nature of language and collective assemblage of enunciation, and creating connections between collective enunciations and reading by focusing on a study that explores how multilingual children acquire multiple writing systems simultaneously.

To understand collective assemblage of enunciations requires an understanding of Deleuze and Guattari's position on language and the social and political nature of language. Their views on language presented in *A Thousand Plateaus* (TP) were a response in part to Chomskian linguistic theory starting in 1960s. The polemic is explored in the first part of this chapter. Moreover, through the introduction of pragmatics and the relationship of speech acts, Deleuze and Guattari incorporated a political/pragmatic nature in language. Since Deleuze and Guattari also perceived language to be social in nature, they created the concept of collective enunciation. However, to understand this concept it is important to explore the concept of assemblage beforehand. Accordingly, an assemblage (*agencement*) is viewed as a coming together and is comprised of, for example, bodies, expressions, and territories. The individual is part of the assemblage. As such, there is no individual enunciation. Lambert stated earlier, '… the subject is not master of the word'. Then what/who is? – Might a response be the dominant social order and its institutions? Bogue (1989) would argue that with language comes the organizing of reality according to a dominant social order, hence the importance of order-words (or words of order: *mots d'ordre*). The function of language according to Deleuze and Guattari is to transmit word-orders and that of the collective order (Bogue, 1989). The words, Bogue might contend, are those of the social dominant order. That is perhaps why Deleuze and Guattari refer to what we say as indirect discourse when we speak. The question might then become, which discourse could emerge to unhinge the territory of language (the territory of literacy that gives primacy to the printed text) that organizes reality according to a dominant social order. What immanent and destabilizing forces could there be? I explore these questions, not so much to elaborate on Deleuzean and Guattarian concepts but rather as an attempt to familiarize readers with these concepts in relation to education (teaching and learning) and multiple literacies. Publications detailing Deleuzean and Guattarian concepts are available (Bonta and Protevi, 2004; Parr, 2002; Patton, 2010).

Once I have explored these concepts, the second part of this chapter highlights their relevance for multiple literacies, especially as I have theorized multiple literacies in terms of reading, reading the world and self (Masny, 2009). In addition, as part of the assemblage of this chapter, vignettes will highlight the rhizomatic social (and political) character of language at work through collective assemblages of enunciation. I will argue that sensations (affect and percept) and relationality (a process of encounters between bodies and milieus/context) that emerge through collective assemblages of enunciation contribute to multiple literacies, reading, reading the world and self. Sense emerges and maps untimely becomings.

Language

This part of the chapter focuses on language and collective assemblages of enunciation. To do so implies that we examine Deleuze and Guattari's stance on language which required creation of concepts as a response to a problem, Chomsky's position on language. As a result, this part of the chapter explores the relationship between 1) the concept of language (a set of order-words – *mots d'ordre*, implicit presuppositions, statements and incorporeal transformations), 2) political (pragmatics) and social processes (collective enunciations and machinic assemblages that can deterritorialize and reterritorialize) and 3) an abstract machine that creates a diagram of assemblages on which language depends.

When Deleuze and Guattari foreground the social and political character of language, the rhizomatic mapping of language is opposed to the Chomskian arborescent tracings of syntax (syntactic trees). When Chomsky elaborated on his theory of Universal Grammar, he was much influenced by seventeenth-century Port Royal Grammar, which was inspired by the work of Descartes. Chomsky proceeded to elaborate his linguistic theory and entitled one of his books *Cartesian Linguistics* (2009). His main thesis is that all languages possess universal structures. To posit such a stance, Chomsky had to think of language as devoid of social and cultural variables related to language. These variables which are considered by applied linguistics as environmental traits contribute to factors of individual differences in language learning. Theoretical linguistics consider these extraneous traits as contaminating variables. Moreover, to theorize language, one posits an ideal native speaker to extract universal structures of language.

Deleuze and Guattari had a different approach to language. The key words to retain are:

- political nature of language
- pragmatics
- relation between speech/statement and action
- social nature of language
- order-words
- implicit presuppositions, and
- incorporeal transformation.

Moreover, while theoretical linguistics is interested in fixing language by according primacy to constants and a secondary role to variation, Deleuze and Guattari had a different and reversed take on constants and variations within phonological, syntactical and semantic systems of language. Variations were primary; variations are virtual and exist on a continuum, for the untimely can never predict for instance how the pronunciation of the word 'shell' is actualized. It would depend on the context. The same could be said about semantics: a word, a sentence can take on different meanings on a continuum. In the end a speech-act is the actualization of virtual variations along continua.

Through speech-acts, Deleuze and Guattari were interested in the relation between the statement and the act, in the relation between action and speech. In other words, a statement produces an act. In addition, phonological, syntactical and semantic aspects of language are accompanied by pragmatics 'To introduce pragmatics into language is to analyze language politically' (Grisham, 1991: p. 45). The political nature of language becomes integral to language. For example, when a teacher asks learners to do something, it is a statement that is politically empowered to act.

With actions stemming from speech, transformations occur. Deleuze and Guattari speak of incorporeal transformations. The latter refers to a statement that results in change. For example: Applying for a job as a teacher. 'You are hired.' The physical body has not altered, hence the notion of incorporeal. Yet pronouncing such a statement that you are hired alters the relationships of bodies, human and non-human encountered in the assemblage. This statement turns into an act, that of a human being, a woman, a mother into a teacher. The transformation has social implications that alter bodies it affects. It is an immanent act actualized once the teacher is in a particular time and space related to the context of teacher. Moreover, there is an implicit presupposition in the words uttered by the director of human resources: the school district liked the application; the school board thinks you are a good fit within the mission of their schools.

The social character of language is seen through language as the 'transmission of order words, from one statement to another or within each statement in so far as each statement accomplishes an act and an act is accomplished in the statement' (TP: p. 79). Order-words in this particular moment reflect a certain dominant social order. Order-words concern commands, questions, promises, and are linked to statements by a 'social obligation'. The notion of social obligation implies that order-words are connected to the dominant social order. Order-words are part of a network that code, overcode, direct, and restrict movements. Order-words are instruments of state. An example in education is 'literacy crisis', which functions as an order-word. It reflects a particular view of literacy and acts in such a way as to establish a state of panic by establishing a crisis. It demands particular actions/interventions. It effects an incorporeal transformation by transforming countries into sub-standard on the world stage and transforms individuals in those countries into (ILL)literate and/or at risk (Masny, 2011a). Finally, Deleuze and Guattari contend that language in its entirety is indirect discourse which refers to speaking in a 'received, common or clichéd style'. In this case, it is not clear who is speaking. Indirect discourse has a collective character because of its clichéd style ('Hello. How are you? Crazy weather out there'). Examples in education are: 'no child left behind', and 'researching best practices'. They produce us. However, as in order-words, indirect discourse can deterritorialize through the becomings of words and statements that are constantly created (example: *mamagachi, la chambre d'ecrivage)*.[1]

In sum, language is a set of statements, order-words, implicit presuppositions and incorporeal transformations that plug into social processes (collective assemblages of enunciation and machinic assemblages, each with their ability to territorialize, deterritorialize and reterritorialize) and into an abstract machine that diagrams the assemblage. For Deleuze and Guattari, the primary role of language is neither to inform nor to communicate, but to produce order-words according to a social dominant reality. In Bogue's (1989: p. 98) words, '... everywhere speech-acts take place a dominant social order is confirmed and reinforced'. Speech and acts, in this way, are territorializing, creating boundaries and relationships within and across territories. These relationships within networks or systems of practices and institutions come together as assemblages. However, territories set up by language can be disrupted, not in terms of agency, but in terms of an assemblage that is deterritorializing and reterritorialized. Assemblages happen as sense emerges while reading the world and self produce readers (human and non-human). The next section of part one of the chapter deals with assemblages in order to understand what the role of an assemblage is in relation to language and collective assemblages of enunciation.

Language, political, social and abstract machines

- Language: order-words, implicit presuppositions, (in)corporeal transformations, statements, indirect discourse, redundancy
- Political: pragmatics, speech-acts
- Social: collective assemblages of enunciation, machinic assemblages
- Abstract machine: diagram of assemblage

Assemblage (*agencement*)

What does it do? An assemblage combines (on the horizontal) both content and expression. An assemblage also incorporates (on the vertical) territorialization, deterritorialization, reterritorialization. These aspects of an assemblage are summarized in the box and graphically displayed in Figure 5.1. It is important to note that content and expression are neither signified nor signifier; rather, they are considered variables of an assemblage (Livesey, 2005). Variables are singular and in flux.

Content consists of non-discursive machinic assemblages of desire, that is, bodies, experiences connecting in a social, educational assemblage, the specifics of which emerge at a particular moment in time and space. Assemblages are populated by becomings and intensities, by various multi-plicities. An example is that of the person going through a hiring process as a teacher. The non-discursive machinic assemblage could consist of a school board building, an office in the curriculum department designed as an interview room, the interview being conducted by a panel of superintendents.

Expression refers to discursive collective assemblages of enunciation (acts and statements including order-words, and incorporeal transformations). Assemblages handle indefinite articles or pronouns, verbs in the infinitive which mark processes, proper names which are events. They can be groups, animals everything that is written with a capital letter (A-WOMAN-BECOMING-TEACHER)(TP). For example, a woman responds to an advertisement for a teacher. The woman is hired. In that statement and in signing a contract, there is an incorporeal transformation of becoming a teacher.

In addition, an assemblage incorporates (on the vertical) territorialization, deterritorialization, reterritorialization. Assemblages change configurations depending on the context or milieu. In that sense deterritorialization is inherent to an assemblage. This means that an assemblage can be a territory that can rupture, deterritorialize and reconfigure as another assemblage that differs in time and space. 'Assemblages combine in a regime of signs or a semiotic machine' containing order-words (TP: p. 83). In a different context, the machine changes and different order-words arise and 'will modify the variables and will not yet be part of a known regime'. Not to be part of a known regime refers to Deleuze and Guattari creating immanent rhizomatic potentialities for assemblages yet to come, becoming.

How do they function? As mentioned earlier, assemblages operate through connections of bodies or experiences by way of (in the form of) content and expression. An assemblage becomes vital to language for language depends on the diagram of an assemblage. The diagram contains the variables of expression and content which are in a reciprocal relationship on a plane of consistency (TP).

What do they produce? Assemblages contribute to sense emerging in reading, reading the world and self and to the power to affect and be affected. Affects are virtual. When they seize each other, they emerge in the actual in a particular way in response to an affective encounter with the immediate environment (Masny, 2012). This process might bring on a deterritorialization and possibly reconfigure the dominant social order. There is a reading, that of the world and self happening. As this non-discursive and discursive assemblage comes together, sense emerges. From investment in reading, a reader is produced; a literate body is produced and invested with incorporeal transformation: You are hired. Welcome to the teaching profession.

How are these variables selected to form an assemblage? Colebrook (2002) suggests that they are selected and assessed according to their [differential] power to intervene in life. Moreover, when these elements/machines (e.g. cultural, social, economical) come together, they form an assemblage. The assemblage is also diagrammatic. Language depends on this diagram of an assemblage. It consists of variables of expression that no longer are separable from the variables of content with which they are in perpetual interaction. 'The variables of content and expression are distributed according to their heterogeneous forms in reciprocal presupposition on a plane of consistency and another in which it is no longer possible to distinguish between them because the variability of that same plane has prevailed over the duality of forms, rendering them indiscernible' (TP: p. 91). An example is that of the school. It is peopled by bodies of teachers, learners, and administrators. These bodies are in school because it has been deemed that the children are of school age and the teachers are certified by the province/state. These pronouncements contribute 'a substance to the form of content. A verbal expression has passed into content. The utterances have transformed' (Massumi, 2002; TP: pp. 66–7).

According to Bogue (1989), collective assemblages of enunciation and non-discursive machinic assemblages actualize the abstract machine that puts the assemblages in relation to each other. In other words, the social processes actualize the diagram upon which language depends.

Assemblage

content (non-discursive machinic assemblages of desire),
expression (discursive collective assemblages of enunciation)
deterritorialization, reterritorialization

Collective enunciations

As has been stated elsewhere (Masny, 2006; also see this volume, Chapter One), Deleuze and Guattari do not assign centrality to the subject and in this way set aside the Cartesian notion of 'I think, therefore I am', the autonomous thinking subject at the centre attempting to be in control. However, the subject is not to be totally dismissed. The subject is an assemblage and part of an assemblage, a multiplicity, the convergence of social, cultural, and educational environments, for instance, at a particular moment in time and space. Each particular assemblage mediates/impacts upon reading, reading the world and self. This collective formation takes place in the mind.

In addition, the subject is part of an assemblage. He or she does not act in isolation. The subject acts in relation to environments, human and non-human. The question that Deleuze and Guattari (EPS; Duff, 2010) are interested in is the following: What can the body[2] do as it enters in relations with other bodies? What is the power of bodies to affect and be affected?

The subject is part of a collective environment. The notion of relationality is critical here.

Deleuze insists that we know nothing about a body until we know what it can do, what its affects are, how they can enter into compositions with other affects, with the affects of another body, because we cannot know in advance what distinctive affects and relations a complex body might become capable of (TP: p. 257). Affect is virtual and therefore a potential for action, 'a dispositional orientation to the world' (Duff, 2010: p. 627). Affects are an effect of encounters, in that every encounter transforms a body's affective capacities. An important aspect of the assemblage is the emphasis on the processes/how the processes of convergence emerge in this context. An assemblage just does not simply happen. Rather it is related to untimely encounters (the vertical axes of the assemblage) and the sensations that attend these encounters in relation to machinic assemblages and collective assemblage of enunciations.

Take, for example, a movie. While at the movie, the power to affect and be affected is there not only through the film being viewed but also by the environment (the social machinic assemblage, an asignifying machine that becomes actualized as seating, people around you, the architecture of the film theatre, the colour scheme, noise, etc.) in which the event is occurring. The power to affect and be affected in the immediate environment is created though the assemblage. There are relationships happening between the different components/bodies of the assemblage. In the virtual, as bodies come together, there are sensations. Resonance is produced along a continuum of amplitude and an affective feeling is produced (Masny, 2012).

Enunciations, according to Deleuze and Guattari, are social in nature. There are no individual statements, there never are (K: p. 18). Every statement is the product of a machinic assemblage and collective assemblages of enunciation. The social nature of language comes through when

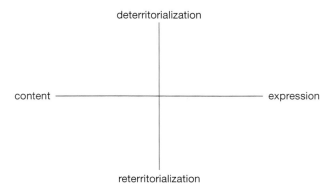

Figure 5.1 Graphic display of an assemblage.

enunciations are collective (p. 80). In other words, the I-subject is not initiating an individual enunciation and using direct discourse. Deleuze and Guattari refer to indirect discourse, a collective assemblage that results in assignations of individuality and their shifting distributions within discourse. Moreover, since the statements spoken belong to a collective enunciation, the relation between the statement and the act is one of redundancy.

Communication and information are secondary to redundancy. Deleuze and Guattari provide the example of newspapers:

> Newspapers proceed by redundancy, in that they tell us what we must think. Language is neither about information nor communication; it is the transmission of order words, either from one statement to another or within each statement, in so far as each statement accomplishes an act and the act is accomplished in the statement. (TP: p. 79)

In sum, readers should not walk away with the notion that we are trapped in order-words and social dominance of reality. That perspective would be nihilistic. Rather, machinic assemblages and collective enunciations can deterritorialize and configure differently order-words, relations of power and social reality. In order for change to happen, it would require going beyond the territories and render the familiar unfamiliar (Conley, 2006). Deleuze and Guattari favour (*préconise*) putting expressions to new uses, bending language to its limits (Roy, 2004). How could this work?

'It could work through experimentation on a language's collective assemblages of enunciations, which in a given context actualize specific circuits of power. And through an activation of the virtual lines of continuous variation immanent within language, which opens vectors of transformation ...' (Bogue, 1989: p. 112) – becoming.

Language, social and political processes are on a plane of machinic assemblage in relationship with reading, reading the world and self on a plane of consistency. How does this work in arts and science education, for instance? As talking groups, what is happening? How do relationality and the power to affect and be affected produce talking groups and the converse?

This entry exits with an instance of mapping literacies as an assemblage. Leander and Rowe (2006) present an ethnographic study of students' various performances in a Language Arts high school classroom. These performances are captured as cartography, a mapping that incorporates an assemblage involving territorialization and deterritorialization as well as collective enunciations (content and expressions). On the horizontal axis, there are machinic assemblages of bodies and collective expressions of enunciation. On the vertical axes, there are cutting edges of deterritorialization and territorial sides or reterritorialized sides. Within that frame, Leander and Row proceeded to map out the performances of the participants that include 'becoming the text ... becoming producers and consumers ... becoming dismembered' (2006: p. 248).

Multiple literacies – multiple writing systems

This section presents vignettes from the study involving Anne, her teacher, and her mother, as well as conversations with the researcher. The vignettes are: Language politics in a French minority context; French and territorialization; Chinese and de/re/territorializations; Mathematics and order-words; Art.

Anne (pseudonym) is 7–8 years old and in Grade 2–3 at the time observations and interviews occurred in the classroom, at home, and at the daycare centre. She was born in Ottawa. She lives in a middle class community where her mother works for the federal government while her father works with the technology industry. From birth, Cantonese is Anne's home language. From age 2, Anne attended a Montessori school in English. At age 4, Anne went to the closest daycare centre which was in French.

As a civil servant, Anne's mother speaks French. Anne's parents felt that, in Canada, it was important to know both official languages. It was then decided that Anne would attend a school near their home where French is the language of instruction and where there is also an after-school daycare centre. Anne speaks all three languages with her mother, using French mainly for homework; Cantonese and English with her father; French in school and at the daycare centre; and, with her friends, any of the three languages depending on the context.

Language politics in a French minority context

In this vignette, the researcher was talking with Anne's Grade 3 teacher, Mrs. Abouji. The conversation turned to her perception of the many different languages spoken by the children, which include far more than just French, the language of instruction.

> *Researcher:* How do you perceive the contribution of the different languages spoken by the children of this class?
> *Teacher:* I really could not answer because French I think that in the school it is a challenge even for children who speak French at home. When they come to school they all tend toward English. As soon as they step out of the classroom, they speak English. So it is very difficult to see the contribution of the different languages the children bring to school. We do not take advantage of other languages because in the classroom, we concentrate on French.

> At times I see some children wanting to teach other children Arab words but that is the extent of it.
>
> R: It seems difficult to integrate aspects of multiculturalism, doesn't it?
>
> T: Yes it is difficult and it is unfortunate because really the other languages, there is a richness and personally, I would like for the children to take advantage of this.

Later in the interview the researcher returned to the question of multilingualism in the classroom, this time focusing on the role of the children's maternal languages.

> R: I was wondering in the case where French is not the home language, how do you see the contribution of the home language in learning to read and write in French?
>
> T: I think that the most important contribution would be at the level of searching for ideas. I don't think it would help for the grammar and writing because it is different. I know Anne speaks Chinese. This is completely different. But the richness in ideas, it would be possible.
>
> R: Does Anne sometimes make connections in class with her mother tongue?
>
> T: No, never. What kind of links for example?
>
> R: Well it could be with reading, writing or even oral.
>
> T: No, never, but I imagine that if there was a text that was related to her culture, of course it would interest her and she would have more background knowledge than other children in the class.

Mrs. Abouji states that the children will prefer to use English and so a complete focus must be put on French (the minority language). Can this statement be an instance of an indirect discourse, a collective assemblage of enunciation, organized by a dominant social order that is characteristic of this particular context in space and time, this particular French minority context? In Deleuze and Guattarian terms, there are political (pragmatic) implications: The teacher's statement turns into an act, a speech act which brings about imperatives regarding the use of French in schools in French minority language contexts. Moreover, would the statement effect an incorporeal transformation of the French language, making it a threatened entity in need of protection? The transformation has social implications that alter bodies it affects. It is an immanent act; the threat of possible disappearance and thought of what might happen ... actualizes in different ways according to particular time and space related to the (minority) context in which French is being used. Moreover, there is an implicit presupposition in the words uttered by the teacher: French is endangered; English is a threat. Children will use French when obliged.

How is this assemblage happening? It involves the coming together of social and political aspects in a complex assemblage. There is the non-discursive content of the assemblage which involves bodies (in a broad sense): the teacher, students, the French language, the English language, other minority languages, the school building, the playground, the classroom, and so forth. There are also discursive expressions within the assemblage: the teacher's commentary, children's talk, school language use policies, Canadian language rights written into law.

What does this assemblage produce? It may be the primacy of French and the exclusion of English as well as other heritage languages. The teacher's speech act (an order-word) is therefore political in the sense that it is pragmatic. The utterance *does* something; it contributes to the ordering (literal hierarchical ordering) of languages in the classroom and simultaneously creates boundaries that territorialize these languages and their use in particular contexts. In this way the speech act demonstrates the political nature of language as it is shaped by a dominant social order; in the French minority context: the focus on French use only. When such language territories are established as part of the dominant social order, what are the implications for reading, reading the world and self across different social contexts: home, school, and community? The collective enunciation could impact the affective powers of multilingual children's bodies.

Order-words are instruments of the state. Mrs. Abouji's comments, as collective enunciations, also offer insights into what Deleuze and Guattari might frame as two order-words currently operating in the policies (i.e. statements) of the Canadian government. These two order-words are brought into a particular relation. On the one hand, there is 'multiculturalism' as a driving force behind government policy. Such policies are speech acts, political and pragmatic, and in the context of schooling they produce incorporeal transformations in the form of inclusive education that views the diverse cultural (and linguistic) backgrounds of students as a rich resource that the 'children could take advantage of', as Mrs. Abouji puts it. On the other hand, there is (Canada has) 'bilingualism' (notably not multilingualism) as another order-word underpinning Canadian government language policy and law. Implicit presuppositions behind such collective enunciations involve the privileging of French and English as official languages (the languages of 'the two founding nations') and the need to protect the French language as a minority language to ensure its preservation. However, order-words – such as multiculturalism and bilingualism – reflect a certain dominant social order in this particular moment only. What might happen when these order-words of the current dominant social order come into a relation? What is the potential for deterritorialization of the current social order as the powers of multilingual Canadians to affect and be affected disrupt, transform, and reterritoralize the assemblage differently?

French and territorialization

In this vignette, Anne is talking about the rules of French in relation to video footage of a classroom observation (year 1 of the study).

> *Researcher:* Let's go to a moment on the video when we talked about a particular grammatical word. What word was it?
> *Anne:* I forgot. It was *manger* (to eat), no, *nager* (to swim).
> *R:* How do you know that it is *nager* (to swim)?
> *A:* Because there are rules in French
> *R:* Can we not do it differently?
> *A:* We cannot do it. That is the rule in French.

Grammatical rules of a language that indicate how the writing system can be used are typically taken as axiomatic. These rules highlight the social character of language – rules are the way a language is used in ways that can be comprehended by different individuals using the same language. What would happen if there were no rules at all governing the possible within a language? Perhaps, after all, 'We require just a little order to protect us from chaos. Nothing is more distressing than a thought that escapes itself. ... We ask only that our ideas are linked together according to a minimum of constant rules' (WP: p. 202). Moreover, the rules of a writing system also highlight the political nature of language, what it does: how it impacts upon what is say-able, write-able. In this way, the rules of a language, the rules of French, can be viewed as collective assemblages of enunciation wherein a rule becomes an order-word that territorializes a language and delimits what is possible when working with, in this case, the French language writing system. Consider the next vignette in which Anne talks about a dictation writing activity after a Language Arts class (year 2 of the study). The grammatical rule being discussed involves the word 'friend' (*ami*) in French, which takes a final 'e' when used to refer to a female person (feminine: *amie*). During the classroom observation, Anne was observed to write *amie*, but then later scribbles out the 'e' when her teacher writes *ami* on the chalkboard.

1) Melissa and Nour went up the stairs.
2) Carla and I like to skate.
3) My friend's cats are dead.
4) The pioneers' methods of transportation are slow.

> *Researcher:* Do you recall the third sentence?
> *Anne:* Ah, my friend's [feminine form] cats died. ...
> *R:* Why did she [the teacher] choose an 'i', why write an 'i'?
> *A:* Yes.

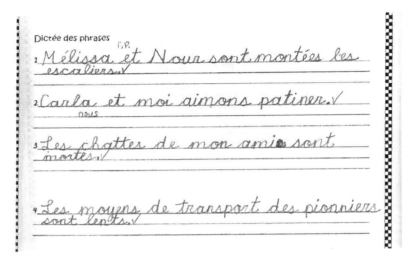

Figure 5.2 Anne's dictation.

R: Why do you think it is like that?

A: We cannot say 'ma [signaling the feminine] *ami* [my friend]', so that cannot signal if it is hum, feminine or masculine.

R: No, but why, when we write, when we say my friend, we write it with an 'i' only?

A: Hummm, because usually when it is feminine we add an 'e'.

R: Yes, but here, here you had a choice. You had a choice between putting masculine or feminine.

A: No I did not have.

R: You did not have a choice? No, why?

A: I don't know.

R: Because, can we write friend [*ami*] with an 'e'?

A: Yes. Because after all the cats who died, cats are in the feminine died [sont mortes], so –

R: Ok, so my friend [*mon ami*, masculine], you removed the 'e'.

A: Ah, I scribbled with my pen.

R: Yes, so for you is this a mistake?

A: No.

R: No, so why did you remove it?

A: Because the teacher removed it.

R: Madame removed it?

A: No, like the teacher em put it like that on the board.

R: Ok, but we can write it with an 'e' as well?

A: Yes, that is what I believe.

R: Yes, you believe; so is it a mistake that you made?

A: No, both are good.

In changing *amie* to *ami*, Anne insists that she 'did not have a choice'. Order-words concern commands, questions, promises and are linked to statements by a 'social obligation'. The notion of social obligation implies that order-words are connected to the dominant social order. According to Conley (2006), they produce repetitions, molar structures and aggregates and reduce differences, thereby making it difficult for deterritorializations to happen (2006: p. 99). Order-words are part of a network that codes, overcodes, directs, and restricts movements.

Does the order-word on the board (*ami*) create the teacher's utterance, a speech act that 'confirms and reinforces' (Bogue, 1989) that order-word, marking out a territory and restricting possible correct responses from the children? There is an implicit presupposition associated with this speech act: 'ami' is the only correct response and any other is somehow wrong. The power to affect and be affected of a teacher-body is also a powerful force working in the assemblage. There is an incorporeal transformation: could it be that children (like Anne) who write 'amie' become transformed from competent writers into error makers?

Anne recognizes in conversation with the researcher that two different responses, *ami* (friend in the masculine) and *amie* (friend in the feminine), would be correct. Does a deterritorialization of the assemblage (French rules, teacher, classroom, *ami*, etc.) take place? Does *amie* simply introduce 'a new set of order-words that simply overlay the previous assemblage' (Lambert, 2002: p. 60), following another grammatical rule? In reading, reading the world and self, might another line of flight (a line of escape, of deterritorialization) be opened? At the outset, Anne maintained that there was only one possible response: *ami*. Is it this kind of refusal of difference and inhibiting of deterritorializations that order-words produce (Conley, 2006)? If rules are collective enunciations that order language and delimit the possible, then how might this organization impact how sense emerges when reading, reading the world and self goes on? Such territorializations accomplished through collective assemblages of enunciation slow down forces of difference and affect. Nevertheless, *ami* is a territory. Then *amie* finally shoots through the territory and deterritorializing *ami* to reterritorializing as *ami* and *amie* (and not in free variation). The in-betweeness from territory to deterritorialization effected a becoming, a difference and it was unpredictable.

The next cluster of vignettes shifts the focus from the use of French at school to the heritage language, Chinese, as it is used by Anne in the home. Again, talking groups are actualized within the context of the political (pragmatics) and the social (collective assemblages of enunciation). What does this assemblage produce?

Chinese and de/re/territorializations

The following exchange between Anne and her mother took place during a video-recorded Chinese character writing lesson at home (year 1 of the study) and was spoken predominantly in Cantonese with some English mixed in. Using an exercise book, Anne's mother was helping Anne to write the characters for the words 'book' and 'professor'.

> *Mother:* Now you write one time of the word, book and professor. You look at the above instruction and follow the steps. You can follow the steps and they start with the horizontal stroke first.
> *Anne:* I don't use those steps.
> *M:* No, you are supposed to follow that. It's not right; it is from left to right.
> *A:* Yeah, but it is so short.
> *M:* No, not that one, the second line.
> *A:* I do this one?
> *M:* And the second line, this is for the second word. You look at the above instruction and follow the steps.

In an interview the next day, Anne and her mother watched and discussed this video footage with the researcher. During that conversation Anne's mother noted that 'if she [Anne] doesn't follow the steps she sometimes may write it from the wrong direction', and she emphasized the importance of writing the character in the right direction: 'It's a good way because that's always, like for the Chinese writing is always from top to bottom and from left to right for within a character'. Once again, the rules of language become important; this time not in terms of grammar, but in terms of producing the written form itself. Anne's mother asserts the importance of doing the steps; the sequence of the character is a statement, order-words that are part of a collective assemblage of enunciation.

Chinese characters are a writing script with an ancient history tied into the aesthetics of calligraphy. A social assemblage, a collective assemblage of enunciation, transforms script into an art form. As Yang Yingshi, a Chinese art critic, describes it: 'Calligraphy is not just a skill, or even an art. It is also a philosophical thing, a ritual and a lifestyle. ... The process of making calligraphy is more important than the product of calligraphy' (Shu Hung and Joe Magliaro, 2006). In short, the stroke sequence matters. The process matters. And yet how might the process of writing a Chinese character (a collective enunciation) work as an order-word of the state? The Chinese government sanctions particular stroke sequences that dictate how characters should be taught (and learned) in school. These standardized writing processes are based on stroke sequences deemed most efficient and most likely to ensure the accurate production of a given character. In this way, the stroke sequence to form the character may be understood as order-words discursively expressed in Anne's mother's statements as she teaches her daughter the correct steps to write the characters. If this is writing territorialized, how might reading, reading the world and self in the process of learning move along the cutting edges of deterritorialization?

In the video of her mini-lesson, Anne acts as the 'teacher' for several of her classmates. She shows them how to write the Chinese character for the word 'long' step by step, emphasizing the importance of each stroke or step in sequence. She makes the first stroke of the character and labels it 'step 1' in French. She begins again, repeating the first stroke of the character and adding the second and labels it 'step 2'. Anne continues in this manner until she has produced all the required steps, in sequence, to write the character 'long'. How is the writing of 'long' indirect discourse, a collective assemblage of enunciation?

In the next vignette Anne, as part of the assemblage, expresses speech acts in her mini-lesson that constitute this collective assemblage of enunciation. In the follow-up interview with the researcher the next day (year 1 of the study), Anne places great emphasis on the necessity of producing the strokes in the correct sequence when writing Chinese characters because 'that is how we write' and that is how others will be able to read what we've written.

> *Researcher:* In order to do this letter [*word small*], you have to start with a line and then what do we do?
> *Anne:* One line here and then another line there [*showing two small lines left and right of the stem-like line*].
> *R:* Ah! One small line, then another small second line and a third? And it is important to do it in this way? Why?
> *A:* Because that is the way we write. If we do it in another way, they might not be able to read what is written. That is why you need different the order of the different strokes, one, two, three, four ...

There is a particular assemblage in which particular bodies come into a relation with powers to affect and be affected: Chinese characters, mother, daughter, home (non-discursive content; bodies) and statements like 'it's a good way because ... Chinese writing is always from top to bottom and from left to right' and 'that's how we write' (discursive expressions;

Figure 5.3 Anne's iconographs for small, tall and long.

collective assemblages of enunciation). A territory: the implicit presup-position that there is a right way and a wrong way to make the character; and incorporeal transformations that produce particular kinds of writers. That is the only way (Anne says) that 'they will be able to read what is written'. Who are 'they'? Does this suggest the inherently social character of language that is a dominant social order? Anne's (as well as Anne's mother's) assertion that stroke order is important may be a discursive expression, a collective enunciation produced by the order-words (fixed, state-mandated stroke sequences) of the dominant social order. The Chinese language is territorialized and that territory is shaped and reinforced with each collective enunciation uttered.

But can a deterritorialization of the assemblage happen? How could a reterritorialization take place on a different territory? What are the implications for reading, reading the world and self? Compared to the language territories marked out in the previous vignettes, the next vignette (after Anne's mini-lesson, year 1 of the study) involves a different assemblage having other potentialities, other relations, other powers to affect and be affected.

> *Anne:* I want to say that it won't be really the right way. And besides we do not really do it this way because it will look all mixed up. It will not look proper. It will be a mess so it is important for beginners to know. But if you are not a beginner, they will leave you do step ten before step one sometimes.
> *Researcher:* Ah, yes?
> *A:* When you are used to it, you can go from step ten to step one.
> *R:* If you are competent, you can skip steps. Is that what you mean? Then would it not be a little confusing. No? Let's continue. Are you a beginner?
> *A:* No.
> *R:* So you skip steps?
> *A:* No not yet [*laughing*]

Here the assemblage is different. Anne's mother is not present in the mini-lesson taking place at school. Anne is the only 'expert' on Chinese characters. This assemblage has Chinese characters, researcher, Anne, school (non-discursive content; bodies) and statements like 'it's [stroke order] important, but that's only for beginners' (discursive expressions; collective assemblages of enunciation). Anne says 'they will let you skip' steps sometimes. Who are 'they'? Does an undefined 'they' again suggest the inherently social nature of all language and collective assemblages of enunciation that produce presuppositions about what is possible in writing?

This is, perhaps, a deterritorialization of the Chinese writing system such that it becomes possible to skip steps in the stroke sequence as long as one is not a 'beginner'. Moreover, Anne does not regard herself as a beginner.

Does she skip steps? 'No, not yet'. What kind of reading, reading the world and self is happening as a product of the assemblage (content and expression)?

Later in the same mini-lesson during which Anne wrote the character 'long' step by step, she writes a second character, the word *grand* ('tall' in French) which requires three distinct strokes in sequence. Anne repeats the character many times in a grid to show how character writing steps are practised. However, she begins skipping steps part way through the exercise and by the time she finishes her grid she is writing the Chinese character for *grand* in the fashion of a cursive writing letter 't' in English/French. Despite her earlier insistence on the necessity of following the steps to write Chinese characters, Anne quickly switches to producing the character using only two strokes that approximate a cursive writing letter 't' in English/French. How might a deterritorialization happen? How might incorporeal transformations be taking place as an effect of the political (pragmatic) and social (collective assemblages of enunciation) of language as writing systems? Collective assemblages of enunciations are everywhere as the indirect discourse that makes up language; however, in the mini-lesson, there are perhaps more deterritorializing forces at work than in the home. Here is what Anne says about writing the character *grand* in the mini-lesson (year 1 of the study):

> *Researcher:* Like this?
> *Anne:* Yes it is like a small case 't'.
> *R:* Hummm. (*in agreement*)
> *A:* 't' cursive writing.
> *R:* Does this mean that in Chinese there is cursive writing?
> *A:* No
> *R:* No?
> *A:* It is only that the word tall under column *a*, it is difficult to do if you are not Chinese (*chinoise*) or Chinese (*chinois*). Because a 't' in small case cursive form it will be easier to do.

In the mini-lesson, as Anne is writing, there is a different assemblage happening than in the home with the mother. The social context is different. The assemblage is different. The content (non-discursive) includes bodies: Anne, a whiteboard, a marker, a researcher, several classmates, Chinese characters. The expression (discursive, collective assemblages of enunciation) includes language: the researcher's talk, the students' talk. This assemblage is different. Assemblages as variables contribute to sense emerging in reading, reading the world and self and to the power to affect and be affected. How reading happens and what reading produces is related to affect. In the virtual, sensations (affect and percepts) seize each other and resonate along a continuum of amplitudes which in turn impact unpredictably those bodies in the assemblage (Masny, 2012). Affect becomes actualized as an affective encounter with the immediate environment that might bring on a deterritorialization and possibly reconfigure the dominant social order.

The relationality between bodies and the powers to affect and be affected within the assemblage are what create the potential of a deterritorialization. To do this might require 'becoming a foreigner' in one's own language, destroying signifieds, exceeding the boundaries/going beyond the territories to render the familiar unfamiliar. This can lead to the formation of atypical expressions which 'constitute[s] a cutting edge of deterritorialization of language' (Conley, 2006: p. 99).

The writing of tall (*grand*) – first as a Chinese character and later as an English/French cursive 't' – is perhaps such a speech act. This speech act is political (pragmatic), that is, it produces an incorporeal transformation. There is a territory about how to write a character using the proper stroke sequence and it becomes deterritorialized at the moment of incorporeal transformation. The entire assemblage (content and expression) deterritorializes the dominant social order that dictates what the process of Chinese character writing can look like and reterritorializes it otherwise, at least for a moment. If Anne writes the characters again at another time she may do them differently. At the same time incorporeal transformations take place: bodies (Anne, writing systems) transform and become *other*.

Mathematics and order-words

Translation: In this bar chart, I notice that:

1) there is only one student who wants to meet the little ugly duck while there are eight students who want to meet Puss-in-Boots;

2) there are three students who want to met Cinderella's godmother and there are three in addition who want to meet Snow White and Tom Thumb;

3) Puss-in-Boots is the most popular character;

4) the little ugly duck is the least popular;

5) Tom Thumb and Snow White each have the same amount of students wanting to meet them.

This interview took place after a mathematics activity in class (year 1 of the study) during which the children wrote sentences based on information from a bar graph. The bar graph was produced by the class and presented the results of a survey they conducted about various fairytale characters.

Anne: I adore mathematics.
Researcher: And when you have to write in math class, is it the same thing as doing an activity in French (language arts) class?

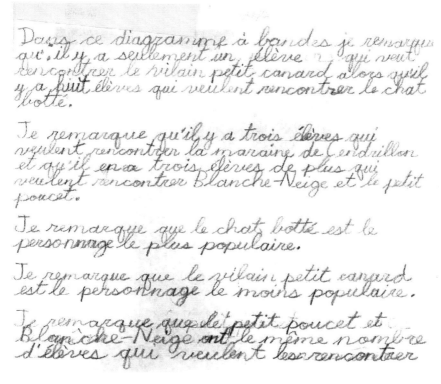

Figure 5.4 Examples of writing in a math activity.

A: It is completely different because I am really good in math but not multiplications, only multiplications.

R: Here you are in the process of writing in a math activity. Can you write sentences like that in activities in the French class?

A: No.

R: No!

A: But you can use words of comparison (*mots de relation*) (e.g. bigger than, the smallest …)

R: What makes you say that you can use these sentences in a French activity?

A: Ah because if you want to write a story, a story about math, then perhaps it will be that …

R: Besides words of comparison (*mots de relation*) that you mentioned that you can use in a math activity and a French one as well, are there other things in addition to words of comparison that you can use in both math and in French classes?

A: Yes, other words of relation: since, when, words that explain.

R: Are there other things that we can use?

A: A number like in math.

R: Let's take a look at what you wrote.

A: I noticed that three pupils wanted to meet Cinderella's godmother and with Puss-in-Boots and Snow White, there were three others, and three more who wanted to meet them.

R: Do you think you could use this sentence in a French activity?

A: Perhaps if I have a story about math.

R: Are there other moments when you could use these sentences [*referring to Figure 5.4*]?

A: No. Not for me.

In this vignette highlighting mathematical language, let us consider the elements of the assemblage. How might the assemblage be mapped? There is the content (non-discursive bodies): paper, pencil, images (asignifying), Anne, the researcher. There is the expression (discursive collective assemblage of enunciation): writing, a bar graph, speaking during the interview. Math is a language and part of the assemblage in which reading, reading the world and self happens. There is an incorporeal transformation.

Also part of the assemblage is the Ministry of Education's curriculum which sanctions the integration of mathematics with other subject areas such as language arts.

> Mathematics is a powerful learning tool. As students identify relationships between mathematical concepts and everyday situations and make connections between mathematics and other subjects, they develop the ability to use mathematics to extend and apply their knowledge in other curriculum areas, including science, music, and language. (Ministry of Education, 2005: p. 3)

In this vignette, the teacher has connected the mathematics activity with the children's experiences of reading storybooks to conduct an in-class survey centred on storybook characters: The Ugly Duckling, Puss-in-Boots, Cinderella's Fairy Godmother, Snow White, The Little Red Hen. This activity can be seen to address two particular curricular outcomes: 1) By the end of Grade 2 children are expected to be able to 'gather data to answer a question, using a simple survey with a limited number of responses' (Ministry of Education, 2005: p. 51) and by the end of Grade 3 they should be able to 'read primary data presented in charts, tables, and graphs (including vertical and horizontal bar graphs), then describe the data using comparative language' (p. 63). In this bar graph reading activity, writing is as important as math; Anne uses words of comparison (*mots de relation*) to describe the data.

To look at how collective assemblages of enunciation may be at work in this assemblage, I want to focus on Anne's response to the researcher's question about whether words of comparison (*mots de relation*) could be used in a French class activity. While Anne is not prepared to say that she could not use these words in a French activity, she seems to accept that you can migrate *mots de relation* in a French activity. She agrees that the words 'when' and 'since', words that she calls explanation/explication words (*mots d'explication*), could also migrate. She says in the end that perhaps you could use these words providing it was a story about/on math.[3] These words are not able to migrate easily, despite the curricular expectation that children learn to use comparative language to describe data and that language should be used across all subject areas. In school settings, curriculum can function as an order-word delimiting what is pedagogically sanctioned. In this particular vignette, the dominant social order would have the words flowing back and forth. Instead, math like 'science gives a reference to the virtual which actualizes it through functions. Science [math] constructs states of affairs with its functions' (WP: p. 118). The math activity relates to a plane of reference while art, story writing, relates to a plane of composition. How does reading, reading the world and self do in the context of this vignette and what does it produce? Could the relationality within the assemblage, powers to affect and be affected, deterritorialize and disrupt the order-word curriculum?

Sensations (percepts and affects) resonate with a particular amplitude within the assemblage and may effect a deterritorialization of the assemblage. At the same time reading, reading the world and self is going on. What is produced? A response: Anne says, 'No'; outside of writing a math story, these words of comparison and explanation could not be used in a French activity. Not for her. On the one hand we can see this utterance as political because it is a speech act that effects an incorporeal transformation in its challenge (disruption, deterritorialization) to curriculum expectations set out by the dominant social order. Yet at the same time, on the other hand, Anne's utterance is not of her own making (as an actively controlling subject). Rather it is an indirect discourse produced from the collective assemblage of enunciation, the inherently social nature of all language. What are the order-words that seem to have the implicit presuppositions that 'math is math' and 'language is language' and there should be no migration of words between math class and French class? It might have something to do with the order-words of a dominant social order of disciplinarity which strike distinct territories between subject areas, resisting interdisciplinary. If there is a disruption of these territories within the assemblage, how is a reterritorialization of the assemblage taking place?

The assemblage (classroom, activity: Anne, artifact, researcher) creates a certain way of becoming (assuming that there is disruption) with the world. This bar graph exercise might be intended to observe functions and 'states of affairs'. Is it the power to think differently, to become different, to create differences? Is the researcher asking that of Anne by inquiring about whether she can use these words in a French activity? Could it be because math has functives (territories) that would be difficult to deterritorialize (a molar)? How could these words reterritorialize as aesthetic words (since this is a story) that have the power to affect and be affected?

The storybooks, their characters, and the stories contained within them also become part of the broader assemblage of content and expression within this vignette happening as part of a mathematics lesson. In this context, the bar graph can be understood as a collective assemblage of enunciation, an inherently social utterance. The bar graph and Anne's sentence 'I notice that Puss-in-Boots is the most popular character' are indirect discourses, shaped not by the children as agents, but as the production of a larger social assemblage. Then, how are these speech acts also political (that is, pragmatic), that is, what are the incorporeal transformations created? Does Puss-in-Boots experience an incorporeal transformation, a change in the state of affairs as opposed to a bodily transformation, as a result of the utterance: 'Puss-in-Boots is the most popular'?

Here there are potential connections to another component of the assemblage. While the teacher may be drawing on storybook characters that are presumably familiar to the children, one might speculate about how it is that Puss-in-Boots wins the popularity contest. What other machinic assemblages of desire and collective assemblages of enunciation (content and expression respectively) are part of the assemblage? In the blockbuster movie *Shrek* (Warner, 2001), an animated film by Dreamworks, and in its sequels (now numbering three) and subsequent mass marketing in the toy, fast food, and theme park industries (to name just a few), Puss-in-Boots plays the ogre Shrek's faithful sidekick. Is it possible that the cinematic Puss-in-Boots trumps the other storybook characters to become an order-word in the dominant social context of a capitalist society? When Puss-in-Boots is named the most popular character, it may be the effect of a collective assemblage of enunciation.[4]

Art

What are order-words in art? What is their role in learning about art, about how to do art? How do they impact reading, reading the world and self in the context of artistic experiences?

In this vignette, Anne is describing her analysis of a painting by Canadian artist Alex Colville entitled *Cyclist and Crow* (Colville, 1981) during a Social Studies class (year 2 of the study). The painting has a washed out appearance in greys, whites, blacks, and browns. It depicts a woman with short sandy blonde hair and wearing dark shorts, a white tank top and white sneakers riding a white Peugeot bicycle in a rural setting. Her face, not visible to the painting's viewer, is turned away to look at a crow flying over the grey-tone field along the edge of which she is riding. The crow's flight parallels the cyclist's trajectory.

In Figure 5.5, Anne is writing up an activity based on the painting by Alex Colville. She has been given a questionnaire with which to analyze the work.

- What are the words that came to mind when you observed the painting? Her response is: the country, sadness, bicycle, bird.
- What questions do you have regarding the work? Her questions are: why is she following the bird? where is she? in the country? is the bird also alone?
- Here is my story that could go with the painting: Introduction: A lady saw a bird. Once upon a time there was a lady on a bike ride. All of a sudden she sees a bird and decides to follow it until she is lost. She goes along the road and through the forest. But she does not find her house. A day has gone by and she is hungry. She still has not found her house. It is night. She lies down beneath a tree and falls asleep. In the morning, she continues to search. After a time, she feels tired. She rests under a tree and falls asleep. When she wakes up it is almost night and she looks for her house. Then it is night. So she rests on the grass. When it is morning, she cannot carry on. She dies of hunger.

The researcher picks up on the word *tristesse* (sadness) used by Anne in her comments upon the painting and asks her about it during the follow-up interview.

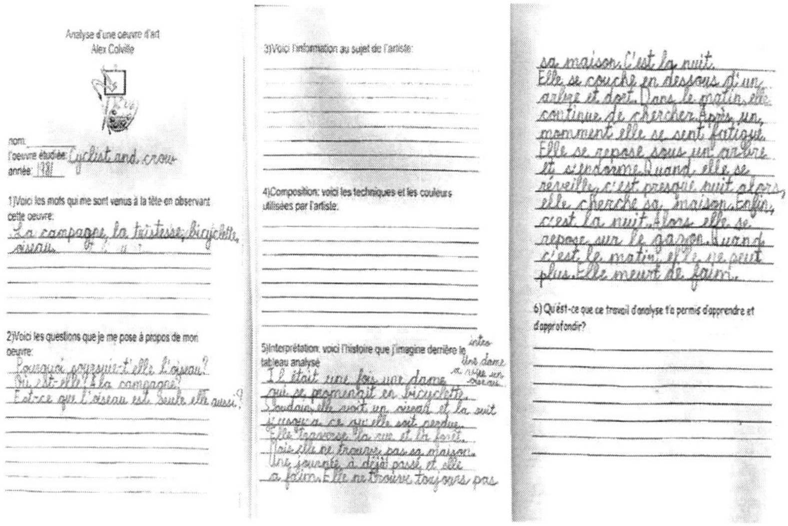

Analyse d'une oeuvre d'art
Alex Colville

nom:
l'oeuvre étudiée: Cyclist and crow
année: 1981

1)Voici les mots qui me sont venus à la tête en observant cette oeuvre:
La campagne, la tristesse, bicyclette, oiseau.

2)Voici les questions que je me pose à propos de mon oeuvre:
Pourquoi poursuit-t'elle l'oiseau?
Où est-elle? À la campagne?
Est-ce que l'oiseau est seule elle aussi?

3)Voici l'information au sujet de l'artiste:

4)Composition: voici les techniques et les couleurs utilisées par l'artiste.

5)Interprétation: voici l'histoire que j'imagine derrière le tableau analysé
intro: Une dame a vu un oiseau.
Il était une fois une dame qui se promenait en bicyclette. Soudain elle voit un oiseau et la suit jusqu'à ce qu'elle soit perdue. Elle traverse la rue et la forêt. Mais elle ne trouve pas sa maison. Une journée a déjà passé et elle a faim. Elle ne trouve toujours pas sa maison. C'est la nuit. Elle se couche en dessous d'un arbre et dort. Dans le matin, elle continue de chercher. Après un momment elle se sent fatigué. Elle se repose sous un arbre et s'endorme. Quand elle se réveille, c'est presque nuit alors, elle cherche sa maison. Enfin, c'est la nuit. Alors elle se repose sur le gazon. Quand c'est le matin, elle ne peut plus. Elle meurt de faim.

6) Qu'est-ce que ce travail d'analyse t'a permis d'apprendre et d'approfondir?

Figure 5.5 Anne's responses to, and her story based on, the Colville painting.

Researcher: So you speak of sadness.

Anne: Because of the black bird. It is sad. The wheels of the bicycle are black. It is sad. The silver is also sombre. Then the green is sombre.

R: Are there other sombre colours for you? ...

A: The green in the back is sombre. Everything is sombre. Even the colour of her skin is sombre.

R: OK.

A: But her sweater is not sombre and her trousers are not sombre. For me, she was sad. It was as if she was sad because of something. I do not know what but she was simply sad in my imagination. And then she goes on an adventure on a bicycle to look at nature and after a bird follows her and she gets lost.

R: Do you like to do this kind of activity in art? Yes?

A: Yes.

R: What do you like in particular?

A: I particularly like to tell a story that comes to mind (*qui me vient à la tête*) when I look at the picture.

Bogue (2003) asserts that to speak is to effect transformations of bodies through language (e.g. French, Arabic, art, music, science etc.). How then might art speak? What language does it speak? 'Painting raises color and lines to the state of language' (FB: p. 74). According to Bogue, the language of painting must be learned. Language in painting is uncoded and is capable of bearing sensation, that is, percepts and affects in the virtual. Deleuze writes that the language of painting is planes, colours and bodies (FB). The language of art may enable 'a passage identifiable entities toward some unknown figure' (Bogue, 2003: p. 111) and thereby disrupt the 'clichés of coded representation'.

> ... painting has close ties with language and its intertwined institutions and practices, and through these ties painting assumes its political function of inventing a people by undoing the fixed codes and static grids that structure the world in conventional configurations. (Bogue, 2003: p. 190)

Deleuze's challenge to creative thinkers is like the challenge facing the artist. He asked her to face her canvas, and like an artist, to begin by wiping away the clichés and the ready-mades of the doxa that stand in the way of her creations; to suspend the chattiness that the dominant ideology of communication encourages, and to opt for the desert of thinking and writing. (Boundas, 2009: p. 1)

The political problem for painters is to undo the clichés, to deterritorialize the collective assemblages of enunciations. The problem is not to fill the 'blank' canvas, but to empty it out (FB). 'The purpose or force of art (and philosophy) thus goes beyond what life is to what it might become' (Colebrook, 2002: p. 14).

Anne's art experience with the Colville painting *Cyclist and Crow* is constituted as an assemblage. There is the non-discursive content of bodies (machinic assemblages of desire): the oil painting, the canvas, different asignifying colours, Anne, classmate, teacher, and classroom. There are also the discursive collective assemblages of enunciation: first, Anne tells us the painting is 'sombre', and second, the painting 'speaks' the language of art (lines and colours). How do these two kinds of speech acts produce incorporeal transformations?

Regarding the first speech act, in which Anne says that the painting is sombre, the painting undergoes incorporeal transformation. Anne, the painting, reading, reading the world and self are expressed as indirect discourse as an effect of sense emerging through a collective assemblage of enunciation. Its order-words are highly coded in the current dominant social order in this assemblage or social context. Dark colours are sombre and bright colours are not.[5] Anne makes a statement: 'the painting is sombre'. It is just as much the mouth and the eyes as it is possibly other elements of the assemblage that produce the statement of sombreness. More precisely, it is the relationality between bodies that encounter each other (paint, colour, eye, nose, mouth, Anne, etc.) within the assemblage that produces sense through the powers of affect. There is an incorporeal transformation of the painting as Anne speaks. In this way sense emerges with the power to affect and be affected. When Anne uses words like 'sombre' and 'sadness', these speech acts are collective assemblages of enunciations produced by the assemblage. The speech act is also seen as political (i.e. pragmatic) by effecting an incorporeal transformation in the painting. It becomes sombre and sad. What are the implications of the incorporeal transformation of the painting? How does pragmatics have a role in producing the painting in certain ways (and not others)? Pragmatics connects with reading, reading the world and self. Reading operates *in situ*, at which point the powers of affect are actualized as affective within the assemblage. The moment of actualization differs each time.

Regarding the second act in which the painting speaks the language of art, Anne undergoes incorporeal transformation. While speech acts have been attributed to humans, speech acts can be non-human as well. Take, for example, studies (Beaulieu, 2011; McGregor, 2003) that explore animal communication and speech acts effected in different social groupings. Non-humans, like humans, can be seen to communicate with vocal language and body language. Would there be conceivably other non-humans expressing speech acts? In art, can a speech act be expressed in a relationship of colours and lines? Painting raises colous and lines to the state of language, according to Deleuze (FB). The language of art may enable 'a passage identifiable entities toward some unknown figure' (Bogue, 2003: p. 111) and thereby disrupt the 'clichés of coded representation'. In the Colville painting, there is the suggestion that 'the coded representa-tions'/order-words are visible: a woman riding a bicycle on a warm day in a non-urban setting with a bird flying about in the distance. However, when these images encounter colours and lines (e.g. the tones of silver, grey, black, green, brown), the coded representations are disrupted. Anne as part of the assemblage in relation to the painting undergoes incorporeal transformation: Anne-becoming-sombre. Sombre itself expresses a deter-ritorializing affect. Forces of affect are at work. Art (affects and percepts) is a contributor in the assemblage. Since art is a language and art expresses, then reading happens and art disrupts and brings on the thought of a story that unfolds in the mind. The painting reterritorializes as a story of a woman cycling in the countryside who gets lost and dies from hunger.

In sum, order-words play a key role on what goes on in the classroom. Anne is critically aware of the dominant social order. Cristelle calls her the inspector in a drawing made by Cristelle of a haunted castle (see Figure 2.2, in the chapter *Cartographies of multiple literacies*). In addition, incorporeal transformations disrupt and change. The relations of bodies – for example, of a person coming for a teacher interview and then being told that she is hired. There is also the example of how Anne, in relation with other human and non-human bodies in an assemblage, speaks of the Colville painting becoming sombre.

What of affect? The power of affect can be seen, on the one hand, as institutionalized power with the use of *ami* and *amie*. In French, the masculine form is the primary/majoritarian marker when both masculine and feminine forms are possible. On the other hand, creative affective powers through deterritorializations happen when both feminine and masculine forms are effected. Anne initially chose *amie* when the expected term is *ami*. That is a deterritorialization.

Exit

What is the significance of this work? Despite the notion that there are no individual enunciations, this does not mean that expression is fixed. Deleuze and Guattari instead focus on collective assemblage of enunciation and the importance of the social character of language. There will always be a social dominant order but it will differ constantly because of creative powers of lines of flight that disrupt a dominant social order at a particular time and space. How does this happen? Enunciation implies collective assemblage. The assemblage of which the subject is a part configures differently each time in reading, reading the world and self. There are multiplicities at work yet one singular event, and each time the assemblage would be different and so the event. In school, there are a multitude of order-words and collective enunciations that happen. In these chapters, there are examples of what the children should be writing and how they should be writing it. One example is Anne regarding the feminine use of the word 'friend' (*amie*). Another example is when Anne is showing a classmate how to write in Chinese. Collective enunciations are at work: the ten steps that have to be followed in calligraphic script. The process of following the numbered steps is disrupted. A line of flight in which a different order is created also creates difference and becoming. There has been a change.

What is the relationship, then, between sense and order-words? Sense, like the collective assemblage, is impersonal (virtual). Sense is the virtual milieu through which we become.

When actualized, it does so in relation to collective enunciation and order-words. It is not that order-words mean the same thing regardless of context. Order-words emerge with different sense depending on the context in which they are expressed. In Deleuzian and Guattarian terms, that 'context' is an assemblage with all of its flows and machines (economic, political, social, etc.). It is important to note that collective enunciations (with their expression and content) are also assemblages, and moreover that assemblages are deterritorialized and deterritorializing (TP).

Collective enunciation and order-words can be virtual asignifying machines. Sense is virtual, in that it is an asignifying machine. Take the example of an image to yield in the face of oncoming traffic. In the virtual there might be many asignifying images. In a particular context of time and space, an image emerges as a signifying machine – in this instance, a triangle. In another context, to yield might be a different image. Be it a triangle or another image, it is an expression of collective enunciation, an order-word.

Sense can also be incorporeal. A speeding car encounters the road sign, to yield. This is an expression. The speeding car now has slowed down. There is a change in the state of affairs. An incorporeal transformation with the car occurred. Incorporeal transformations are becomings. Moreover, an act of becoming is an event, since becoming takes the car onto a different path.

Sense as an event happens through encounters, encounters of/through communication: language human and non-human, and organic matter. Language is about creating a world of sense that interacts with other material worlds (ECC: p. 111). Sense gives meaning to language. For instance, art speaks and effects a deterritorialization. The assemblage (a particular time, place, artist, social machine, etc.) disrupts the clichés, removes them from the canvas. The assemblage comes together in order to read and disrupt and bring on the thought of what could potentially stem from the canvas. A deterritorialization happens as a result of affects released in the relations between bodies within the assemblage (e.g. Anne, the painting, etc.). Anne and the painting (themselves assemblages) are part of a larger assemblage which is deterritorialized/deterritorializing. There is a reterritorialization as a sombre story about a woman losing her way in the countryside. The assemblage is transformed. It is not what it was. It is different.

The language of art for Deleuze is lines and colours. In the Colville painting, black and silver are affects in the virtual and become actualized as 'sombre' when they emerge through collective assemblages of enunciation. In art – a bloc of sensation – colour becomes a mode of expression, a creative force, an affect that is more than a passive emotion. 'Sensation [affect/percept] is thus the action of forces on the body' (FB: p. 34). Sensation is the power to affect and be affected. Within the assemblage, sensations resonate with various amplitudes (FB: p. 33). The resonance that is happening between the different components of the assemblage in the virtual gets taken up in the actual as an emotion: sombre. Sombreness is created by the assemblage. Sombreness creates a story. The virtual sensation of affect unpredictably created in the actual an affective feeling of sombreness through incorporeal transformation (when Anne says, it is sombre). Reading the painting intensively, the painting became sombre. As well, reading as immanent brought on the *thought of* a story.

What might be disconcerting is the implication that, as humans speak, for instance, that which is effected is a product of the social order. While it might be disconcerting, it is not deterministic. Order-words produce molar structures; however, the power of affect can disrupt and 'molecularise the molar structure' (Conley, 2006: p. 99). There are always deterritorializing forces operating so sense may emerge in ways that disrupt.

References

Beaulieu, A. (2011). The status of animality in Deleuze's thought. *Journal for Critical Animal Studies*, IX(1/2), 6–88.

Bogue, R. (1989). *Deleuze and Guattari*. New York: Routledge.

—(2003). *Deleuze on music, painting, and the arts*. New York: Routledge.

Bonta, M. and Protevi, J. (2004). *Deleuze and geophilosophy: A guide and glossary*. Edinburgh: Edinburgh University Press.

Boundas, C. V. (2009). Introduction. In C. V. Boundas ed., *Gilles Deleuze: the intensive reduction* (pp. 1–4). London: Continuum.

Chomsky, N. (2009). *Cartesian Linguistics* (3rd edn). Cambridge: Cambridge University Press.

Colebrook, C. (2002). *Gilles Deleuze*. New York: Routledge.

Colville, A. (1981). *Cyclist and Crow* [Painting]. Available online at http://artmight.com/Artists/David-Alexander-Colville-1850-1927/Colville-David-Alexander-Cyclist-and-Crow-end-135578p.html (accessed 27 January 2012).

Conley, V. A. (2006). Borderlines. In I. Buchanan and A. Parr (eds), *Deleuze and the contemporary world* (pp. 95–107). Edinburgh: Edinburgh University Press.

Duff, C. (2010). Towards a developmental ethology: Exploring Deleuze's contribution to the study of health and human development. *Health (London)*, 14(6), 619–34.

Grisham, T. (1991). Linguistics as an indiscipline: *Deleuze* and Guattari's pragmatics. *SubStance*, 20(3): 36–54.

Lambert, G. (2002). *The nonphilosophy of Gilles Deleuze*. New York: Continuum.

Leander, K. M. and Rowe, D. W. (2006). Mapping literacy spaces in motion: A rhizomatic analysis of classroom literacy performance. *Reading Research Quarterly*, 44(4), 428–60.

Livesay, G. (2005). Assemblage. In A. Parr ed., The Deleuze Dictionary (pp. 94–6). New York: Columbia University Press.

McGregor, P. K. ed. (2003). *Animal communication networks*. Cambridge: Cambridge University Press.

Masny, D. (2006). Learning and creative processes: A poststructural perspective on language and multiple literacies. *International Journal of Learning*, 12(5), 147–55.

—(2009). Literacies as becoming: A child's conceptualizations of writing systems. In D. Masny and D. R. Cole, *Multiple Literacies Theory: A Deleuzian perspective* (pp. 13–30). Rotterdam: Sense Publishers.

—(2011a). *International literacy testing: Powering the world*. Paper presented at the 4th International Deleuze Conference, Copenhagen, June.

—(2011b). Multiple Literacies Theory: Exploring futures. *Policy Futures in Education*, 9(4), 494–504. Available online at http://dx.doi.org/10.2304/pfie.2011.9.4.494 (accessed 24 January 2012).

—(in press). Multiple Literacies Theory: Discourse, sensation, resonance and becoming. *Discourse*, 33(1).

Massumi, B. (2002). Introduction: Like a thought. *A Shock to Thought: Expression after Deleuze and Guattari*. London: Routledge. Available online at http://www.brianmassumi.com/textes/Introduction%20to%20A%20Shock%20to%20Thought.pdf (accessed 27 January 2012).

Ministry of Education (2005). *The Ontario curriculum, grades 1–8: mathematics, 2005*. Available online at http://www.edu.gov.on.ca/eng/curriculum/elementary/math18curr.pdf (accessed 27 January 2012).

Parr, A. ed. (2002). The Deleuze dictionary. New York: Columbia University Press.

Patton, P. (2010). Deleuzian concepts: Philosophy, colonization, politics. Stanford: Stanford University Press.

Roy, K. (2004). Overcoming nihilism: From communication to Deleuzian expression. *Educational Philosophy and Theory*, 6(3), 297–312.

Shu Hung and Magliaro, J. (2006). Writing with water on stones. *Theme Magazine*, 6. Available online at http://www.thememagazine.com/stories/yang-yingshi/ (accessed 27 January 2012).

Wikipedia (2011). *Stroke Order*. Available online at http://en.wikipedia.org/wiki/Stroke_order#Stroke_order_per_polity (accessed 27 January 2012).

Notes

1 The paintings of Francis Bacon deterritorialize. Painting is a language (FB). It contains clichés and order-words. They are on the canvas more or less

actually, more or less virtually. Painting can deterritorialize the language of painting, that is, clichés, order-words, indirect discourse, through the creation of different affects. The affects are actualized in the paintings' affective power. Bacon's paintings challenge representational art by distorting figures such as the dog, the chimpanzee, a series of head portraits.

2 A body can be any: animal, sounds, mind, idea, linguistic corpus, social collectivity (SPP: p. 127).

3 In Masny (2011b), another participant in the study, Estrella, performed a scientific activity in class. She then had to write up the experiment. At the interview, Estrella was asked if she could use the scientific terms in a story. The answer was no unless it was a story about science. For instance, 'cement' would not be used in a story. Moreover, Estrella would not use the word 'soft' (*fait doux*) in a story for it belongs to the realm of the experiment (based on the videotaping: one outcome of touching the mixture was that it was soft).

4 Notably, at the time of writing (summer 2011) Dreamworks is making a spin-off animated feature film due out November 2011 in which Puss-in-Boots will be the central character. It seems his popularity extends beyond Anne's grade 3 class.

5 Notably these order-words look different in other social contexts, such that white may be considered a sombre colour reserved for mourning.

CHAPTER SIX

Mapping power and literacies

David R. Cole

Introduction

Questions of power and powerlessness drive many recent studies in education (see Anyon, 2009). This is due in part to the stated aim of those in power to empower citizens through education and to give enhanced life opportunities to those who are educated. The questions that confront this chapter include: What does it mean to become more powerful due to literacies? How do literacies empower? What are the relationships between multiple literacies and power? To answer these questions one may turn to the philosophy of Gilles Deleuze (1994) as a means to reconcile power concerns with the life of education. This life can often leave one with a sense of powerlessness, as educative practices are squeezed between political concerns and economic outcomes. It is as if the life of educative practice may be drained by the drives that flow through it. For example, the Global Financial Crisis (GFC) has caused ripples and waves of new debt and credit retardation around the globe. Educational programmes have been cut – e.g. philosophy courses in the UK, due to the lack of direct economic outcomes. Certain professions have been downgraded – e.g. architecture in Ireland, due to a halt in new construction. Education is therefore not a universal right or dream of enlightening the masses, but connected to the truths of capital investment as it narrates and directs the lives of those trapped in social strata. Education is not necessarily a way out of these strata, but often involves being inculcated by the forces that are indeed forming the strata. In the case of literacy studies, many of the new literacies are responses to developments in new capitalism, i.e. educating students to become e-workers under global, digitally inter-related market conditions (e.g. Lankshear and Knobel, 2003). One might argue that this is fitting, in that students need the skills to survive these new times of internet-augmented consciousness and 'i-creativity' (see Araya and Peters, 2010). Yet one may also question the ethos of the new literacies in that digital revolutions in schools may be preparing future generations for lives of office work sat behind monitors or flexi-work with network-enhanced laptops, or merely sitting in call-centres. What happens to the affect of these generations? How does one stave off or understand the commercialization of life and thought when one is endlessly working in cyberspace? This chapter suggest that a possible escape route from the tentacles of global capitalist control society is through applying Deleuzian philosophy to questions of power and literacy in education. This is because Deleuze gives the analyst the ability to look at life through an immanent, material lens (see Deleuze and Guattari, 1988). Literacies may be subdivided and differentiated internally, until they reach a zero point or undifferentiated plane of emergence. It is here that the drives of literacy learning and power may be understood as pre-normalized singularities or 'strange attractors'. These attractors are ruptures in the ways things work, and therefore point to the pragmatism of the process, in that Deleuzian analysis helps one to get behind what is happening and not be caught out by ideology, rhetoric or by taking a pre-determined or normative stance on data. It is through this rupture analysis that multiple literacies may be set free and education will become populated by the multiple in literacy learning that explains the workings of power as a process.

English teachers and power

This chapter will take a specific example of a set of teachers of English and a rupture point in their lives to demonstrate Deleuzian analysis. This example will be used to look at the ways in which power and multiple literacies flow through the lives of these English teachers, both in terms of their literacy acts (teaching) and the work of their cohorts. One of the most prevalent ways in which power works in education is by separating out and segmenting knowledge areas so that their corresponding synergies and connective augmentations are nullified. This chapter takes secondary English teaching as an example of these complicated social processes, and presents research that brings disparate fields of investigation together. On the one hand, teachers may be polarized and challenged by curriculum changes and governmental mandates that could impinge upon their everyday practice. On the other, every teacher in the profession will bring their interior and emotional life to bear on their ways of working (affect), and this aspect of teaching has not usually been connected to curriculum change. This chapter on mapping multiple literacies proposes a conjunction of educational affect and discursive identities, through an analysis of the ways in which teachers perceive curriculum change and their personal teaching and learning realities. The analysis that is presented represents a means to understanding a Deleuzian intervention in literacy studies as facts of curriculum change or rupture points are analyzed simultaneously with the affective dimensions of these changes in literacy. This investigation has been worked into the teacher training of pre-service (or trainee) secondary English teachers, so that they may realize and discuss how such concerns are understood conjointly, and so that the data analysis is not retained as a form of Royal or state science (Deleuze and Guattari, 1988), from the outside looking in.

Teaching English in secondary schools brings together internal and external influences. The most pressing external influence on teachers and students is often the particular curriculum design that is being used in the zone that places and contextualizes English within a knowledge system. Animating this design are social forces such as the importance of English to the community and the ways in which English may explore identity through literature (see Doecke *et al.*, 2006). Internal influences on the English teaching and learning that happens in the classroom are more entwined, as particular teachers will bring their own motivations and conceptual understandings about English to bear on their teaching as well as the requisite expression of socialities that concur with these understandings (see Kress, 2006). This chapter puts the field of knowledge about English teaching into play through the curriculum changes that have recently been happening on the island of Tasmania, Australia, due to the introduction of a new framework called the *Essential Learnings* (see Figure 6.1), and explanations about the affective aspects of teaching English from secondary practitioners. This writing aims to join the internal and external dimensions of English teachers' professional lives in a non-dualistic manner, and to the benefit of the student trainee teachers undertaking the research, the readers of this article and the main researcher who has brought this evidence and thinking together. This joining exemplifies the value of research as a nexus for understanding interrelated aspects of English teaching (Cole, 2007a) and exploring the ways in which emergence may be represented to challenge positions that could separate affect from identity and change, i.e. mapping multiple literacies.

Notes on methodology

The Bachelor of Teaching course that pre-service trainee English teachers follow in Tasmania is a postgraduate qualification, and this course includes aspects of educational research training. This project has been designed for them as part of this training and therefore is a form of direct action research (Martin *et al.*, 2006). The student teachers learn through doing, in

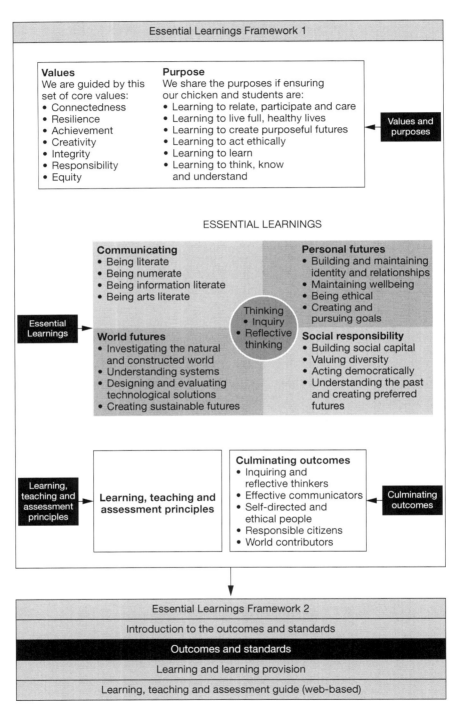

Figure 6.1 The Essential Learnings Framework 1 (Department of Education, Tasmania, 2002).

this case talking to in-service English teachers and gauging their opinions and ideas with respect to curriculum change, affect and emotion. Fifty-eight secondary English teachers were interviewed for this project in their place of work for up to an hour and a half at a time. These teachers constitute a random sample of different ages, ethnicities and genders. The student teachers were required to write up their research in the manner of a mini-thesis, by building literature reviews, coding, doing analysis and critical evaluation of the themes that emerged from semi-structured interviews and any observations that they undertook in the schools. In this way, the quality of their research was monitored and evaluated by the main researcher, who marked and discussed the results with the students. This project gained full local ethics clearance, in terms of the students using the data for their own projects, and the aggregation of the evidence that is represented by this book chapter on multiple literacies and power. Students supplemented their data with self-reflective diaries and notes from teaching on four practicum experiences over two years. The teachers who were interviewed read an information sheet about the research and signed a consent form to take part. The students designed an appropriate research instrument, which included open-ended and informational questions about affect, emotion and curriculum change (see Gubrium and Holstein, 2002). Specific questions that ran through the research designs included: 'What is the reaction of the teachers to curriculum change in Tasmania?' and 'Discuss the affective factors that permeate your English teaching'. The students' analysis of the data depended on their ability to make qualitative distinctions in the transcripts (see Upton, 2005), and to isolate themes in the research that corresponded to curriculum change and affective proclivity.

   This research report and MLT chapter has been organized by the lecturer and main researcher running the course with the consent of the students and teachers, and provides an overview of the results obtained over four years. The sections that follow differentiate between different types of English teacher. This set of categories relates to curriculum change, the effects of the Essential Learnings and multiple literacies as identity formation and divergence. These teacher types are not sketchy characterizations of typical English teachers (see Marshall, 2000) or crude stereotypes, but constitute a discourse analysis (Fairclough, 1992) of the related identity resources available to English teachers in Tasmania during the research and time of change. The resultant Discourses are wholly interrelated and may coexist in the same subject, yet for the purposes of representation have been separated by the main researcher from the evidence as it was presented by the students after intense discussion. The data that is included in the Discourses serves as evidence, and is related on many levels to the power and identity structures that were present (see Cole, 2005) in the English teaching system of Tasmania. These following sections therefore show the multiple literacies of the teachers in terms of their reading and articulation of the curriculum changes that were happening at the time. The distinction used here between

Discourses and discourses works in this Deleuzian report to distinguish between the governmental forms of communication – Discourses – that carry power concerns and identity constructions, and everyday forms of language use – discourses (Gee, 2003). This distinction functions as a process of mapping power though multiple literacies as the Discourses are examples of government-produced language identity resources. The overall research question for this section is: What are the categories of English teacher identity that one might discern after the introduction of the Essential Learnings?

The Essential Learnings (ELs)

The Essential Learnings was implemented in the Australian state of Tasmania in 2002 after eight years of public consultation and debate (Watt, 2005) and is parallel to other Australian curriculum designs such as the Victorian Essential Learnings (VELs). The ELs is a knowledge framework based on constructivist and integrated curriculum principles (see Dowden and Nolan, 2006). According to the ELs, the teaching of English as a knowledge area was to be integrated into the Essential Learning of Communicating. The teaching of English is henceforth reorganized through this model – Being literate, as part of the area of Communicating, is valued alongside numeracy, information literacy and arts literacy. Teachers should accordingly design units of work around generative themes, and include communicative opportunities under these themes through which the students will improve their (multiple) literacy skills. The ELs was assessed through standards that related to each element in the framework; for secondary English teachers, the standards of Being literate were of primary concern. For many years, English was taught in Tasmanian secondary schools in a traditional manner, with a fixed and rigidly demarcated curriculum model, i.e. as subject English. This teaching was constituted by the study of classic and contemporary English texts from years 7 to 10, and marked against a set of state-wide English standards. According to the guidelines of the ELs, English teachers should now shape their lessons to suit communicative outcomes, and this has resulted in three distinctive reactions that one can use to understand English teacher identities (Discourses) and the corresponding multiple literacies amongst the teachers with respect to this curriculum change. These categories were arrived at through discussion and debate between the student researchers and the course leader.

Essential learners

These teachers are thoroughly convinced that the ELs is a step in the right direction. They agree with the Essential Learnings because it restructures the teaching of English with respect to social and cultural factors. According to this perspective, English in the secondary context will become more aligned and integrated with the primary area of literacy, which enables learners to communicate effectively using words whilst thinking critically about text. For example:

> Teacher A: The ELs has given me the chance to really start planning some relevant lessons for the kids. I work in a school with a severely disadvantaged cohort. They have no money, and they come from families with no money. Now we don't have to go through the motions of studying an irrelevant novel or planning gap-fillers to use up the time. We can do work that will help this group in the real world – to earn money by improving their literacy skills!

It could be argued that the ELs provides continuity and scaffolding between primary and secondary language learning. Essential learners may well be sympathetic to whole language philosophy, and integrate critical literacy into their everyday English teaching through interdisciplinary units of work. The new knowledge framework (ELs) fits in with a socially constructed view of English teaching. There is a focus on context in literacy according to the ELs that combines well with the introduction of multiple literacies and MLT.

Neutral pragmatists

The English teachers in this group identify curriculum changes as exterior to their personal beliefs about English teaching. As such, they take on board some of the tenets of the ELs without being overly concerned about implementation. Neutral pragmatists go about their business of teaching English through text and organizing the curriculum according to traditional definitions of English such as teaching the classics, yet they are able to fit in and adapt their lesson ideas with the ELs. For example:

> Teacher B: I'm most familiar with Communicating, Being Literate and Being Arts Literate. I've sat down, and written my own rubrics – and that takes a lot of time, and it takes a lot of time to assess, 'cause you sit there with your school's understanding of it, and the actual ELs folder understanding of it, and whatever you've done with the rubric, and it takes probably five times as long to mark things. We are progressing, and getting there. I will work my way through this new system. It's hard to hand down to the kids as well, because they look at these numbers and they're not exactly sure what they mean.

The pragmatists will use aspects of critical literacy and child-centred learning, yet will not usually articulate a specific mandate to make changes in the curriculum through their teaching and learning. These teachers perceive the new knowledge framework to be an outside influence, to be tolerated and worked with, but without transformative power, which is located in their experience of classroom English practice and the agreements that they have come to with their students. The neutral pragmatists continue to do what they want in their literacy lessons, whilst being seen to conform to the ideas of the ELs.

Defenders of the canon

The third reaction to the introduction of the ELs that the research in this chapter has uncovered is that this curriculum change is a threat to subject integrity. These English teachers not only consider this reform to be a matter of interference with their teaching practices, they also believe it to be wrong. This is because the ELs impinges on their beliefs about the canon of English literature and language, and the appropriate pedagogies to get this body of work across. The teachers in this group are vocal opponents of the ELs, perhaps supporting other, more traditional curricula, where the subject disciplines are rigidly differentiated into specialist subject areas. For example:

> *Teacher C:* I'm worried about social engineering, and I'm worried about that in ELs and critical literacy ... in the ELs, for example, there are these world futures and personal futures. Now, somewhere, someone's decided, if you're going to assess someone on world futures, someone's obviously got an idea about what they would like the world to be like ... but if I buy that teachers are able to sell a worldview – what happens when it's not one I like?

These teachers may hold a cultural heritage or skills-based approach to teaching English that is shaped by direct instruction and the pivotal role of the English teacher to pass on truths about English cultural life. These teachers are also the most conservative and the perhaps least likely to take on board multiple literacies and MLT in their pedagogy.

Interdisciplinary subject area

One of the most prevalent educational issues that this research has identified is the contrast between interdisciplinary knowledge and the preservation of the subject disciplines in the secondary context (see Shulman, 1986). The ELs lends itself to working across subject areas, and developing integrated units of work around generative topics. The intense discussion and analysis of the transcripts has shown that English teachers fall into two Discourse and multiple literacy categories with respect to interdisciplinary work.

Vocational project managers

These teachers fully embrace interdisciplinary working. The reorganization of English into communication studies suits them as they enjoy the real-life contexts and the freedom to explore the media. Such teachers may take pedagogies from the perspective of multiliteracies (see Cole and Pullen, 2010), which is a parallel, earlier development to MLT, so that students use research and critical analysis to examine social phenomena through their reading and writing projects. For example:

> *Teacher D:* We were doing a unit of work on autobiography. The issue of motorbikes came up! We decided to follow this theme, and did research into the sales and branding of motorbikes. We looked at the gender stereotypes around motorbikes. Students found out about biker gangs, we looked at where they lived, what they believed in and what types of people they were. We did market research and critical analysis of the image of bikers and the associated gender divisions.

It could be argued that opening English up to the interdisciplinary style of planning and teaching is a response to new cultural conditions. Students will have to become literate in different (multiple) ways in the twenty-first century, and their repertoires of literate activities should be aligned with these changes (see Cole, 2007b). Interdisciplinary work gives English teachers the freedom and flexibility to explore this terrain, and to teach students relevant skills for today's workforce. Vocational project managers believe that English should be aligned to new workplace arrangements and the communication skills necessary to succeed in these environments, e.g. using new software packages to get one's message across.

Tireless bookworms

These English teachers accept the fact that the world is changing, but simultaneously believe that the basis for secondary English teaching and learning is print literacy. Students should therefore have the opportunity to study written text in a direct manner, learning about written effects such as metaphor, verisimilitude and hyperbole. Bookworms will search out reading opportunities for their students and design pedagogies that enhance the reading experience. For example:

Teacher E: Last year I read a book called *Hana's Suitcase* by Karen Devine. I found it so moving that I wanted to share it with my class. Even though I only had one copy, I was determined to use this book and we worked our way through it together and it has turned into one of the best teaching experiences that I have ever had. I believe that the class felt that this book had moved me, and they were too.

Bookworms will organize writing exercises that test the skills of their students to work in different genres (e.g. Derewianka, 1998). They will look at interdisciplinary work with suspicion, as it may constitute a threat to their understanding of reading and writing print text as primary. Bookworms will use many discursive and oral strategies in their English teaching, but these lesson segments and connectives will not usually be too far removed from a printed text source such as a script or a speech, therefore eliminating many of the digitally mediated multiple literacies.

Critical literacy

The issues with regard to the status and use of critical literacy in English get to the heart of the changes and rupture points that these Discourses and multiple literacies explore. The ELs has put critical literacy at the centre of 'Being literate', and therefore prioritizes its potential and usage. This is perhaps an ironic counterpoint to traditional notions of textual authority and the mandates that emerge from government and bureaucratic offices. It could be suggested that most system control centres would not overtly encourage critical exploration of controversies and the thorough questioning of text, especially those suggested for study by the centres. After close and animated scrutiny, it was found that the English teachers were divided according to two opposing Discourses or multiple literacies to questions about critical literacy.

Textual revolutionaries

This research chapter on power and multiple literacies found that there are English teachers who are wholly in agreement with the critical literacy approach to English teaching. Not only does critical literacy fit in with these teachers' beliefs about making a difference in the classroom, critical thinking also gives their lessons a purpose and meaning beyond any confined inter-action with the students. Such teachers will seek out text that can be used for the purposes of social justice and egalitarianism. They will not shy away from exploring the media, and addressing issues such as racism, misogyny and the environment. Textual revolutionaries will include post-structural thinking in their approaches to text (see Mellor and Patterson, 2004).

Teacher F: The problem with English teaching has been for many years that it has not addressed fundamental social problems. Therefore there was no point to it other than improving the student's level of English and perhaps some polite edification through reading. Now we have a framework that encourages me to make a difference – I really appreciate that.

The textual revolutionaries will highlight the ways in which those in power have constructed meaning, and they will look for different positions in English teaching to make sense of text such as post-colonialist, feminist or environmentalist perspectives. These English teachers will be politically motivated in terms of making a difference in society, and they will use this objective as an animating force in English classrooms. They believe wholeheartedly that it is a teacher's job to educate their students to be able to articulate their own opinions, especially if this means going against the norm (Cole, 2007c) or standing up for fundamental rights. These teachers may use non-normative strategies of mapping multiple literacies as a practice of English teaching, and introduce the Deleuzian literacy studies of this book. This materialist practice includes questioning textual authority, understanding authorship and the deployment of affect in the construction of meaning.

English 'royales'

Counter-arguments against critical literacy were not found to be prevalent in the cohort of English teachers questioned for this research. Perhaps this was because the teachers in Tasmania were acting through the Discourse and literacy of pragmatic neutrality, as they thought that it would be imprudent to speak out openly against critical literacy. Those who did, however, spoke about the suffocating and conformist English teaching agenda that critical literacy can produce. These teachers indicated that changing the world through English teaching is unrealistic and idealistic. These English teachers believe that students need sets of values that may be delivered through quality literature. For example:

Teacher C: You should remember that English isn't just about language and literacy skills – it is about ideas. In the absence of philosophy being well taught in schools, English can be a quasi-philosophy at times – it's about coming to terms with issues in life and the textual responses to these issues. It is not about giving students one certain answer or point of view.

The English 'royales' are sceptical with respect to politically motivated teaching and suspicious about leading the students to a pre-conceived position on a text. These teachers are aligned with the defenders of the canon, and select their texts from English literature to give students a panorama of writing throughout history; they do not acknowledge the impact of multiple literacies, context or social-cultural factors in their practice. These teachers would probably not use Deleuzian literacy studies, as they perceive English teaching to be constructed outside of the influence of French philosophy.

Emotions and teaching English

The second part of the research in this chapter presented the greatest challenge for the pre-service students. The aim was to examine the emotional side of English teaching. The level of emotions was tackled as a way into discussion about deeper aspects of English teaching, and as a bridge to affect, which is a central part of Deleuzian literacy studies (see Chapter Three). Once the teachers' ideas with respect to the ELs had been ascertained, the researchers were asked to pursue the emotions involved with teaching English. Clearly, this could lead the interview in a number of different directions (see Strauss and Corbin, 1998). The pre-service students used open-ended questions to allow teachers to tell their stories, and to explore how emotion permeates their practice. The teachers were encouraged to speak about their personal emotions, student emotions, emotions in the books that they were studying, or emotions that might be produced in the classroom due to the examination of text related issues. The second part of the research depended upon the quality of the relationship that the student-researcher had managed to strike up with the teacher, and was not designed to be psychoanalytic. It should be noted that the representation of emotional phenomena in English teaching came about in the context of a trainee teacher interviewing a fully trained teacher. This creates a certain angle to the data, in that the teachers may well have added pedagogic value to their 'emotionality' as they spoke to the trainees. The analyses that follow about emotions and English cannot be differentiated into Discourses, literacies or interrelated teacher types. This is because the emotional factors that are being represented here are thoroughly entwined in that there are no unambiguous labels or clear categories to separate opinion (see Chevellard, 1991). The following headings were arrived at after discussion between the pre-service students and the main researcher. In a parallel manner to the Discourse types, these headings are highly interrelated, and represent a qualitatively themed analysis of the data on emotions and secondary English teaching in Tasmania during 2004–7. The primary research question here is: What are the ways in which emotion works in your English class?

Maturation

The research has shown that teachers construct English teaching differently as they mature into the job. At the beginning of their careers, many of them were trained to use emotions in the text to create lively and interactive learning environments. Perhaps they were responding to reader response or the personal growth theory of English teaching (see Sawyer, 2004). Whatever the precise reason for the initial integration of emotional textual stimulation into their practice, they tend to personally value these tactics less as they have matured. For example:

> *Teacher G:* My ideas have changed over the years – when I was an early teacher, I did a lot of teaching that I hoped was affecting students in an emotional and empathetic way – now I'm moving away from that model. I'm still looking at literature in the way it has an effect on students, but I don't want my students to be affected by the characters and the work in the same way. I actually want them to be more involved with the writer, the intended audience, the gaps and silences in the text, the purposes within the text.

Teachers at the beginning of their careers also found it more difficult to speak about ways of working with text to enhance emotion, both in terms of their own emotions and emotions that come about due to reading texts. For example:

> *Teacher L:* I have just started teaching and I have had a terrible time getting the kids to talk about anything! I remember having great discussions at school about characters in books and important issues. My students just don't want to say anything.

Perhaps because the emotions of beginning teachers are sometimes under pressure in the classroom context, textual emotions may be difficult to locate, address and articulate (see Holland, 1968). The interview transcripts point to a complicated relationship between the use of emotions in English as a textual practice, the understanding of how to use emotions by particular English teachers and the articulation of emotion in their work. This relationship must take into account the ways in which habit and conditioning make emotions part of the automatic working in the classroom (Varela *et al.*, 1993) – which also points to maturation as being pivotal in terms of English teaching and emotion. This is reinforced by the ways in which English teaching may become easier as practitioners mature into the job. At the beginning of their careers, English teachers could find it hard to separate their emotional involvement with a lesson from the emotions that would be stirred up from reading a text (see Doecke, 2006).

Gender

The interviews show that gender has a part to play with respect to emotion in English, in terms both of students reacting to texts and of gendered emotional relationships in the English classroom. For example, boys sometimes found it difficult to take on role-plays, or to empathize with characters in the text. Girls, however, more frequently have no problem in identifying with characters, understanding the emotions with respect to the text, and completing work that requires them to analyze relationships in the text. Gender therefore plays a role in secondary English in that engagement with literature requires emotional processes that may be gendered. For example:

> *Teacher H:* ... it can be a struggle with boys to get a deep response out of them. It just usually requires you to pull back or alter the task in some way so that they are not obviously traumatized by the experience.

> *Teacher I:* Something I find interesting though is that girls, perhaps because they are conditioned, are more likely to identify with the obvious male characters and feel quite happy talking about that identification, the emotions and the situation than boys do with female characters.

Teachers commented that work around gender stereotypes and relationships between genders can have a positive impact in English classes, in that the emotional proclivities stirred up by gender in the classroom may be resolved and articulated through the third person of the text. Teachers willing and able to use textual emotion positively in the classroom will stimulate differences through these practices (see Cole, 2007a); those perhaps preferring a quiet life will yearn for single-sex English classrooms! The results of this research do not point to binary gendered opposites in English teaching, but show how classroom experience may be intensified through understanding the roles of gender in English studies.

Power

The third heading for emotions and English that this research and the debriefings picked up was power. Many pre-service students have benefited from these discussions as they have come into teacher training with misconceptions about teacher power and the use of power in the classroom. They have found out that teachers feel empowered through an emotional connection with their job; they would also feel disempowered if this emotional connection is broken. The power of the English teacher was prevalent and articulated when he or she worked with a group with definite objectives and processes. The disempowered teachers were often working through power differentials. For example:

> *Teacher K:* At the end of the year, the grade 11 class wrote a letter about the behavioural problems that we had been experiencing. They said that there had been a personality clash. I don't believe in personality clashes myself. The secret to survival in that class was one boy who took an age to come around. Once he was on board and working with me, the rest of the group complied. They realized that I was the one with the power, and that the student was engaging in a power-stunt.

This teacher shows how power problems in the classroom may resolve themselves through dialogue and emotional alignment. The disempowered teacher may be unconnected to the will of the group, and feel a gulf between their expectations, curriculum matters and the class reality. Clearly, this emotional aspect of English teaching has a lot to do with behaviour management. Teachers who perceive their job to be a daily battle with teenagers will feel disempowered; those who understand their working lives as a synchronized movement towards enhanced communal literacy are more likely to revel in their existence (see McWilliam, 2000).

Affect in English teaching

The students and the main researcher discussed affect and its relationship with teaching English before doing the fieldwork. Affect was distinguished from emotions by understanding that emotions are connected to the personality and makeup of the teachers, whereas affect is a network of connections between people and text and reading that may provoke emotions (Holland, 1968). The affect level of English teaching is a non-representative part of mapping multiple literacies, and an important aspect of Deleuzian literacy studies (see Chapter Three). It was agreed that affect is useful with respect to talking about how English classrooms work on a depersonalized level, and in contrast to emotions (Keen, 2006). It was hoped that discussing affect would elicit non-reactive responses from the English teachers, whereas directly asking the teachers about their emotions could close down the discussion; emotions and affect should both produce useful information on current English practice and identity as they run through embodied practice. Affects can only be differentiated via interrelated themes, which do not define Discourses, literacies or identity resources, as the conversations that emerged around them are not structured as constituting types. The headings below were arrived at after open analysis of the interview transcripts between the pre-service students and the main researcher. The research questions here are: What affect helps to make your classes work? What affect might cause difficulties in your English teaching?

Creativity

Many teachers spoke to the students about how to be creative in the English classroom. This can be a personal goal in terms of not endlessly repeating the same photocopied lessons, as well as being a social objective (see Houtz and Krug, 1995) that relates to the contemporary heightened requirements of literate creativity. Students need to be skilled in creativity in their language usage, as the communication abilities demanded of them in the contemporary workplace are becoming increasingly disparate (see Cope and Kalantzis, 1995). Affects are related to these global changes in English teaching and the corresponding identities that improved creativity demands, as teachers have to continually work on the level of impact and relevance with the students. Affects are expressions of desire (Semetsky, 2007) that may be differentiated from emotions in that they relate to the atmospheres and drives that the English lessons can produce and have running through them. For example:

> *Teacher H:* ... so sometimes very deep affective learning can come out
> of life writing and I have to try and say you are not writing just
> to be cathartic and for your own personal counselling here, there
> has to be an awareness of audience as well as learning outcomes
> and a valid learning experience going on. At this level, teenagers
> sometimes don't know the difference and I feel I've got to be the one
> that arbitrates.

This teacher shows how affect may be connected to creativity, and the ways in which language use alters when engaging with audience in creative writing. In an increasingly diverse demographic environment and with the acceptance that this diversity should be used and celebrated (e.g. Graham, 2007) in teaching, English teachers should look at new ways to make their lessons appealing to new audiences. For example, the use of technology shows one possible route and the affect that is produced through multi-media is an important zone for English teachers to teach their students to write about and explore: for example, the affect of media studies, film, advertising and the Internet (Cole, 2005). Furthermore, the increasing prominence of the multiple literacies of family literacy, personal literacy and English as a second language as part of mainstream English practice (see Cardiero-Kaplan, 2004) demonstrates how English teaching is evolving and affect is part of this evolution. The students found that some teachers were reluctant to talk about such changes in English, as it can involve new skills and multiple literacies for them to learn. However, those who did accept changing demographics would engage in discussing the use of affect to get their classes to work creatively through building positive literate relationships (see Chapter Three). Examples that were given of using affect for creativity included: scenarios for vocabulary, working with communicative competence and engagement, and exploring the cultural perceptions and desires that are brought to the English classroom by the students through the media, popular culture and ethnicity.

Rebellion and dissonance

The last category of affect that this research chapter with English teachers has uncovered involves rebellion and dissonance in the classroom. Critical dissonance is a research methodology for teachers that encourages the educators to critique and explore the social consequences of their knowledge (see Cochran-Smith, 2003). Several English teachers agreed with this way into the contemporary English curriculum as it enables inquiry-based learning and teaching for understanding:

> *Teacher J:* The way I work through a book is a semi-reflexive process. I gauge the ways in which the class might react before I bring literature into the room. It's a kind of experimentation. I have to set all of these ideas up before we start reading a text or they won't learn.

This way of using affect taps into pervasive affects of rebellion and dissonance (Cole, 2005, 2007b, 2007c) that may be present in their teenage cohorts. Teachers may structure lessons around literature that expresses these ideas, or introduce the topics of rebellion and dissonance through examining current news events. These lessons should not have a negative feel, but use the desires of the participants (affect) to engage with the texts to the advantage of the English teacher. Many of the pre-service students were impressed and surprised at this development in English teaching, as it marks out the ways in which the profession is evolving as the nature of textual authority changes in society. This point also shows how English teachers now need to work with cultural seduction in and through language that deploys affect to make their classes work (see McWilliam, 2000).

Polarization and emergence

The teacher identity Discourses and literacies that have been put into play by the rupture of ELs and brought to light through this research may be represented in the diagram below (Figure 6.2). Polarization is represented in this figure by the arrows that jut out horizontally through the teacher identity Discourses or literacies. Polarization is a useful term to use in this context as it describes the ways in which the Discourses may be connected to the friction or antipathy between groups involved in curriculum reform. This figure points to the fact that there is lateral movement between

Discourses and literacies, in that they are not sealed or constituted by privileged spaces. The diagram could be added to indefinitely to show how polarization may also work along different axes, yet this complexity would make it impossible to understand as a summary or map of multiple literacies of this research project.

Polarization is the most conspicuous aspect of this mapping of Discourses as the teachers are forced into positions by the introduction of the new knowledge framework. It could be said that many of these teachers had been happily performing their jobs for many years without having to consider their identity positioning. In many ways, and as has already been discussed, the introduction of critical literacy as a headline government objective may augment polarization (see Hargreaves, 1994). Most governments content themselves with functional or linguistic, rationally defined discrete learning outcomes (cf. Eisner, 1994). These outcomes do not produce polarities, in fact they often work to do the opposite and to neutralize debate. I am sure that many English teachers, especially those who endorse critical literacy, have welcomed the *Essential Learnings* for exactly the reason that serious critical examination of text and text choice is now on the agenda. Many teachers may have been working in their English lessons to produce critical

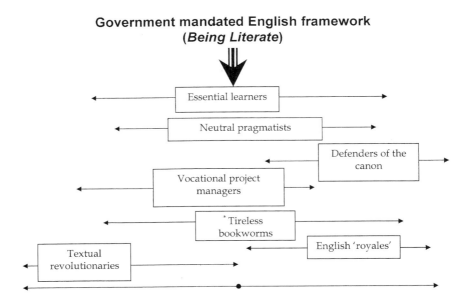

Figure 6.2 The English teacher identity Discourses and relative positions that have been produced after the introduction of the Essential Learnings.

thinkers for many years; this is for the first time in line with explicit governmental outcomes.

The emotional and affective factors that this research has uncovered may be represented in Figure 6.3. The through-line of the diagram is a spiral that oscillates between personal English teaching development and the ability to articulate one's philosophy of English teaching (see Arnold, 1991). At the top of the spiral is one's power as an English teacher at any given time during a career. Below this, the factors of maturation and gender also heavily influence one's emotional state and the consequent textual emotions that one may be able to induce at a given point through the application of affect. Running through these emotional factors in English teaching are the affects of rebellion, dissonance and creativity. Creativity goes through the whole of the figure, and to a certain extent defines the emergent qualities of the teacher (cf. Tochan and Munby, 1993). These qualities include the ability to work through change, the establishment of shifting yet positive learning relationships and inspirational teaching with elements of spontaneity and surprise. It should be noted that emergence is non-linear and includes retardation as well as development (Casti, 1989).

Power should not be thought of as the goal of English teaching, though it is always part of the pedagogic and professional roles that one might inhabit. Figure 6.3 is an attempt to represent the complicated nature of emotion in English teaching, and this point has been discussed in detail throughout the course of the project by the main researcher and the pre-service students. This discussion had the aim of looking at the nature of complexity in English teacher identity, and asking what we may learn from this (Purcell-Gates, 2004). The overall impression was that lessons learnt from life – for example, communicating with one's children or taking on roles of responsibility in the community – will help with understanding how Figure 6.3 might help to structure and restructure English teaching development.

Multiple literacies of English teaching

This research has given pre-service students an insight into English teaching in Tasmania. On one level, this project shows how changes due to curriculum reform can polarize English teachers and make them shift with respect to their job positioning; on another, it gives them an introduction to the emotional and affective parts of the daily work. As Muchmore (2001: p. 28) has explained when investigating the personal pedagogies of an English teacher, there is a 'complex and multi-layered system of beliefs' to understand. It is only when the teacher is challenged in some way that transformation of these beliefs happens (Tann, 1993), and the relationships between these beliefs come into the light and may be articulated. In terms

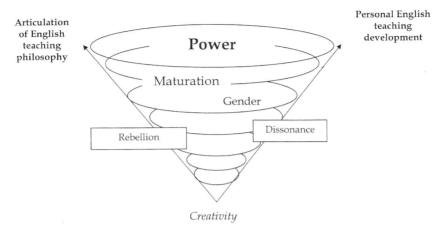

Articulation of English teaching philosophy

Personal English teaching development

Power

Maturation

Gender

Rebellion

Dissonance

Creativity

Figure 6.3 The emotional and affective journey of the English teacher. English teacher identity emergence.

of Deleuzian literacy studies, the change in curriculum represents a rupture point, through which one may discern non-normative ways of working. The Discourses that this project has found are indicative of the multiple literacies that the teachers are working through after this rupture point. The introduction of the ELs works on this level as it has shaken up the idea of what it means to teach English in many teachers' minds, and this process has enabled the questioning of cultural and social assumptions. Excerpts from the pre-service students' self-reflective diaries relate to these points:

> *Student A:* I was actually teaching today when one of the interviews came back to me. The teacher had been speaking about the ELs and how it was attacking the subject fidelity of English. He wanted more Shakespeare in the curriculum! The kids in the room were bored by the literacy project that had been set, and I was wondering if I could ask the colleague teacher if I could use a different text.
>
> *Student B:* The project has really helped me to think about my emotions and those in the English teaching classroom. Before I just thought it was a matter of going in there and getting through the text in a professional manner. Now I realise that I bring a whole lot more of 'me' in there.

The knowledge that the students have gained by taking part in the research is connected to the drives of the students as well as being discursively based (see Masny, 2006). This means that they are assimilating ideas about the construction of English not only as public output, but also as personal experience. On this level, the forces of identity in Figure 6.1 are activated by polarized beliefs (e.g. Leach and Moon, 1999), as described in Figure 6.2. This aspect of the synthesis and analysis of English is concerned with having the will to carry on, and takes into account the ways in which English may be recast through the unconscious, the imaginary and the multiple. These long-term goals deal with the possibility that exterior and interior factors in English teaching would not form a dualistic system of division between the inner and the outer in the minds of English teachers. The benefit of this research is to address this possible dualism early on, and to set a course for English teaching careers where the interior and exterior are aligned and reconciled to enhance the power of future teachers through multiplicity.

Conclusion

Deleuzian literacy studies do not tend towards discourse analysis, as the linguistic entanglements that pass through teaching and learning contexts are just one part of the multiplicity of factors that could impinge upon any power concerns that are present. Yet the discourse analysis above does serve as a map of the multiple literacies that the teachers involved with study articulated after the curriculum change of the ELs. These multiple literacies relate to political positioning with respect to the new curriculum model, as well as involving the identity resources of the teachers. Politics and identity are mixed up in the teachers in the manner of a *bricolage*, which the research in the chapter has only begun to discover. As a postscript to this chapter and research report, the ELs was scrapped in 2008 after the incumbent government lost a local election. Many of the Discourse categories that the teachers were acting through during the period of the fieldwork will have now faded back into meshed and hidden opinions and drives. These flows may bolster or detract from the emotional and affective zones of the English teacher's job on the island, as the Discourse categories settle and merge with affective and creative ways of working with text (see Chapter Three). The power of literacy in Tasmania will henceforth follow the positioning of pre-ELs curricula, with a focus on helping low-income, low-literacy families, basic skills and structured literacy intervention. This cloud of power concerns in Tasmania will tend to block the move to multiple literacies and Deleuzian literacy studies as have been argued for throughout this book.

References

Anyon, J. (2009). *Theory and Educational Research: Towards Critical Social Explanation*. New York and London: Routledge.
Araya, D. and Peters, M. A. (eds) (2010). *Education in the Creative Economy: Knowledge and Learning in the Age of Innovation*. New York: Peter Lang.

Arnold, R. (1991). *Writing Development: magic in the brain*. Buckingham: Open University Press.

Cardiero-Kaplan, K. (2004). *The Literacy Curriculum and Bilingual Education: a critical examination*. New York: Peter Lang.

Casti, J. L. (1989). *Nonlinear System Theory*. New York: Academic Press.

Chevellard, Y. (1991). *Le Transposition Didactique: Du savoir savant au savoir enseigné*. Paris: La Pensée Sauvage.

Cochran-Smith, M. (2003). Learning and Unlearning: the education of teacher educators. *Teaching and Teacher Education*, 19, 5–28.

Cole, D. R. (2005). Education and the Politics of Cyberpunk. *Review of Education Pedagogy and Cultural Studies*, 27(2), 159–70.

—(2007a). Teaching Frankenstein and Wide Sargasso Sea Using Affective Literacy. *English in Australia*, 42(2), 69–75.

—(2007b). Techno-shamanism and Educational Research. *Ashé: Journal of Experimental Spirituality*. Available online at http://ashejournal.com/index.php?id=277 (accessed 31 January 2012).

—(2007c). Virtual Terrorism and the Internet E-Learning Options. *E-Learning*, 4(2), 116–27.

Cole, D. R. and Pullen, D. L. (eds) (2010). *Multiliteracies in Motion: Current theory and practice*. New York and London: Routledge.

Cope, B. and Kalantzis, M. (1995). *Productive Diversity: organisational life in the age of civic pluralism and total globalisation*. Sydney: HarperCollins.

Deleuze, G. (1994). *Difference and Repetition*, (P. Patton, trans.). London: The Athlone Press.

Deleuze, G. and Guattari, F. (1988). *A Thousand Plateaus: Capitalism and Schizophrenia II*, (B. Massumi, trans.). London: The Athlone Press.

Derewianka, B. (1998). *A Grammar Companion for Primary Teachers*. Sydney: Primary English Teachers.

Doecke, B. (2006). Teacher Quality: beyond the rhetoric. In B. Doecke, M. Howie and W. Sawyer (eds), *Only Connect: English teaching, schooling and community* (pp. 195–209). Kent Town, SA: Wakefield Press (AATE).

Doecke, B., Howie, M. and Sawyer, W. (eds) (2006). *Only Connect: English teaching, schooling and community*. Kent Town, SA: Wakefield Press (AATE).

Dowden, T. and Nolan, P. (2006). Engaging Early Adolescent Students in their Learning Via Student-centred Curriculum Integration. Paper presented at the *Australian Association for Research in Education Conference*, November 26–30, Adelaide.

Eisner, E. (1994). *Cognition and Curriculum Reconsidered*. New York: Teachers College Press.

Fairclough, N. (1992). *Discourse and Social Change*. London: Polity Press.

Gee, J. P. (2003). Literacy and Social Minds. In G. Bull and M. Anstey (eds), *The Literacy Lexicon*, 2nd edn (pp. 3–15). Frenchs Forest, NSW: Pearson Education Australia.

Graham, L. (2007). Done in by Discourse ... or the Problems with Labelling. In M. Keefe and S. Carrington (eds), *Schools and Diversity*, 2nd edn (pp. 46–65). Frenchs Forest, NSW: Pearson Education Australia.

Gubrium, J. E. and Holstein, J. A. (eds). (2002). *Handbook of Interview Research: context and method*. Thousand Oaks, CA: Sage.

Hargreaves, A. (1994). *Changing Teachers, Changing Times: teachers' work and culture in the postmodern age*. New York: Teachers College Press.

Holland, N. N. (1968). *The Dynamics of Literary Response*, 1st edn. New York: Oxford University Press.

Houtz, J. C. and Krug, D. (1995). Assessment of Creativity: resolving a mid-life crisis. *Educational Psychology Review*, 7, 269–300.

Keen, S. (2006). A Theory of Narrative Empathy. *Narrative*, 14(3), 207–40.

Kress, G. (2006). Reimagining English: curriculum, identity and productive futures. In B. Doecke, M. Howie and W. Sawyer (eds), *Only Connect: English teaching, schooling and community* (pp. 31–42). Kent Town, SA: Wakefield Press (AATE).

Lankshear, C. and Knobel, M. (2003). *New literacies: Changing knowledge and classroom learning*. Buckingham and Philadelphia: Open University Press.

Leach, J. and Moon, R. (1999). *Learners and Pedagogy*. London: Paul Chapman.

Lyotard, J.-F. (1991). *The Inhuman: reflections on time* (G. Bennington and R. Bowlby, trans). Cambridge: Polity Press.

McWilliam, E. (2000). Stuck in the Missionary Position? Pedagogy and Desire in New Times. In C. O'Farrell, D. Meadmore, E. McWilliams and C. Symes (eds), *Taught Bodies* (pp. 27–39). New York: Peter Lang.

Marshall, B. (2000). *The Unofficial Guide: researching the philosophies of English teachers*. London: Routledge.

Martin, G., Hunter, L. and McLaren, P. (2006). Participatory Activist Research (Teams)/Action Research. In K. Tobin and J. Kincheloe (eds), *Doing Educational Research: a handbook* (pp. 123–48). Rotterdam: Sense Publishers.

Masny, D. (2006). Learning and Creative Processes: a poststructural perspective on language and multiple literacies. *International Journal of Learning*, 12(5), 147–55.

Mellor, B. and Patterson, A. (2004). Poststructuralism in English Classrooms: critical literacy and after. *International Journal of Qualitative Studies in Education*, 17(1), 83–98.

Muchmore, J. A. (2001). The Story of Ana: a life history study of the literacy beliefs and teaching practices of an urban high school English teacher. Paper presented at the *Annual Meeting of the American Educational Research Association*, Seattle.

Purcell-Gates, V. (2004). Ethnographic Research. In N. K. Duke and M. H. Mallette (eds), *Literacy Research Methodologies* (pp. 92–114). New York: Guilford Press.

Sawyer, W. (2004). Seminal Books on English Teaching. In W. Sawyer and E. Gold (eds), *Reviewing English in the 21st Century* (pp. 23–36). Melbourne: Phoenix Education.

Semetsky, I. (2007). *Deleuze, Education and Becoming*. Rotterdam: Sense Publishers.

Shulman, L. S. (1986). Those Who Understand: knowledge growth in teaching. *Educational Research Review*, 57, 4–14.

Strauss, A. and Corbin, J. (1998). *Basics of Qualitative Research: grounded theory procedures and techniques,* 2nd edn. Newbury Park, CA: Sage.

Tann, S. (1993). Eliciting Student Teachers' Personal Theories. In J. Calderhead and P. Gates (eds), *Conceptualising Reflection in Teacher Development* (pp. 53–69). London: Falmer Press.

Tasmania Department of Education (2002). *Essential Learnings: learning together*. Hobart: Tasmania Education Authority.

Tochan, F. and Munby, H. (1993). Novice and Expert Teachers' Time Epistemology: a wave function from didactics to pedagogy. *Teacher and Teacher Education*, 9(2), 205–18.

Upton, P. (2005) Re-positioning the Subject: trainee English teachers' constructions of grammar and English. Ph.D. thesis. *University of Nottingham*.

Varela, F. J., Thompson, E. T. and Rosch, E. (1993). *The Embodied Mind: cognitive science and human experience*. Cambridge, MA: MIT Press.

Watt, M. G. (2005). Looking back at Curriculum Change in Tasmania: Is the Essential Learnings Framework Promoting Successful Curriculum Reform? Paper presented at *"Blurring the Boundaries: sharpening the focus"*, ACSA Biennial Conference, University of the Sunshine Coast, 21–23 September.

CHAPTER SEVEN

Mapping the literacy of digital futures

David R. Cole

Introduction

One of the obstacles connected to the discourse and movement that is framed around the 'new literacies' (e.g. Coiro *et al.*, 2008) is that there are ubiquitously and continuously new digital learning products. Consequently, to frame the future of digital literacy around the current learning options that are available includes consistent obsolescence. Publications that examine the latest in e-learning and computer assisted learning (CAL) products almost immediately become out of date when in print. This is because the global learning market constantly produces novel ways to learn (see Pullen and Cole, 2009), as commercial suppliers have teams of research and development software designers working on the latest digital interfaces to make new devices. Governments may try to catch up with these processes by funding research into the new digital environments through which the youth of the country are learning; however, this research is necessarily one step behind the latest developments. For example, a government may commission cutting edge research into social media. The findings are henceforth synthesized and reused to make a government website that mimics the ways in which young people are using social media. Six months after the experiment, the funding for the website is withdrawn due to lack of usage. What has gone wrong? Why have users not participated in this carefully orchestrated e-government project? The truth of the matter is that users demand new experiences from mediated social environments. The time lag between commissioning the research, doing the research and assembling the social environment for e-government is critical. The ways in which young people are socializing on the Internet has already moved on when the government site appears. The other factor that makes the site unappealing is that Internet users are highly sensitive to e-context (see Gee, 2005); anything that appears to be counterfeit would not be appealing. Even the whiff of political or governmental presence makes the website less attractive unless the users are doing research on government or interested in a career in politics. This chapter on the future of digital literacy therefore does not take a static or projective look at the current state of digital learning, but examines emergent features of multiple literacies that are currently connecting and diverging through digitalization.

The theoretical backdrop to this chapter in Deleuze and Guattari (1988) and Multiple Literacies Theory (MLT) gives it a platform in time. Deleuze has been described as a philosopher of the future (e.g. Sellers and Gough, 2010). This future orientation is due to Deleuze's engagement with issues around time through the various strands of his philosophical project. For example, Bergson (1994) argued for a subjective concept of time that could not be bracketed as 'inner sense', or as purely relying on intuitive data. The philosopher David Hume (1739) considered the construction of the self to be reliant on fleeting sensations that may stick in time through mechanisms such as the memory or appetite. Nietzsche (1961) considered the notion of time to be central to his philosophy, and worked to understand how one might conceive of the possibility of eternal return that allows for and promotes difference. Deleuze (1989) took these philosophical strands and wove them into something new – an idea of time that encourages the future to be present in the instant. Ronald Bogue (2008) has executed a means to understand this notion of time with respect to the writings of Marcel Proust. Proust wrote characters that reminisced and lived through infinitely delicate 'thread works' of memories, coincidences, loves and narrative streams (consciousness). Deleuze contends that Proust's novels are not nostalgic. The future is present in the instant, in that time has been fragmented by the writer into terribly fragile, looking-glass moments whereby one may understand someone's entire life through a casual glance or a few chords from a piano piece. This is because the instant holds time, the writer's consciousness has conceived of the entire life of a character as a moment, and that moment can lead both backwards and forwards, depending upon what one is looking for. Reading Proust's novels is an art form, and Deleuze challenges us to apply this craft and skill to philosophy. To use Deleuze's philosophical conception of time in the context of the literacy of digital futures is perhaps even more difficult, given the enormous and somewhat inconsistent field of operation that we are examining.

The art form that we need to acquire as a practice to understand this chapter has at least three main characteristics:

1   The map of the literacy of digital futures that this chapter describes is time-based. This time basis for thought means that the ways

in which the themes and ideas are organized do not represent a spatial arrangement. This fact has vital consequences for one's understanding of what literacy looks like and how it relates to learning. This time-based point relates to the major artefacts of learning in the future, such as developments in the sociality of the Internet and new ways in which virtual reality envelops thought; these both play with one's sense of time (see Cole, 2005b).

2   Literacy in this context is not a holistic or sequential notion that leads to either greater general intelligence or improved mastery of subject areas relying on the manipulation of language or communication skills. The multiple futures that are present in the instant, that is, our focus for understanding questions that relate to the self and power through education, require multiple literacies. These multiple literacies are completely differentiated, and it cannot be assumed that one leads to improvement in another. For example, the intense research and writing that has gone into understanding visual literacy has shown how it can be an exciting means to introducing new subject knowledge areas, in that it provides a motivational platform for teaching and learning (e.g. Debes, 1968). Yet the designation of multimodality, that is, the switching between different modes of meaning making, such as the visual and the linguistic, would suggest that there is a crossover effect between understanding virtual dynamics and language (see Cole, 2005a). This chapter should be read through the lens of multiple literacies, whereby literacies develop separately in their own spheres of intensification. Crossover, blended and hybrid learning are certainly all possible in and through the digital futures of this chapter, but these changes happen as a secondary effect, given the primacy of intensified multiple forms of literacy.

3   The impact of the literacy of digital futures in terms of social life is a speculative yet important aspect of this writing. In line with interpretations of Deleuze's philosophy as a type of speculative materialism (see Cole, in press), this writing feeds into understandings about how global capitalism is changing and the ways in which these systems relate to education. Much of the technological mediation in education is due to flows of capital and investment, combined with the expansion of techno-products in global markets. This chapter accepts these facts, and they lurk in the shadows of literate futures, colouring the ideas that are presented in this writing with capital, and subsequent variegated shades of privilege, race, class, gender and ethnicity.

Digital machines and connectivity

The change from analogue to digital functioning in education is imminent. This means that print literacy forms of education are becoming progressively more out of date as digital technology proliferates. This has real and practical effects, such as challenging and changing the use of textbooks in the classroom. The style, content, layout and possible rate of consumption of digital text can make a print-based textbook archaic to a generation schooled on the Internet and through digitalization. Reading and understanding the print-based textbook corresponds to linguistic, visual and interpretive literacies, yet the lack of digital content in the book will act as a film, whereby the digitally immersed user perceives the static and two-dimensional aspect of the experience as primary. The traditional school textbook may mimic digitally uploaded content; yet, in a parallel way to which the e-government website inevitably fails to draw in its target audience, the print textbook mimicking a digital text is a poor imitation. One might say that the experience of working through a textbook is different in kind to that of working through digitally connected texts. Teaching and learning with digitally connected texts includes literacies such as digital literacy, Internet literacy, video literacy and hyperlink literacy (see Cole, 2005b). These multiple literacies represent an expanded focus and increase in the distribution of energies for learning with respect to print literacy.

Another means to explaining this intensification in the reading process is through positing the computer as a machine, and understanding how that machine connects the user to other machines and ultimately to a plethora of digital machines that have been built to exchange code (e.g. Cole, 2007b). The agent plugs into this world of interconnection, and the relationship with digital machines has started. This is an irreversible relationship, even if the agent loses touch with computers, or switches off during ICT class. This is because digitalization lives on in the memory, and is a restructuring of thought processes in that the synthesis that digital texts represents is not open to decay in the same way that remembering a page of a textbook fades after one has taken the requisite examination. Research into this cognitive field is in its infancy, though neuroscientists (see Small and Vorgan, 2008) have found that:

- Memory processes are altered through the use of digital text in contrast to print-based text. The user tends to remember the pathways and sites for the collection of information (for example the *urls*), rather than recalling all of the information itself. Also, short- and long-term memory processes are realigned given the ways in which the digitalized memory acts to remember pathways and sites over specific detail and subject matter.

- There is intensification in speed in the neural activity when the agent is engaged in reading digital texts. Research has shown that the brain's communication routes 'light up' between different parts of the brain, e.g. the linguistic and visual processing centres of the brain, as reading takes place. Similar neural maps are seen when the agent reads digital texts that are parallel to print-based texts; the difference here is that the interconnections are accelerated and the brain activity flickers between requisite processing centres.

- The brain registers more 'background noise' when the agent is engaged in reading digital texts rather than with print-based text. The reasons for this are not known, though the hypothesis is that there is a requisite amount of parallel processing going on when one is reading a digital text, perhaps to understand what one is going to do next as well as understanding the visual data on any particular screen of information.

- There is no evidence to suggest that linguistic processing is in any way diminished through immersion in digital texts. It can be stated that the increased amount of neural activity that the brain exhibits when processing a digital text, and henceforth moves between texts very quickly, means that the connection to linguistic explanation may be muted. The practice of reading comprehension of print literacy is therefore inappropriate as pedagogy if applied in a linear fashion to the educational use of digital texts.

These neuro-chemical and electrostatic factors connected to digital engagement, as discovered through research, spread out and affect the behaviour and habits by which children learn through digital texts. The drawback for teachers employing digital texts in a school context is the school itself – or as Deleuze and Guattari (1988: p. 67) put it:

> As in school: there is not just one writing lesson, that of the great redundant Signifier for any and all signifieds. There are two distinct formalizations in reciprocal presuppositions and constituting a double-pincer: the formalization of expression in the reading and writing lesson (with its own relative contents), and the formalization of content in the lesson of things (with their own relative expressions). We are never signifier or signified. We are stratified.

In other words, the school works as a palimpsest, through which various writings are carried out, often erasing and hiding the other levels of writing – or strata. This paradox is particularly striking in the case of reading digital texts at school, as the machinery of schooling, i.e. conformism to rules and preparation for integration into systems of capital, can lead in different directions to the lessons available online and through reading digital texts.

The point is not that there are necessarily different value sets online that may contradict the school environment, but that the ways in which levels of influence may be determined are reversed and complexified given the ways in which authorship works on the Internet. At school, the rules are determined through a central body, usually including government edicts, the principal, senior teachers and possibly a small student contingent. On the Internet, the authors of digital texts may be hidden, or the text may be cut and pasted from somewhere else. There is no central body coordinating and regulating the flows of information on the Internet (see Cole, 2007b), even though national governments have tried to censor and ban sites. Digital connectivity leads to web or 'astral works', which are luminous, nodal framings that link and picture circuits of intensity, as represented in Figure 7.1

These astral works are present in our lives through the ubiquitous digital connectivity that has emerged since the 1980s. Schools and systems of schooling were, for the most part, built and designed before the unfolding of digitalization. The challenge, therefore, is to readjust the ways in which schooling happens to account for the new digital connectivity and machinery that has burrowed inside of and redefined consciousness, and has started to transform social life. For example, the idea of specialization

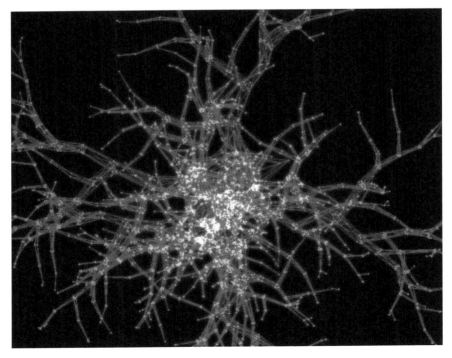

Figure 7.1 Representation of digital connectivity.

in subject knowledge areas is put under pressure through the fact that most specialist knowledge may now be found on the Internet. The notion of a specialist teacher is therefore made redundant, as is a transmission model of teaching and learning. The questions that concern us become: What should we do with our specialist knowledge? and: How can we use specialist knowledge (to better society)? Deleuze and Guattari (1988) talk about abstract machines that are at work inside of thought processes and through the history of ideas. The digital machines that transmit connectivity are impregnated with countless abstract machines, such as those connected to text, imagery, concepts, philosophers, scientists, writers and artists. The digital machine is therefore an aggregating machine, which collects and transmits all other abstract machinery in coded form. These codes could lead to increasing the strata, or, to the haves and have-nots of the digital divide (see Shields, 2003), yet the strata can also remain as code. The literacy of digital futures as figured in this chapter is therefore crucially about keeping the code flowing – and not as coded stratification. This movement involves extracting and animating the multiplicities embedded in digitalization and understanding how to translate these processes to social life – this is explained below under the rubric 'cyber-revolutions'.

The cyber-revolutions

The overriding social process that is present in the literacy of digital futures is that of revolution. Revolution does not necessarily mean the violent overthrow of a political system or class – here it involves the dynamics of social life that are engendered through digitalization, hence cyber-revolutions. In 1995, I was part of a team that organized a conference called *Virtual Futures: Cyber-Revolutions* at the University of Warwick, UK. We took the philosophy of Deleuze and Guattari as a framing for the idea of social change being driven by digital technology. The conference drew a huge crowd of philosophers, futurists, cultural theorists, conceptual artists, musicians and scientists. The cyber-revolution was demonstrated through the ways in which we were able to pull the event together through email, and use the Internet to simultaneously broadcast and record what was happening. In contrast to most academic conferences, it could be stated that a form of social change did take place at this conference. *Virtual Futures* showed us how diverse interests in the future could be combined on the social plane, and this conference gave us a glimpse of what that future might look like. No aristocrats were killed during Virtual Futures (to the best of my knowledge), though we did notice worried university officials wandering around, trying to work out what was happening.

Cyber-revolutions have now transmigrated from university-organized conferences to everyday life in post-industrial society. Recently, I saw a photograph in the New York Times[1] that illustrates Prensky's (2001) notions of digital natives and digital immigrants. These notions bear a direct relation to cyber-revolutions, as these behaviours indicate tendencies of social change. This photograph visualized a family of four spending a quiet evening at home reading. The father sat in his chair reading a print-based newspaper, while the mother was reading a print-based novel. The children, two teenagers, are perched on the couch, looking at their laptops. This image portrays a familiar dichotomy in a technological society and shows how the cyber-revolutions may function in family units. Many students today are digital natives, or agents who have lived with digital technologies all of their lives and do not choose print-based resources, but elect to read and socialize online. Contrariwise, the parents and teachers of the students have to adapt to the digital environment, but retain the 'digital immigrant accent' (Prensky, 2001). One's accent may be shaped by their preference for traditional, print-based texts, as seen in the image of the family. Prensky argues that 'The single biggest problem facing education today is that our digital immigrant instructors, who speak an out-dated language (that of the pre-digital age), are struggling to teach a population that speaks an entirely new language' (2001: p. 4). This new language forms part of the literacy of digital futures and has the cyber-revolutions embedded within it as an impetus for social change.

The idea of cyber-revolutions works on the micro level to affect the macro. There is a multiplicity of different ways in which cyber-revolutions work, given the unprecedented digital options that agents now have to make changes in their lives. On a straightforward and individual level, the Internet can work as an important portal to find jobs around the world, and therefore facilitates the global movement of people. On an organized and collective level, the global Internet encourages new social groups to emerge and to solicit support without normative factors of control directly interceding, such as those exerted by the family, religion or the school. Elsewhere, I have examined these processes by understanding and articulating ideas that relate to cyberpunk, techno-tribalism and virtual terrorism (see Cole and Pullen, 2010). Many of the new social groups do not survive beyond a few meetings, or the publication of a statement of intention. Yet the point here is that the rapid and dispersed growth of new social movements that are facilitated through digital mediation leads to an expanded sense of literacy connected to life-worlds. This literacy, imbued with the accent of digital natives, represents a competency in reading about and organizing cyber-revolutions, and in understanding how they function. The literacy of cyber-revolutions includes the inclusion of affinity-spaces (Gee, 2005), which is the way in which groups come together and how they gather collective momentum. The notion of affinity-spaces is complemented by virality, whereby certain websites may become extremely popular, often for a very short period of time, and they 'go viral'. The 'viral-affinitive' therefore represents a motor for cyber-revolutions, and is an example of concept creation for the literacy of digital futures. This concept is also part of science fiction landscape in education, whereby the future is written into the present as a bundling of time related tendencies.

Science fiction landscapes in education[2]

The science fiction landscape of digital futures is present in the ways that education is run by neo-liberal capitalist democracies that universally deploy digital technology for learning. Technology is a means to levelling diversity, ignoring affect and framing entire heterogeneous populations by deploying digital learning tools that do not recognize difference (they are machines). Technological deployment and digital mediation in education are complemented by the tendency towards global capitalism, whereby cultural input is commodified due to capital process. Simultaneously, projective fantasies and the illusions of difference are present in the education of the populace as a form of control. Ursula K. Le Guin (2000) imagines parallel science fiction circumstances in *The Telling*, a novel in her series of 'Hainish' stories. This series supposes that, half a million years ago, intelligent humanoids from the planet Hain spread across the galaxy and settled on a hundred habitable worlds, including Terra (Earth). Le Guin designates that travel between the worlds has resumed and that an interplanetary federation, the 'Ekumen', coordinates the exchange of goods among the worlds. Representatives of the Ekumen go to each planet when it is rediscovered and invite peoples of Hainish descent to participate in the federation.

In *The Telling*, Sutty is a Terran Observer for the Ekumen, who travels to the planet Aka to continue studies initiated by the first Observers who made contact with the Akan people 70 years earlier:

> It was a simple fact, but one remarkably difficult for the Terran mind to comprehend. No aliens. No others, in the deadly sense of otherness that existed on Terra, the implacable division between tribes, the arbitrary and impassable borders, the ethnic hatreds cherished over centuries and millennia. "The people" here meant not my people, but people – everybody, humanity. "Barbarian" didn't mean an incomprehensible outlander, but an uneducated person. On Aka, all competition was familial. All wars were civil wars. (Le Guin, 2000: pp. 98–9)

The Telling demonstrates something important about the literacy of digital futures. This is that difference may be levelled through industrial-style education, the universal deployment of computers and the imposition of a digital learning style. Perspectives are changed through technology, and questions about otherness and the ways in which different groups are treated in education is altered. For Sutty, the Akans demonstrate a planar society lacking in difference; for the Akans, this perception does not exist.

The literacy of digital futures includes the levelling of differences through technology, and understanding that this plane of becoming tends towards one global (capitalist) society, a homogenized mode of communication (English), and the consequent internalization of otherness. *The Telling* and Ursula Le Guin's (2004) collection of short stories, *Changing Planes*, are science fiction landscapes that encapsulate an affective politics of literacy futures around difference. The entrapment, sense of control and communicative homogenization of educational technology is a counterpoint to the thought experiments of Le Guin's writing. The premise of *Changing Planes* is described in the first story, 'Sita Dulip's Method':

> ... [t]he airport is not a prelude to travel, not a place of transition; it is a stop. A blockage. A constipation. The airport is where you can't go anywhere else. It is a non-place in which time does not pass and there is no hope of any meaningful existence. A terminus: the end. The airport offers nothing to any human being except access to the interval between planes. (Le Guin, 2004: p. 2)

Sita Dulip realized that the experience of waiting in airports for delayed and cancelled flights represents 'a specific combination of misery, indigestion, and boredom' (p. 5) – and this facilitates 'interplanary travel', 'by a mere kind of twist and a slipping bend, easier to do than to describe, she could go anywhere – be anywhere – because she was already *between planes*' (p. 3). After setting out the method of interplanary travel, the book becomes a travel guide to civilizations that exist on different planes. Le Guin invents permutated worlds, and, in *Changing Planes*, a series of invented planets disrupt ideas about what is normal. For example, the inhabitants of Frin share their dreams. The people of Asenu become silent when they reach adulthood, which leads scholars to generate exegeses of the few words spoken by the Asenu. On Islac, genetic engineering has produced a huge range of beings, some of whom are the result of weird desires, such as chess-playing cats and talking dogs: 'There are talking dogs all over the place, unbelievably boring they are, on and on and on they talk about sex and shit and smells, and smells and shit and sex, and do you love me, do you love me, do you love me' (p. 13). *Changing Planes* demonstrates micro tendencies in the literacy of digital futures that are embedded in global capitalism. The literacy of digital futures simultaneously includes the communicative homogenization of global capitalism, along with the individualization of fantasy and permutation by market-led consumerism. This is a paradox in the literacy of digital futures, as the reading of one global capitalized system connects to emergent local multiple literacies through the imagination.

One of the most intriguing stories in *Changing Planes* is 'The Nna Mmoy Language', in which the Nna Mmoy people do not address each other by name but by 'ever-varying phrases [for] a thousand social and emotional connections' (p. 153). No interplanary visitor has yet understood the Nna Mmoy: 'Though their monosyllabic language is melodious to the ear, the "translator-mat" has so much trouble with it that it cannot be relied upon even for the simplest conversation' (p. 144). This is because 'the meaning of each word is continuously modified by all the words that precede or may follow it in the sentence ... And so, after receiving only a few syllables, the translator-mat begins to generate a flurry of alternate meanings that proliferate rapidly into a thicket of syntactical and connotational possibilities so that the machine overloads and shuts down' (pp. 145–6).

> Each syllable is a word, but a word with no fixed, specific meaning, only a range of possible significances determined by the syllables that come before, after, or near it. A word in Nna Mmoy has no denotation, but is a nucleus of potential connotations that may be activated or created by its context. Texts written in Nna Mmoy are not linear, either horizontally or vertically, but radial, budding out in all directions. Literary texts carry this poly-directional complexity to such an extreme that they resemble mazes, roses, artichokes, sunflowers, fractal patterns. (Le Guin 2004: p. 145)

With *Changing Planes*, Le Guin creates a science fiction of language that is impossible to translate, and sets parameters about the limits of learning. The literacy of digital futures has similar processes at work, as its processes move towards the language of global capitalism and individualized consumer fantasy. The narrator of 'The Nna Mmoy Language' quotes a friend who offers further understandings of Nna Mmoy:

> We talk snake. A snake can go any direction but only one direction at a time, following its head. They talk starfish. A starfish doesn't go anywhere much. It has no head. It keeps more choices handy, even if it doesn't use them. (Le Guin 2004: p. 148)

> Learning Nna Mmoy is like learning to weave water ... Their lives don't start here and run to there ... like horses on a racecourse. They live in the middle of time, like a starfish in its own centre ...
> What little I know of the language ... I learned mostly from children. The children's words are more like our words, you can expect them to mean the same thing in different sentences. But the children keep learning; and when they begin to read and write, at ten or so, they begin to talk more like adults; and by the time they're adolescents I couldn't understand much of what they said – unless they talked baby talk to me. (Le Guin 2004: pp. 150–1)

The introduction of Le Guin's works in education, to understand the literacy of digital futures, is a type of *defamiliarization*. The word defamiliarization has been attributed to the German poet Novalis (Friedrich von Hardenberg). The concept of defamiliarization was also used by other Romantic poets such as Wordsworth and Coleridge, and is associated with Surrealism. Russian formalist Victor Shklovsky (1917) introduced the concept of *ostraneniye*, or 'making strange', to literary theory. This idea is useful in that the literacy that we are learning about in digital futures is a process of 'becoming other'. This means that we cannot project what is normal to us to understand the becomings that digital envelopment entails. A further example to illustrate this process is contained in *Dr Strange* (see Figure 7.2).

Dr Strange has to become-other to himself to enact his destiny and to save the world. Understanding the literacy of digital futures includes overcoming, and represents a similarly difficult task, though without the triumphalism and closure of *dénouement* in terms of being a world saviour. The future is contained in the present through the associations of the unconscious, and these have to be constructed (Deleuze and Guattari, 1988). This means taking a strange new path to understanding literacy, such as the science fiction landscapes in education suggest, and these push the literacy imagination to its limits. This path could also be described as an apprenticeship in signs (Bogue, 2008), and the signs that new digital media suggest open up tremendous panoplies for the mind. For example, the ways in which small cameras attached to computers may be used to record and upload material onto sites such as YouTube produces new options for expression and learning. This is an addendum to science fictional landscapes in education and involves students using video in new ways to express themselves, which I have termed cam-capture literacy in the following section of this chapter.

Digital literacy case studies

Cam-capture literacy in middle schools

Cam-capture is video recording using small cameras attached to computers. The literacy of this process is part of mapping multiple literacies and a sign of digital futures. Cam-capture literacy in the research context of middle school education (grades 6–9) may be understood as a dynamic composite of three primary literacies: visual, information and personal.

Visual literacy

Cam-capture involves students being engaged in thinking through visual aspects of their representation. As the students talk, perform and look into

Figure 7.2 Page from the comic book *Dr Strange*.

the camera they are presenting themselves and their ideas to an audience. This is the primary mode of literacy that cam-capture gives rise to, and it is direct, formative and immediate (see Callow, 1999). Cam-capture presents face-on images, similar in kind to portrait photography. A secondary type of visual literacy that one may discern happens when the students discuss matters in pairs or groups and the recording captures a real-time discussion, or a scripted scene that the students may have prepared earlier. Users in this secondary context are able to record social and integrated behaviours and analyze these images.

Debes (1968) described visual literacy as gaining knowledge and experience about the workings of visual media coupled with a heightened conscious awareness of those workings. Visual literacy is 'what is seen with the eye and what is consequently seen with the mind' (1968: p. 1). This includes the ability to successfully decode and interpret visual messages and to encode and compose meaningful visual communications (Bamford, 2003). Cam-capture, as an integrated part of literacy teaching and learning, directly relates to these visual processes. If one surfs through the complex networks of the Internet and perhaps encounters social sites full of recorded digital videos, such as YouTube, one may be struck by the amount and diversity of footage that is available to view. Furthermore, such activity may take place outside of educational contexts. Cam-capture literacy is an opportunity for this motivational process to be brought into schools. Students viewing the videos that are present on YouTube are digesting visual cues and cultural norms when they log on and watch. They are also learning about new ways to represent themselves and how to integrate their identity development with the mediated digital environment (e.g. Gee, 2004). The visual lessons that students learn from recorded videos will depend upon their level of involvement in cam-capture processes, and in having the confidence to select and present images that resonate with an audience. This vital learning (Ansell Pearson, 2002; Deleuze, 1988) is a contemporary literacy that may be aligned with multiple literacies theory, the literacy of digital futures, and the teaching of visual analysis and representation.

Information literacy

Underneath the surface and analytical aspects of visual literacy lies the more expansive notion of information literacy. Students will learn how to use the computer software and editing tools when they execute cam-capture episodes. Every time they switch on the computer, they enter into an informational relationship with their machines in terms of locating files and performing logical steps to enable them to make choices. In addition, information literacy includes learning how to perform critical analysis so that the students may successfully process information and make perceptive decisions about their videos (Lemke, 1984; Leu, 2000).

Information literacy requires learning how to distinguish between various types of information – identifying what Burbules and Callister (2000) have defined as 'misinformation; malinformation; messed-up information and mostly useless information'. This process will alter the ways in which students present themselves through cam-capture and the resultant cam-capture literacy that they learn. Cam-capture participants make critical choices about what they are presenting and discussing in self-recorded videos. This 'criticality' can only be gained through research and reflection (Bingham, 2005) with respect to other cam-capture videos. Questions that students may ask include: What video episodes held my attention? Why were some self-recorded videos successful and others not? What messages did the videos present? These textual and critical questioning modes offer deconstructive moments in the classroom context and in the development of the self – that have been located and defined as pedagogic devices to encourage social interaction and literacy purpose (Luke, 2000). The reflective abilities (cf. Bransford, 1979) of the users may be used to critically examine the context and placement of cam-captured episodes on the Internet. Critical website questions that induce information literacy in the context of cam-capture literacy include: Who is the author of the video and what do we learn about them? Why has the video been placed on this site? How does the self-recorded video relate to other sources of information available on the website? Has the self-recorded video been successfully integrated into the other messages and signs that the author is presenting on the site? What are the narrative elements of the video and how do they relate to understanding that one may gain about the story of the author or the site generator?

Information literacy is a central part of multiple literacies as a social movement and digital future, as it presents a pedagogical perspective on text related to critical framing. Students will become skilled at analyzing the contents of the self-recorded videos through critical practice – as well as uploading their own productions with a critical and contemporary edge.

Personal literacy

Information and visual literacy may be blended and focused through the understanding that cam-capture not only requires analytical, logical and evaluative skills, but also 'radically alters space, time and subjectivity' (Dery, 1994: p. 19). This strong claim for the effects of 'digitalization' may be understood in the context of the subjective realities that cam-capture gives access to and the ways in which this process can be relayed into social and cultural life (Cole, 2007b, 2005a). In the educational context, this is fundamentally a question of power – or the ways in which the individuals or groups involved with cam-capture understand how to use this technology to transform their situation.

Personal literacy is the process of expressing desires and complex emotive states in an articulate manner (see Fiumara, 2001). Yet as Gerald Coles (1999) has noted, the procedure of reading and writing about emotions is hindered by 'focusing on literacy learning as if children's minds were information-processing mechanisms' (1999: p. 8). Educators should therefore position cam-capture as a positive enunciation of emotional content in order to create the transformational possibilities of empowerment (Arnold, 2005) and personal literacy. Moreover, children using cam-capture as part of their literacy education are learning how to represent their personal nature to an audience and their group identity as a whole. Group dynamics may be overlooked or misrepresented in terms of literacy learning. Cam-capture gives the users a flexible and immediate resource to work on group messages. For example, a teacher who encounters students antipathetic to mainstream literature choices (Millard, 1997; Sefton-Green, 1999; Wilhelm and Smith, 2001) may use cam-capture with these students to express alternative textual preferences. This evidence counts as an important articulation of personal literacy, yet these ideas may be shaped through group values – in this case the rebellion against print literacy. Students and teachers should view and discuss the cam-capture tapes together to come to decisions about their cultural identities and future textual choices.

Personal literacy is dealt with by multiple literacies through the concept of the creative unconscious. The unconscious refers to the social future of the group involved with any set project as well as particular design briefs such as architecture, town planning or story telling. Cam-capture literacy provides a link between the unconscious of multiple literacies and the personal expression of desire captured on video, which will criss-cross between school and life in transversal becomings (Cole, 2005b) of the participants in the literacy of digital futures.

Complex tripartite cam-capture literacy

Cam-capture literacy would be a straightforward matter to record and understand if it were a simple joining of the three aspects of literacy described above. On the contrary, students recording videos are also doing complex identity work (Cole, 2007a) that involves activation of their modes of creativity including the imagination, memory and synthetic thought about who they are and who they would like to become. As such, cam-capture literacy may be recast thought the lens of interlinked visual, informational and personal processes and represented through use of the diagram in Figure 7.3.

Figure 7.3 summarizes the background to the concept of cam-capture literacy. This figure also helps to bridge cam-capture literacy with its research context – which is middle school literacy. In this context, the

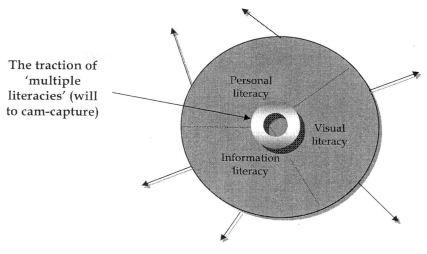

The traction of 'multiple literacies' (will to cam-capture)

Personal literacy

Visual literacy

Information literacy

Figure 7.3 The tripartite representation of cam-capture literacy. The arrows denote the placement of this figure in the chaotic field of middle school development – and the figure is 'moved' by multiple literacies.

students are involved with personal, visual and informational development as an ongoing part of education.

This tripartite background to cam-capture literacy feeds into and complements research that has been carried out into student-generated video (Schuck and Kearney, 2004) and how to enliven the middle school curriculum. Schuck and Kearney found out that students are emboldened and engaged in learning when given the chance to make their own videos (2004: p. 41). Dowden (2007) has analyzed the ways in which middle school curriculum can affect student outcomes, and has come to the conclusion that an integrative curriculum is the best way forward for the middle years (2007: p. 65). Cam-capture tends towards integration, as it gives students the opportunity to reflect and analyze their practice across the visual, informational and personal fields. Students may also be empowered through cam-capture, that which Schuck and Kearney describe as having 'beneficial effects in terms of student voice, pedagogic structures and ownership of the learning process' (2004: p. 88).

Socio-qualitative research analysis – the cam-capture zones

This analysis represents a multi-layered representation of the self-recorded literacy videos ($n = 512$) and the construction of zones. The power of the zones is dependant on the energy and participation of the students and their cam-capture expression (see Robertson *et al.*, 2007). The following zones are interlinked and did not yield statistical data as to the number of students or types of students that figured in each zone. Rather, the zones are constructed as proximal resource centres that student 'dip into' at any point in their recordings about middle school literacy practice and these give rise to the literacy of digital futures:

1 *Boredom.* The videos elicited the deeply felt emotion of boredom. Boredom permeates all of the literacy practices of the middle schools involved with the research, as the students perceive them. Boredom is not a superficial surface effect to the deeper processes of education or mere reactivity on the part of the students, but exists on every level of their lives at school. It could be said that boredom as a cam-capture literacy zone is vital as an organizing and originating principle – and a useful sign for educators to enable the transformative potential of new technology to help with middle school literacy practice and digital futures.

2 *Time.* The pace of the self-recorded videos differed dramatically from student to student. Some rushed through their speeches at such a rate that their words are barely audible. Others spoke so slowly and deliberately that the videos seemed to be recorded at half-speed. Few students were able to talk naturally or directly at the camera, which indicates the determinate factors of time and pace in cam-capture literacy. Consequently, it could be said that the time of cam-capture literacy exists in a different zone to non-mediated time (Cole, 2005b).

3 *Face.* Many of the students had prepared their images in advance before the video. The girls had put on make-up; boys combed their hair and straightened their shirts. The video cameras are small and only frame the face and shoulders of the students, which means that the students became self-conscious with respect to these parts of their bodies that represented everything about them during the recordings. Some students preferred to be framed in profile and tilted their heads to one side of the camera, as they thought that this would look cooler. The notion of face is an important cam-capture zone.

4 *Inarticulation.* The self-recorded videos produced by this project demonstrate that these middle school students are linked by their communal inability to talk about middle school literacy. Most of the students had great difficulty articulating any worthwhile phrases about their literacy practices. If the students were given direct questions to answer by the researcher or teacher, such as 'What helps me to get better at literacy?', they were often left speechless. If they were asked 'What am I good at in literacy?', they would maybe be able to say 'reading' or 'writing', but usually without any further elaboration. Some would follow up their comments

with 'I'm bad at spelling'!! Very few of the students could critically analyze their literacy skills in any depth. Rather than perceiving this to be a negative feature of the population in the socio-economic strata of the sample and their consequent self-reflective skills, inarticulation is hereby integrated into the cam-capture literacy zones. This zone can be a positive aspect of expression when other parts of representation are also important – for example, image or the power of a discourse. In terms of cam-capture literacy, inarticulation can help to add atmosphere and tenor to the expressions, in the same way that musicians use silence as an important part of musical expression (Moffett, 1981).

5 *Teacher intervention and power*. Several teachers in the four sample schools, who perhaps thought that the students were not taking the research seriously, sat by the computers and quizzed their best students about what they had just been studying in the previous literacy lessons. These videos resemble reading comprehension sequences, with the students mechanically responding to prompts. The students register noticeable relief and satisfaction if they think that the teacher is pleased with their performance – and seem to be nervous about the experience. This zone signals an important aspect of cam-capture literacy, in that it is not about getting the answer right, but about using the technology as a source of social empowerment. The students who were made to record these videos were not using the technology to improve their personal literacy, but were being asked to fit into the pre-determined power structure as organized by the school and the teacher. This zone therefore also defines the ways in which cam-capture literacy involves breaking free from power inhibition in one's expression by recording videos.

6 *Chaos and form*. In contrast to the previous zone, there were a number of videos that were made by students during recess. These recordings featured tapes of students dancing and making shapes with their bodies. The students moved the camera to look around the room in rhythmic bursts; the camera operator also made sweeps around the room to produce novel effects. During these recordings, one can hear laughter and other students talking in the room. There were also videos that include the random filming of the students in the classroom or the library during their leisure time, and a disconnected narrative from a student off-camera who doesn't appear in the video. Sometimes the narratives are silly, rude and provocative. This cam-capture zone defines the ways in which the technology was used an experimental aspect of the students' lives at school. The freedom to experiment with cam-capture led to them to change the role of the technology and to test its efficiency to produce different effects.

   7 *Self-consciousness*. This cam-capture zone is intimately connected
   to 'face', and ran through most of the self-recorded videos. The
   students usually came across as being self-conscious when they
   spoke about the repetitive nature of their literacy lessons, or how
   they could get better at reading, writing or speaking English. The
   cam-capture zone of self-consciousness denotes the idea that the
   author of the clip is aware of a viewing audience and to a certain
   extent is worried how they will appear on the video.

The cam-capture literacy zones are useful due to the ways that they
define how one may understand the middle school socio-qualitative context
of the study (Freebody, 2003). This context has been characterized by
low achievement in print literacy according to recent test results. The
cam-capture literacy zones are starting points and possible ways of working
through this situation, and should be perceived as educational aids that
can make a difference in the lives of the students, teachers and parents.
For example, the zone of boredom could be turned into an excellent
thematic unit of work, whereby students and teachers examine this theme
through literature and relevant resources in an effort to uncover the
sources of boredom and to address the consequences in terms of learning.
To this extent, the cam-capture literacy zones are a social and educational
movement and a subsequent aspect of mapping multiple literacies. The
zones also give a vocabulary and matrix for the literacy of digital futures
because this type of literacy creates entangled webs of interconnection with
mainstream literacy practice (school) and the future.

Future trends of cam-capture

The cam-capture zones are present in schools, even when the computers are
turned off or have been consigned to dusty cupboards by English teachers.
Students will, for example, bring the transformations that are present in
the cam-capture zones of 'time' and 'boredom' to bear on reading comprehension exercises that are set with respect to any class text. The challenge
for the future is to find synchronous and synergistic ways (Cole, 2006)
of combining real-time reading comprehension with computer mediated
reflection and the recording of relevant cam-capture episodes that mesh
with the practice of reading and responding to a text. The cam-capture
zones should work through and parallel to the practices of the reading
comprehension teacher to encourage a technologically enhanced reading
experience and an empowering group atmosphere (cf. Holland, 1998).
   The simplest way to encourage full integration between the cam-capture
zones and traditional literacy practices such as reading comprehension is
by using mobile electronic devices in the classroom with video recording
facilities and relevant software. Students may synchronously record their

thoughts about the reading comprehension exercise, and send their video messages by email during the lesson. This will take away the sense that the reading exercise is a personalized or subjective test. Traditional print literacy reading comprehension therefore changes, from test-based or an assessment focused on individual literacy skills, to a technologically mediated experience that encourages transversal communication. This case study on cam-capture literacy in the middle school serves as a research-based example of mapping multiple literacies and the literacy of digital futures. The next section serves to exemplify a specific social trend involving young Muslims in Australia, and the literacies involved with this trend as they help us to understand the future.

Young Muslims in Australia on Facebook

In a recent government sponsored research project in Australia (Collins *et al.*, 2010), it was found that large numbers of young Muslims are using social networking sites such as Facebook. In fact, 82 percent of the 15–18 age group when asked said that their primary focus on the Internet was to socialize. Of the 18–25 age group, 63 percent responded similarly, which points to the ways in which social life is evolving under the influence of social media. The sample of 323 young Muslims was taken from the Sydney area, and the urban focus of the research prejudices the study to a certain extent, in that all respondents would have access to computers. Yet this sample points to a tendency in Australia that is important in the context of the literacy of digital futures. This tendency is that a dichotomy is appearing between the ways in which young Muslims are socializing on the Internet and in 'non-mediated life'. Young Muslims read the world and life differently through their Facebook sites than through the experiences and media that are not mediated digitally online. The mainstream media in Australia (newspapers and TV) often transmit messages of conflict and war with respect to Muslims, and this stands in contrast to the messages of support and community that young Muslims may receive through social networking. Young Muslims can obtain stories from and about Islamic countries from a different (i.e. pro-Muslim) perspective, and avoid the Western filter of the War on Terror that realigns stories about Islam. The problem is not one of objectivity for young Muslims; it is rather to do with the forces that are positioning the stories of war and conflict in their lives. One of these forces is sensationalism, and the need for impact that the mainstream media requires to drive ratings, including news stories. The post-9/11 world is a hostile, *Islamophobic* (see Schmidt, 2004) one for many young Muslims, one that they did not create. Their reaction is to use the social networks to seek out new ways to understand who they are and what position they occupy in society.

Market driven media in Western democracies are relentlessly looking for news stories to increase and maintain their audiences. The War on Terror is a central narrative and organizing factor for Western democracies that ensures funding for the military and maintenance of 'the fear of the other'. Young Muslims are caught in the middle of these forces and are involved in the narrative, both as consumers of the news and as potentially marginalized others. The ways that Muslim youth are handled in democratic Western countries such as Australia are a critical signpost to understanding the literacy of digital futures. This is because the group dynamics and issues to do with the voices that young Muslims listen to are vital if they are to avoid radicalization. Research has shown that radicalization also often happens online, where networks of radicalized youth can share views and possibly escape detection (e.g. Abbas, 2007). The voices that young Muslims may listen to online tell of war against the West, and the struggle against the infidels that has been waged across millennia through Islam. These are very powerful forces for young Muslims, especially as they hear about the War on Terror as a ubiquitous narrative in the mainstream (Western) media. The digital world is an escape route from victimization and a source of power and unity for young Muslims. With respect to Deleuzian literacy studies, the way that young Muslims are using social media is their plane of immanence, and an organizing factor for the unconscious. The imaginative and associative aspects of using digital media fit in well with religious aspirations, as the user is able to roam free in their mind, and go wherever their desires take them on the Internet. In an Islamophobic (outside) world, the Muslim imagination will be drawn to voices of brotherhood and harmony through the interconnectedness of being online.

In terms of mapping multiple literacies, the young Muslims are involved with political, visual, rhetorical, religious and affective literacies. The affective literacies are especially important to young Muslims using Facebook, as the affective contrast in environmental and digital realms is a powerful driver in their learning. It is also true that young Muslims are not a group apart, but are invested in generalized youth culture in Australia, with its mixture of inter-generational and cultural issues, including those connected to music, education, TV and film. Youth culture in Australia is a powerful affective and collective organizational factor that is present through the use of digital media, and invites 'buy in' from the agents who view and participate. In this respect, young Muslims are incorporated along with every other group identity in contemporary Australia. Yet the religious 'push' that Islam gives these individuals in Australia makes them likely to question certain aspects of Australian youth culture, especially those that involve the use of alcohol. Young Muslims read and participate in the parts of Australian youth culture that are appropriate from their Islamic perspective. This means that they are trained to be able to differentiate between actions that define a moral code for life. This is a powerful reading practice that is reinforced through religious observation and extra-curricula classes. This practice can help young Muslims to succeed and to find a path in their lives that avoids immoral temptation. However, many young

Muslims in Australia will come to question the virtue of these choices that they derive from religion, as they live in a predominantly secular society. This questioning will result in engagement with affective literacies, and a potential loss of certainty. These affective literacies find an appropriate place on Facebook, as the open questioning of faith is taboo in strict Muslim society. Facebook invites relativity, as comments and opinions are transitory or expressed without forethought or understanding of potential consequences.

There is a politics of affect which is produced through young Muslims using Facebook in Australia. By excluding affect from their calculations, neo-liberalism and civil society may be at odds with the often-violent resurgence in contemporary revolts against the state. Ignoring or repressing affect, wallowing in it, or taking it for granted have ultimately the same consequence: affect remains a mystery; and politics itself is rendered opaque, as may be understood through young Muslims on Facebook. The return of affect in education (see Chapter Three) demands of multiple literacies theory (MLT) an adequate conceptualization of affect's politics, and its relationship to the state. Deleuze enables us to rethink the notion of the 'return' of affect as politics through his formulation of materialisms in his first two texts authored jointly with Félix Guattari (1988). History may be cast as narrative that emphasizes regularity and predictability; in Massumi's (2002) words, history comprises a set of 'identified subjects and objects' whose progress is given 'the appearance of an ordered, even necessary evolution ... contexts progressively falling into order' (p. 218). Such an appearance is projected by the same political operation that nullifies pre-personal multiplicity and the mobility that is characteristic of affect. Narrative history results from the selection, confinement and capture of an affective flow that is in fact unpredictably mobile and in continuous variation. In Deleuze and Guattari's (1988) terms, 'all history does is to translate a coexistence of becomings into a succession' (p. 430). In this translation, affects become emotions, singular collectives become identifiable individuals, and the state arises, imposing its order upon culture. As a result of these transformations, the affective – now constituted as the emotional – is represented as reactive, secondary, the essence of passivity; events provoke sadness, happiness, or in the case of young Muslims, frustration. Affect's primacy and excess is translated into the secondary residue that is emotion. History has to be remapped in view of the affective flux that resonates through (and resists) its linear orderings. Part of this remapping includes the designation of multiple literacies and the literacy of digital futures. Young Muslims in Australia on Facebook represent an important 'flow' of affective energies that can escape the control of the state, and therefore signal future tendencies about society and the politics of control.

Notes from the 'digito-sphere'

Using Deleuze as a theoretical backdrop to understanding the literacy of digital futures enacts what one might call the 'digito-sphere'. This is the way in which the influence of digitalization comes together and gathers strength in areas of intensification such as education or business. In *A Thousand Plateaus* (1987), Deleuze and Guattari talk about the 'mechano-sphere' (p. 71), which is the aggregate of numerous abstract machines working together, and could be summarized as a figure to comprehend the ways in which the forces of modernism have merged in social institutions such as schools and factories. The point is not that factories are entirely functionally synchronous, or that schools have been designed to work by clockwork. The way to understand how schools and factories have been set up to work is by looking at the tendencies in play, or the emergent forces that define their existence and the players in their folds. The most powerful forces in motion are those that tend towards mechanization, the way objects 'fit together' and give precise, analogue and casual explanations about the various forms within their domains. For example, a defective product may be examined and the anomaly traced to a section in the production process. The production line can be temporarily halted, the machine that is responsible for the defective aspect of the product may be fixed, and the production line will be switched back on again. The factory could be defined through these processes of examination and regulation, and the ways in which the whole is segmented into processes that are lined up successively. The same ways of working have defined schooling.

Nowadays, businesses that rely on digital technology have begun to overturn the factory mentality. Clocking-on and clocking-off timecards have been replaced by flexitime arrangements. Control of the production line has been replaced by mastery of digital media and code. The analogue connection between successive parts of the production line has been replaced by digital astral works, which can lead in any direction (see Gough, 2007). This means that digitalized education simply cannot function in the same way as the factory production of qualifications, goods and services has in the past. Perhaps the 'digital revolution' in education inevitably leads to regimes of 'lifelong learning' that in some ways are even scarier than the factory production of delimited minds. Whatever the final truth of the matter, the emergent tendency and force is towards the 'digito-sphere'. This is where the abstract machinery of every aspect of learning through digital media begins to join together and merge into discernible planes that carry along the agent, for example, when they are surfing on the Internet. Multiple literacies theory is a positive way to understand the movement towards the digito-sphere as digitization signifies a development in multiple literacies (e.g. Leu, 2000); for example, Internet literacy, information literacy, visual literacy and social literacy are potentially activated simultaneously when using Facebook. These practices are mostly performed out of school, but impinge upon traditional print literacy in that students use and develop literacy learning resources when they negotiate simultaneous multiple literacies.

The challenge for contemporary education is to fully activate the 'digito-sphere' through learning and not through the control mechanisms of the state. This has already happened in areas of business that rely on simultaneous international deal-making. E-workers now turn on their screens, follow global business trends, and take positions with client's capital to make profit. Such precision and directness in deal-making would have been unimaginable in the days before the Internet and digital platform for international trade. These deals create (and lose) wealth rapidly, directing global capital. These actions take place in the 'digito-sphere', where the intentions, thoughts and desires of the traders are aligned with the capabilities of their electronic machines. In comparison, schooling is outdated and sluggish, still relying on textbooks, examinations and the oral transmission (and understanding) of data. The 'digito-sphere' permeates the classroom in that banks of computers line physical spaces of enclosure and signify a possible escape from drudgery and ordering by capital flows. In Australia's New South Wales, the state government has unleashed the 'digito-sphere' into schools by ordering laptop computers for grade 9 students and by fixing interactive whiteboards (IWBs) to the walls. Exactly what teachers are going to do with these computers and IWBs is not yet clear, though the possibility of being e-entrepreneurs may now be a step closer for some Australian teenagers. In so doing, students will leave behind their digital immigrant teachers, who are still stranded in the 'mechano-sphere' with its abstract machines and concomitant behaviours.

Conclusion

This chapter necessarily represents the most disparate mapping of literacies amongst the multiple literacies of this book. As has been stated above, the use of printed words to express this disparity includes redundancy and obsolescence as digitized multiple literacies spread out and become other. This chapter therefore embraces the most difficult set of concepts for a practising teacher to take in and to use in the classroom, as the ideas are already inculcated in emergent and contingent multiple literacies of future populations. Perhaps it is therefore better to let students be the experts in this field, and show the teacher how the literacy of digital futures is written into any task that one might designate. The teacher's role is not to instruct about nor correct the details of a digital product, but to act as a conduit for the literacy of digital futures to emerge through teaching and learning practice (as Deleuzian). For example, the ways in which social media are currently being deployed for the purposes of online activism cannot be arrested or readily assessed. Rather, the educative life and literacy of this process should be harnessed to animate debate and action around issues of interest to the cohort. The examination and use of such websites as 'Wikileaks' could be included in this discussion work, and an affective set of political practices to enhance educative experience could be assembled ...

References

Abbas, T. (2007). Ethno-Religious Identities and Islamic Political Radicalism in the UK: A Case Study. *Journal of Muslim Minority Affairs*, 27(3), 429–42.

Ansell Pearson, K. (2002). *Philosophy and the adventure of the virtual: Bergson and the time of life*. London: Routledge.

Arnold, R. (2005). *Empathetic intelligence: teaching, learning, relating*. Sydney: University of New South Wales Press.

Bamford, A. (2003). The visual literacy white paper. Commissioned by Adobe Systems Pty Ltd, Australia. Available online at http://wwwimages.adobe.com/www.adobe.com/content/dam/Adobe/en/education/pdfs/visual-literacy-wp.pdf (accessed 1 February 2012).

Bergson, H. (1994). *Matter and Memory* (N. M. Paul and W. S. Palmer, trans). New York: Zone Books.

Bingham, C. (2005). The hermeneutics of educational questioning. *Educational Philosophy and Theory*, 37, 553–67.

Bogue, R. (2008). Search Swim and See: Deleuze's apprenticeship in signs and pedagogy of images. In I. Semetsky ed., *Nomadic Education: Variations on a theme by Deleuze and Guattari* (pp. 1–16). Rotterdam: Sense Publishers.

Bransford, J. D. (1979). *Human cognition: Learning, understanding and remembering*. Belmont, CA: Wadsworth.

Burbules, N. C. and Callister, T. (2000). *Watch IT. The risks and promises of information technology*. Boulder, CO: Westview Press.

Callow, J. (1999). *Image matters: Visual texts in the classroom*. Newton, NSW: Primary English Teaching Association.

Coiro, J., Knobel, M., Lankshear, C. and Leu, D. (eds) (2008). *Handbook of Research on New Literacies*. New York: Lawrence Erlbaum Associates.

Cole, D. R. (2005a). Learning Through the Virtual, *CTHEORY*, 1 (EJ) EJ. Available online at http://www.ctheory.net/articles.aspx?id=445 (accessed 1 February 2012).

—(2005b). Reading in the future: literacy and the time of the internet, *Reconstruction*, 5(2) EJ. Available online at http://reconstruction.eserver.org/052/cole.shtml (accessed 1 February 2012).

—(2006). Techno-shamanism and Educational Research. On-Line literary e-zine, *Sage of Consciousness* available at http://www.sageofcon.org/ez7/nf/dc.htm (accessed 11 March 2011).

—(2007a). Cam-Capture: An eye on teaching and learning. In J. Sigafoos and V. Green (eds), *Technology and Teaching: A casebook for educators* (pp. 55–68). New York: Nova Science Publishers.

—(2007b). Virtual Terrorism and the Internet E-Learning Options. *E-Learning*, 4(2) 116–27.

—(in press). Matter in Motion: The Educational Materialism of Giles Deleuze. *Educational Philosophy and Theory*, forthcoming special edition on the future of educational materialism.

Cole, D. R. and Pullen, D. L. (eds) (2010). *Multiliteracies in Motion: Current theory and practice*. New York and London: Routledge.

Coles, G. (1999). Literacy, emotions, and the brain. An invited contribution to *Reading Online*. Available online at http://www.readingonline.org/critical/coles. html (accessed 1 February 2012).

Collins, J., Jakubowicz, A., Pennycook, A., Ghosh, D., Cole, D. R., Al-Momani, K., Hussain, J. and Chafic, W. (2010). Voices Shaping the Perspectives of Young Muslim Australians. *Cosmopolitan Civil Societies Research Centre*, University of Technology, Sydney, 1–154.

Debes, J. (1968). Some foundations of visual literacy. *Audio Visual Instruction*, 13, 961–4.

Deleuze, G. (1988). *Bergsonism* (H. Tomlinson and B. Habberjam, trans). New York: Zone Books.

—(1989). *Cinema 2: The time image* (H. Tomlinson and R. Galeta, trans). London: Athlone Press.

Deleuze, G. and Guattari, F. (1988). *A Thousand Plateaus: Capitalism and Schizophrenia II* (B. Massumi, trans.). London: The Athlone Press.

Dery, M. (1994). *Flame-Wars: The discourse of cyberculture*. Durham, NC: Duke University Press.

Dowden, T. (2007). Relevant, challenging, integrative and exploratory curriculum design: Perspectives from theory and practice for middle level schooling in Australia. *The Australian Educational Researcher*, 34(2), 51–72.

Fiumara, G. C. (2001). *The mind's affective life: a psychoanalytic and philosophical inquiry*. Hove: Brunner-Routledge.

Freebody, P. (2003). *Qualitative research in education*. London: Sage Publications.

Gee, J. P. (2004). *What video games have to teach us about learning and literacy*. Basingstoke: Palgrave/Macmillan.

—(2005). Semiotic social spaces and affinity spaces: From the age of mythology to today's schools. In D. Barton and K. Tusting (eds), *Beyond communities of practice: Language, power, and social context* (pp. 214–32). Cambridge: Cambridge University Press.

Gough, N. (2007). Changing planes: rhizosemiotic play in transnational curriculum inquiry. *Studies in the Philosophy of Education*, 26: 279–94.

Greene, M. (1995). *Releasing the imagination: Essays on education, the arts and social change*. San Francisco: Jossey-Bass.

Holland, E. (1998). Spinoza and Marx. *Cultural Logic* 2, 21–47.

Hume, D. (1739 [1978]). *A Treatise of Human Nature*. Edited, with an analytical index, by L. A. Selby-Bigge, 2nd edn. Oxford: Oxford University Press.

Le Guin, U. K. (2000). *The Telling*. New York: Harcourt.

—(2004). *Changing Planes*. London: Victor Gollancz.

Lemke, J. (1984). Action, context and meaning. In Toronto Semiotic Circle Monograph, *Education and Semiotics* (pp. 107–21). Toronto: University of Toronto Press.

Leu, D. J. (2000). Our children's future: Changing the focus of literacy and literacy instruction. *Reading Online* (EJ). Available online at http://www.readingonline.org/electronic/elec_index.asp?HREF=/electronic/RT/focus/index.html (accessed 1 February 2012).

Luke, A. (2000). Critical literacy in Australia: A matter of context and standpoint. *Journal of Adolescent and Adult Literacy*, 43, 448–61.

Masny, D. (2006). Learning and creative processes: a poststructural perspective on language and Multiple Literacies. *International Journal of Learning*, 12(5), 147–55.

Massumi, B. (2002). *Parables for the Virtual: Movement, Affect, Sensation*. Durham, NC: Duke University Press.

Millard, E. (1997). *Differently Literate*. London: The Falmer Press.

Moffett, J. (1981). *Active voice – A writing program across the curriculum*. Montclair, NJ: Boynton Cook.

Nietzsche, F. (1961). *Thus Spoke Zarathustra: A book for everyone and no one* (R.J. Hollingdale, trans.). London: Penguin Books.

Prensky, M. (2001). Digital natives, digital immigrants. *On the Horizon*, 9(5), 1–6.

Pullen, D. L. and Cole, D. R. (eds) (2009). *Multiliteracies and Technology Enhanced Education: Social Practice and the Global Classroom*. Hershey, PA: IGI Global Publications.

Robertson, M., Webb, I. L. and Fluck, A. E. (2007). *Seven steps to ICT integration*. Camberwell, Australia: ACER Press.

Schmidt, G. (2004). Islamic identity formation among young Muslims: the case of Denmark, Sweden and the United States. *Journal of Muslim Minority Affairs*, 24(1), 31–45.

Schuck, S. and Kearney, M. (2004). Students in the director's seat: Teaching and learning across the school curriculum with student-generated video. *Teacher learning and development group*. Available online at http://engage.wisc.edu/dma/research/docs/Kearney-StudentsDirectorsSeat.pdf (accessed 1 February 2012).

Sefton-Green, J. ed. (1999). *Young people, creativity and new technologies*. London: Routledge.

Sellers, W. and Gough, N. (2010). Sharing outsider thinking: thinking (differently) with Deleuze in educational philosophy and curriculum inquiry. *International Journal of Qualitative Studies in Education*, 23(5), 589–614.

Shields, R. (2003). *The Virtual*. London and New York: Routledge.

Shklovsky, V. (1917 [1965]). Art as technique (Lee T. Lemon and Marion J. Reis, trans). In L. T. Lemon and M. J. Reis (eds), *Russian formalist criticism: Four essays* (pp. 3–24). Lincoln: University of Nebraska Press.

Small, G. and Vorgan, G. (2008). *iBrain: Surviving the technological alteration of the modern mind*. New York: HarperCollins.

Wilhelm, J. and Smith, M. W. (2001). Literacy in the lives of young men: Findings from an American study. *English in Australia*, 132, 17–26.

Notes

1 www.nytimes.com/2008/07/27/books/27reading.html?_r=1andpagewanted=alla
   ndoref=slogin.

2 This section has been inspired by Noel Gough's (2007) use of SF in his
   rhizomatic plays with curriculum theorizing.

CHAPTER EIGHT

Conclusion: Exits

Diana Masny and David R. Cole

In this chapter we want to consider what the implications are for mapping multiple literacies in life, and how, while being distinct, they are inter-twined with concept creation, problems/paradoxes in life, teaching and learning, curriculum and assessment, experimentation and creativity, and exiting with the pedagogy of the concept. With the publication of this book, concepts such as reading, literacies, affect and power have been reterritori-alized. Since they could be taken up in teaching, learning and curriculum, they participate in institutionalized literacy practices. However, it is the nature of Multiple Literacies Theory (MLT) to deterritorialize concepts through reading intensively and immanently as they (reading the world and self) circulate through collective assemblages of enunciation.

Concept creation

Throughout these chapters, Deleuze and Guattari (WP), with their own perspective on concept creation, have provided us with the potential for experimenting with our own concepts. In this regard, we echo the statement made by Colebrook (2002: p. 17): 'Concepts are not amenable to dictionary style definition, for their power lies in being open and expansive. For this reason, we have to understand them through the new connections they make.' In these chapters, we saw how the different connections happen. As one concept is created it connects with another and another, etc. Concepts do not operate in isolation.

In this book, we have considered concept creation in relation to reading and we could not do any linkage without considering the creation of the concept, sense. Sense is not about what a text means, nor is it about interpretation. Recall that Deleuze and Guattari referred to searching for meaning/significance in the text as interpretosis (WP and TP). In contrast to these ideas, sense is virtual and actual. Sense is an event and has the potential to become. Sense in this process actualizes in unpredictable ways. This has tremendous implications for how teaching gets taken up and what and how learning happens. For one, it opens avenues for creativity and affect (see Chapter 3) and what they contribute to the learning equation (for example, making complex mathematics more accessible and open).

How important is concept creation in teaching and learning? Concept creation is the result of looking at a problem/paradox to see how it functions and what it can produce (not solve). What problems produce is the creation of concepts. And the creation of concepts allows us to think differently about a problem. Concept creation is a deterritorialization. It disrupts the statement and presuppositions that make up the problem statement in order to look at the problem differently. An example of concept creation is the following: In response to the problem created when the researcher asks the children about how multiple writing systems work when they are writing (see Chapter Four), Anne has the thought of computer chips in her brain and Cristelle has the thought of little secret men on a trampoline. Are the chips and the little men forms of concept creation in response to the problems produced when the notions of multilingualism and multiple literacies connect?

With regard to the problem of reading, the emphasis on literacy (printed materials) in education has been a major concern, especially since provinces, states and countries refer to literacy rates as a benchmark for economic and social prosperity. The chapters of this book are filled with paradoxes; institutionalized power of literacy is a tracing that can be put on the rhizomatic map, unhinging an institutionalized power of reading in order to create a different concept that allows us to think differently. However, reading as a concept cannot stand alone. In Chapter Four, *What is Reading?*, reading was presented as intensive and immanent. Moreover, reading operates in relation to the world and self. What self is this?

In order to look at this question of self, we refer to Chapter Five, *Cartographies of Talking Groups*, to consider what language is and the social character of language. Language consists of speech acts, order-words, (in)corporeal transformations, statements and indirect discourse. The basic unit of language, order-words, is an expression of the dominant social order. The social character of language refers to collective assemblages of enunciation. An assemblage consists of different desiring machines and social machines. The individual is part of the assemblage. Reading self is reading the relationship of the encounters among the parts of the assemblage. In teaching and learning, it is reading self, that is, reading what encounters are going on in the assemblage of which the teacher and a learner are part, that produces an expression in response to the problem at hand, whether it be a math activity, an art activity, or some other pedagogical activity.

Reading perceived as intensive and immanent provides a different way of exploring reading than what psychological, applied linguistics and language arts-based research have provided. In the context of these chapters and their vignettes, there are immanent potentialities for all sorts of unpredictable responses to problems through reading.

Teaching and learning

'We never know in advance how someone will learn ...' (DR: p. 165). Deleuze also would argue that 'there is no more a method for learning than there is a method for finding treasures' (DR: p. 165). This also has implications for formal learning. The curriculum produced might claim to be tied to no specific teaching method or learning method. In other words, it is up to the teacher to integrate the curriculum/learning outcomes with their own specific approach to teaching. Deleuze (DR) considers that learning and teaching would happen in an environment that would require 'do with me' and not 'do as I do', favouring an apprenticeship. If we take Deleuze's example of learning to swim, 'doing with me' might not suffice because, as the apprentice swimmer sets foot in the water and begins to swim with the instructor, reading self and the world intensively and immanently in the assemblage are different in each case and therefore the experience of swimming is different.

> For learning evolves entirely in the comprehension of problems ... learning to swim or learning a foreign language means composing the singular points of one's own body or one's own language with those of another shape or element which tears us apart but also propels us into a hitherto unknown and unheard-of world of problems. To what are we dedicated if not to those problems which demand the very transformation of our body and our language? (DR: p. 192)

From this quote, we want to know what the problem in learning to swim is; what the problem in learning a language is. Learning is a process in that, when one's own body (as in swimming) encounters another element or when one's own language encounters another, there is disruption/deterritorialization. This encounter propels the swimmer or the language learner into an unknown and unpredictable world of problems. This is not seeking the comfort zone of a territory or the world of certainties (e.g. Chapter 7). This is seeking becoming. It is problems to which education teachers, learners, assessors and curricularists should turn their attention for it is in problems that learning happens. Lines of flight in becoming are events that take us along unknown paths. For instance, when Anne faces the problem of speeding up the writing of a Chinese iconograph, she begins forming it differently (modeling a cursive 't' in English). When Hello Kitty and her teacher are faced with the mystery of why there is no colour in the little storybooks, they contact the publishing house to make inquiries (see Chapter Five). In each case, paths were opened up that had been unknown in advance of the learning event.

In the classroom, each learner and teaching situation is different. Nevertheless, the learning outcomes are the same for all. The power of an educational institution makes reading an overcoded practice. Learning to read in relation to a particular curriculum often is created in relation to an arborescent (tree-like) system. A tracing has been created. In Chapter Two, *Cartographies of multiple literacies*, we see how Deleuze and Guattari describe a tracing as a dualistic and hierarchical system, a territory. They suggest that transformations happen by putting the tracing on the map, a rhizomatic one that includes lines of flight that shoot through the segmentarity lines of the tracing. Lines of flight are becomings that transform learning and teaching.

> All of tree logic is a logic of tracing and reproduction. It consists of tracing, on the basis of an overcoding structure or supporting axis, something that comes ready-made. The tree articulates and hierarchizes tracings; tracings are like the leaves of a tree. ... What distinguishes the map from the tracing is that it is entirely oriented toward experimentation in contact with the real. (TP: p. 13)

Experimentation and creativity

Experiment is the operative word. Each learning situation and each teaching situation could be an invitation to 'experimentation with the real'. Experimentation is an event, a moment for territories to deterritorialize and eventually reterritorialize, only to deterritorialize once more. Each moment a disruption, each moment the disruption is different. This movement 'describes becoming through difference' (TP: p. 14). From reading, reading the world and self, an assemblage transforms. In the classroom, an unpredictable moment disrupts and learning/teaching happens differently. Experimentation is about creativity happening in the classroom. While each assemblage is different, creativity offers potentialities to disrupt overcoded learning and teaching practices (e.g. Chapter 6). This also means that the rhizome is constantly in motion.

Creativity also extends to interdisciplinarity, a move away from the disciplines in which school systems are conditioned to the silo effects of disciplines. While there may be curriculum projects that advocate interdisciplinarity, therein lies a paradox. Sure there is the 'intermingle' mandate of the curriculum; but at the same time think about what happens in schools:

children have different notebooks for each subject area, they have different time periods for each subject area, those times are separated by bells ringing and the teacher's voice saying 'time for math now children, put away your artwork', and sometimes there are different teachers for certain subjects. The bells and the teacher's voice may work like indirect discourse, collective assemblages of enunciation produced out of an order-word that distinctly separates the subject areas and resists disruption. Recall the vignettes in the Chapter Five: for Anne and Estrella, math is math, science is science, and writing a story is writing a story. You could not use science words in a story. You could not use math words when writing a story. Perhaps the curriculum asking for an intermingling of art, math, science, and language is supposed to have a deterritorializing effect on order-words like 'subject area' and 'discipline'. But, as we know, order-words can be resistant to deterritorializations. 'Schools in the present day are interesting sites of transition and tension between forces of knowledge capital and demands of accountability on the one hand and traditional disciplinary structures on the other hand, within which familiar "subjects" are maintained' (Lines, 2008: p. 134).

Curriculum and assessment

In an actual learning environment of the classroom, how can a curriculum predict learning outcomes? Is curriculum a learning plan if it is a learner-centered curriculum? A teaching plan if it is teacher-centered? Since this is an era of accountability, the curriculum might be an accountability plan. Learning outcomes in the curriculum find their way onto report cards and appear in many provincial/state tri-annual literacy tests. While the curriculum drives teaching and learning, curriculum has been disrupted/deterritorialized by assessment. Does this imply by extension that teaching and learning has also been deterritorialized by assessment? Seeking to comply with teaching, learning and curriculum may be a pathway to complying with accountability structures. 'Curriculum language that initially informs teacher planning once again returns to frame learning for the intention of reporting to authorities and parents' (Lines, 2008, p. 133).

Assessment is an order-word that resists deterritorialization. While pedagogical changes in the classroom can be achieved through experimentation and creativity, these changes can be molarized, subsumed by the 'standardized criteria of assessment value' (Lines, 2008: p. 134). Herein lies a paradox. Tracings in terms of assessment are important since they bring structure to a system. We operate with rules under the umbrella. In WP, Deleuze and Guattari refer to the umbrella which protects us from chaos, from disruptions. The umbrella is the world of certainties. At the same time, rhizomatic maps are just as important, otherwise there would be no creation. For instance, when curriculum promotes interdisciplinarity and when curriculum and interdisciplinarity are open to experimentation and creativity, teachers and learners might engage in such activity that disrupts order-words and creates opportunities for expansive modes of thinking. These innovations might be disrupted by the normalizing force of assessment. Once more it is time to put the tracing on the map that allows lines of flight to happen.

Pedagogy of the concept

As in Chapter One, we enter and exit in the middle for mapping literacies, as a process of becoming continues. It continues with the pedagogy of the concept. Just as problems are important to education, so could be the pedagogy of the concept. Deleuze and Guattari devote the introduction to WP to concept creation and conclude their introduction with the pedagogy of the concept. Pedagogy is critical for thinking whereas professional commercial training is a disaster for thought (WP). The pedagogy of the concept 'analyzes the conditions of creation as factors of always singular moments' (WP: p. 12). In teaching and learning, assessment and curriculum, there should be what Lines describes as 'aha' moments, when encounters in the assemblage (teacher, learner, classroom, materials, etc.) resonate (affect and percepts) in the virtual and actualize affectively. On the one hand, pedagogy of the concept is about teaching and learning creatively with concept creation. On the other hand, it is about creative responses to problems that happen in life. Daignault (2011) understood these singular moments in the classroom as parenthetical remarks, an accident that would turn into an event, a moment of deterritorialization and becoming.

Deleuze was not interested in dualisms such as literacy or illiteracy. He was interested in multiplicities. Cartographies of multiple literacies bring together tracings and maps, segmentary lines, lines of flight, roots and rhizomes. There is no hierarchy here. It is not a question of, for instance, tracings or maps; rather it is about tracings and maps. Mapping multiple literacies is about exposing the paradoxes in education not to destroy tracings or life under the umbrella of certainties (WP), but rather to be on the lookout (être aux aguets) for accidents, parenthetical remarks to be expressed and that become events of transformation, a movement outside the umbrella. For instance, assessment as a normalizer is a way of life. It provides an umbrella of certainties about how well schools are doing with regard to learning outcomes. However, it is just as important to explore what the problem of assessment is, and what and how it produces. Let's step outside the shelter of the umbrella and read the problem of assessment intensively and immanently. If we can extend this way of reading problems/paradoxes to teaching, learning, curriculum and life, then there are potentialities for the pedagogy of the concept and accidents-as-events. Should we not be looking at problems/paradoxes in a way that opens up to transformations? In exploring a problem related to curriculum as a normative force (a tracing), Waterhouse (2011, 2012) has created a concept, rhizocurriculum, to explore the problem/paradox of curriculum in terms of rhizomatic cartography.

Literacies in terms of reading, reading the world and self are multiple, expansive and becoming. While literacies are about mapping becomings, there are also literacies that are tracings as overcoded literacy practices. Literacies are expressed as collective enunciations in an assemblage. Alongside a dominant social order that frames collective enunciations, there are, however, potentialities for deterritorializations. Deterritorializations refer to the disruptions of territories as events that take off on new lines of flight, different becomings. Mapping multiple literacies through reading, reading the world and self are connected to events that hinge on problematization, experimentation, creativity and concept creation.

References

Colebrook, C. (2002). *Gilles Deleuze*. New York, Routledge.

Daignault, J. (2011). In conversation with Jacques Daignault and Diana Masny. *Policy Futures in Education*, 9(4), 528–39. Available online at http://dx.doi.org/10.2304/pfie.2011.9.4.528 (accessed 24 January 2012).

Lines, D. (2008). Deleuze, education and the creative economy. In I. Semetsky (ed.), *Nomadic education: Variations on a theme by Deleuze and Guattari* (pp. 129–42). Rotterdam: Sense Publishing.

Waterhouse, M. (2011a). Deleuzian experimentations in Canadian immigrant language education: Research, practice, and policy. *Policy Futures in Education*, 9(4), 505–17.

—(2011b). *Experiences of multiple literacies and peace: A rhizoanalysis of becoming in immigrant language classrooms*. Unpublished doctoral dissertation, University of Ottawa. Available online at http://hdl.handle.net/10393/19942 (accessed 17 January 2012).

INDEX